The Liturgy, the Family, and the Crisis of Modernity

Os Justi Studies in Catholic Tradition

General Editor: Peter A. Kwasniewski

The Liturgy, the Family, and the Crisis of Modernity
Essays of a Traditional Catholic

Joseph Shaw

S Justi
PRESS

Cover design: Julian Kwasniewski

On the cover: Fountains Abbey Church, Yorkshire, England.
From the West Door looking east. Taken by the author.

Os Justi Press
Lincoln, NE
https://osjustipress.com/

Inquiries to
info@osjustipress.com

Hardcover ISBN: 979-8-37304-984-9

Paperback ISBN: 979-8-37234-738-0

Domine, dilexi decorem domus tuæ,
et locum habitationis gloriæ tuæ.

I have loved, O Lord, the beauty of thy house;
and the place where thy glory dwelleth.

—Psalm 25(26):8

Contents

Part III: Family

Introduction

Six of the chapters in this book have been previously published in English, and two others in translation. In addition, seven have been presented as talks, but not until now printed. The remaining three have been specially composed for this collection, though I have written about these topics extensively on my own blog, LMSChairman.org. Since most of the chapters of this book were conceived as stand-alone pieces, they can be read as such, and I have not impeded this benefit by removing arguments and ideas which are found in more than one place across the collection. What I have done is to correct and sometimes expand the pieces, and introduce some cross-references.

These papers are efforts to address particular aspects of the great debate of our time: the crisis of modernity, particularly as it affects the Catholic Church. This encompasses the linked crises of faith, culture, and sexuality.

What I mean by the "crisis of modernity" can be described in this way. It is often observed that the project of Enlightenment rationalism, coupled with capitalism and building on the Protestant Reformation, weakens the ties that bind individuals to each other: to family, village or city, religious communities, nations, and so on. Many regard this is as a positive development: as a liberation from expectations, habits, and norms that inhibit the freedom of individuals to go their own way. Certainly, the things that bound together local, national, and religious communities in former times were far from perfect. The negative results of the loss of these ties, nevertheless, are increasingly making themselves felt. As I note in chapter 7, the sociologist Hillary Putnam summarises these negative consequences as the "loss of social capital."

The Liturgy, the Family, and the Crisis of Modernity

As I see it, the long process has become a crisis, as more and more fundamental social connections are undermined and severed. The crisis can be seen in particular with the family and the liturgy. A purely rationalistic and individualistic family is a contradiction in terms. Something with emotional bonds and commitments is necessary to sustain the family, and there is no satisfactory alternative to the family as a means of bringing up children. In a similar way, a purely rationalistic and individualistic religious rite is a contradiction in terms. A set of words and rituals in some sense "given," not self-created, is essential to the idea of the worship of something beyond ourselves.

The development of the process of the dissolution of bonds, which characterises modernity, has not (yet) entirely destroyed these institutions, but it has brought them close enough to collapse to give us an insight into the inevitable consequences. This is why I call it a crisis: it is a moment when we may be able to gain the wisdom to avert the final stage, or we may simply plunge into it.

The theme of part 1 of this volume is the transformation of culture. This transformation means that, for those of us on the wrong side of it, a special effort is required to understand the traditional Mass: what it is for, what are its principles of development, and how worshippers are supposed to engage with it. As I note in chapter 1, this distance does not make this Mass less attractive, but rather a revelation: a message from another world, which cuts through those aspects of modern culture that isolate us from our own spiritual instincts, and from the supernatural. I develop an understanding of the traditional Mass in chapters 2, 3, and 4. In chapter 5, I turn to the non-Catholic philosopher Byung-Chan Hul, who sees pre-modern ritual culture as an antidote to modernity's mechanised and commercialised narcissism—an idea that would have appealed very much to the Catholic apologists who evangelised industrial Britain and America with such success a century ago. In chapter 6, I confront the Enlightenment argument directly: whether destroying tradition liberates or impoverishes us.

In part 2, I focus on the era of the revolution itself. Chapters 7 and 8 assess the sociological effects of the Second Vatican Council and the liturgical reform, and their effect on Catholic belief. This leads to my responding to some particularly bitter critiques of the ancient Mass and its adherents, which try to connect them with racism (chapter 9), sexual repression (chapter 10), and clerical sexual abuse (chapter 11). In regard to this abuse, chapter 11 examines one of the roots of this problem within the Church—clericalism—and chapter 12 addresses the way abusers have been able to take advantage of the adoption, particularly by the educational establishment, of the morality of consent.

In part 3, I turn to issues surrounding the family and the sexes. I start with another aspect of the historical development of the crisis in the Church, which is critical to its complete understanding: the well-documented way in which religion came to be seen as feminine (chapter 13). This is followed by discussions of the male and female roles in the Church and the economy of salvation (chapters 14 and 15), the effect of feminism on sexuality (chapter 16), and the role of the family in recovering, maintaining, and transmitting culture to future generations.

With this final essay I return to the hope I expressed in the first one. A sober assessment of the problems our society faces and of the abject condition of the Church at the current moment seems overwhelming; nevertheless, we all have our work to do. We cannot bring back past generations, but we can ensure there is a new one.

> *Pro patribus tuis nati sunt tibi filii.*
> Instead of thy fathers, sons are born to thee.
> Psalm 44:17 (45:16)

Joseph Shaw
January 6, 2023
Feast of the Epiphany

Part I

Liturgy

Discovering and Rediscovering the Traditional Mass

Finding the Old Mass

God has been good to me: I stumbled over the traditional Mass twice before I really appreciated it.

One Lent in my childhood, it must have been in the early to mid 1980s, my mother proposed to me that we get up early to attend a daily Mass. This pious resolution did not long survive contact with reality, but for a few days we went to one of London's great churches, the Oratory of St Philip Neri, at seven in the morning, and walked its considerable length to the chapel of St Wilfrid, which is to the right of the high altar. This was closed with a curtain, enormous, thick, opaque, and sound-deadening, which we had to struggle through to enter the crowded but tiny chapel, where an old priest, Msgr Alfred Gilbey, was celebrating the traditional Mass. When this nefarious activity, the celebration of this form of the Mass, was not taking place, which is to say for the rest of the day, this curtain was drawn aside and hardly noticeable.

Msgr Gilbey died in 1998, at the age of 97, so he must have been in his eighties at this time, and it was his age which allowed him to freely celebrate the ancient Mass. My family knew him, and no doubt this encouraged the choice of this Mass for our devotion, despite it being so well hidden. However, the combination of our always being late, and the speed of Msgr Gilbey's celebration, meant that we invariably arrived about half-way through. What is clearest in my memory is his saying the long, traditional formula for the

This was first published in Polish translation in Tomasz Rowiński, ed., *Odwieczna Msza Świadectwa* (Wrocław: Rosa Mystica, 2021).

distribution of Holy Communion, quietly, rapidly, repeatedly, and without break or pause, as he went down the kneeling line of Communicants.

It was, for me, a deeply mysterious, though not unattractive, liturgical experience. It must have been in my mind when, in about 1988, I used a newly acquired bank account of my own to respond to an advertisement to join the Latin Mass Society. I had had no chance to attend the ancient Mass since those first experiences, and there was no immediate prospect of attending one again. But the 1980s in Britain was a decade of reaction, and just as in dress, architecture, and politics, much of what had been done in the 1960s and 1970s was being critically reassessed, the idea of a group preserving a form of the liturgy which had been casually cast aside in those decades appealed to me a good deal. I read the messages from the then Chairman, the late Christopher Inman, expressing both his frustration and the extraordinary perseverance characteristic of the movement in those years. I didn't really understand the background, but I sympathised with him all the same.

I remained an inactive member of the Society for more than a decade, seeing in their quarterly lists of traditional Masses none in Oxford, where I arrived as an undergraduate in 1991. The real situation, as I eventually discovered, was that Masses were being celebrated by a retired priest, but the archbishop had insisted that they not be advertised. However, before this changed, I had another curious encounter with the Old Mass at the other side of the globe.

While I was studying for my doctorate I made a trip to New Zealand, and while crossing the country from north to south I stayed the night with a cousin I had never met before. I realised it was her looking for me at the railway station, thanks to her remarkable family resemblance to my mother. She was not a Catholic but found out on my behalf about Mass times which would fit my itinerary. She gave me the details of a Saturday evening Mass in the Cathedral at Christchurch. Sensing my conservativism, she remarked "You'll find us very informal here." When I got there—late, again—I slunk into a pew at the back and gradually became aware of an old priest celebrating in Latin with his back to the nave, a considerable distance away. It was the traditional Mass.

It was a year or two after this, the autumn of 2001, that I found the situation in Oxford had changed: a traditional Mass was finally being advertised as taking place, on Sundays. The location, however, was obscure, and my first attempt to find it was a complete failure. This failure, however, was partly one of credulity. I could not at first believe, what the following Sunday I found to be a fact, that this Mass, taking place with the permission of the archbishop, was celebrated in a small meeting-room in a nondescript municipal building, the West Oxford Community Centre, which local groups could hire by the hour.

There, at last, I attended the traditional Mass: not arriving late, or seeing it from a great distance, but with about twenty people crowded into a plain box of a room, where the young priest had to vest in front of us and celebrate on a portable altar.

I came out of that ridiculous room—we later moved to a larger one, which doubled as a basketball court—with but one thought: "This is it." This is what I had been looking for, the real thing, Mass as it ought to be, and as I wanted always to attend it from then on.

The philosopher Alasdair MacIntyre expressed my feelings well: "Upon encountering a coherent presentation of one particular tradition . . . such a person will often experience a shock of recognition: this is not only, so such a person may say, what I now take to be true but in some measure what I have always taken to be true."[1]

Recognising worship

Our experiences are conditioned by what we already know and have experienced before. My own liturgical experiences, with the exceptions just noted, were of the *Novus Ordo*, with a strong bias in favour of liturgical "conservatism": liturgy celebrated somewhat more in continuity with the pre-Vatican II tradition. I had encountered progressive liturgies at my Catholic school and had no wish to repeat the experience, a sentiment shared, I think, with my school-fellows, who mostly ceased to attend

---

[1] Alasdair MacIntyre, *Whose Justice? Which Rationality?* (London: Duckworth, 1988), 394.

church altogether after they left. Another Oratory of St Philip Neri was founded in Oxford at around the time I arrived as an undergraduate, and I usually attended their Novus Ordo Latin celebrations on Sundays, though I also attended a variety of other Masses, particularly with my parents in the vacations. As far as liturgical abuses and theological confusion were concerned, I was living a sheltered life, though aware, to an extent, of this shelteredness.

I became interested in the question of liturgical abuses, and read an aptly titled book called *Mass Confusion*[2] about it. It seemed that while priests tended to find their way through the texts, give or take the odd addition of their own, the rubrics were effectively meaningless. They were not only ignored by progressive clergy, they were fudged by conservatives in favour of what was done in the older missal: genuflecting as they crossed the sanctuary, elevating the Host above, and not beside, the Chalice, and the like. I wouldn't necessarily criticise these deviations, but it was undeniably a state of lawlessness. I realised that I had almost certainly never witnessed the *Novus Ordo Missæ* celebrated in complete accordance with the rules. But this problem was a mere detail in a much bigger picture.

Apparently something very big and very strange had happened to the Church in the years immediately before my birth in 1971. The institution taken for granted in the novels of Evelyn Waugh or the apologetics of Msgr Ronald Knox, the Church to which both my parents had converted in the 1950s, had suffered some disfiguring calamity. I was used to defending the orthodox Catholic position, as I understood it, against liberal Catholics and non-Catholics, but I was only groping towards what the Church truly, historically, was like: what generations of Catholics had regarded as normality, in the liturgy and in everything else. Notwithstanding the peculiar setting, it was this that I saw in that little meeting room in the West Oxford Community Centre: a long-lost normality.

---

[2]   James Akin, *Mass Confusion: The Do's and Don'ts of Catholic Worship*, 2nd ed. (San Diego: Catholic Answers, 1999).

This I recognised, though without having seen it properly before, rather as I recognised my New Zealand cousin, by a kind of family resemblance to what I did know. It fitted in to the works of Waugh and Knox, to the architecture of old churches and the ethos of old prayers, like a piece of jigsaw puzzle temporarily mislaid under a rug. This Mass was what was needed for the rest to hang together and make sense.

One disorienting aspect of this shock of recognition was that I had always been the most conservative Catholic of my acquaintance, and usually attended the most conservative liturgy available, and yet I had encountered something which represented, if one must think in these terms, a whole additional wing of the spectrum of opinion which I had not properly taken in until that moment. I had been in the centre-ground of the Church all those years, and never realised it! I did not remain there long, however. I found my fellow-worshippers incomparably better-informed and better-read than I was, and with the help of their recommendations I began to read up on the situation, starting, as is usual, with the works of Michael Davies. With this, and continued exposure to the traditional Mass, which I was able to attend almost every Sunday and Holy Day, I stopped being a "conservative" Catholic and became instead a traditional Catholic: a "trad." That is to say, a Catholic who wishes to live in continuity with previous generations.

Asking the wrong question

This implied a programme of the restoration of continuity, the restoration, indeed, of tradition, which seemed Quixotic, even hopeless. Oxford had then, and still has, many well-filled Catholic churches on Sundays, and various programmes of conservativism and progressivism were being undertaken in and around them, by articulate, self-confident, and highly educated people. At the time I made the traditional Mass my usual Sunday option, in 2001, it seemed that Pope John Paul II had stabilised the crisis in the Church, and defeated Communism as well. The Oratorians had arrived just in time to save from destruction the altar-rails at St Aloysius, a formerly Jesuit church, though not the collection of relics. (These, donated to the Jesuits a century earlier, had been destroyed in a crematorium.) I was a member of a Benedictine house of studies in the University,[3] where I saw a stream of conservatively-minded young monks do studies with the Dominicans down the road, in preparation for their ordination. The little group meeting for Masses in the Community Centre was not part of any of this. It seemed that all the clever people, the establishment people, the people with prospects, were part of a theological and liturgical project which took its start from Vatican II, but the Community Centre congregation were not only shut out of the physical churches, but self-excluded from this project. Their mistake, if indeed it was a mistake, was to notice the wrong thing and to ask the wrong question.

What they noticed was the sense that the Mass being celebrated in this little room was an act of *worship.* That is to say, it was a mysterious and awesome communication with the divine, directed wholly towards God, not to the congregation. A service which falls short in doing this also falls short in satisfying the psychological need, and the objective obligation, that humans have to worship God.

The question they seemed to ask was this: what possible justification could the Church's leaders have for doing away with this form of the liturgy, which had been the beating heart of the Church's inner life, her spirituality, for a dozen or more centuries? Ambiguous and slippery as they are, the documents of the Second Vatican Council do not present any such justification, and indeed they were promulgated before the enormity of the liturgical reform was apparent.

They nowhere say, for example, that the entire spirit and atmosphere of the ancient liturgy leads people away from true religion and must by expunged, regardless of the cost. This was indeed the view of a handful of influential liturgical writers of the 1940s and '50s (and since), but this idea is not expressed in Council documents. My conservative Catholic friends, again, would defend the superiority of the reformed Mass, but would never express themselves as strongly as that. And yet, nothing weaker could begin to explain or justify the reform which had actually taken place: the extirpation of Latin, the wholesale rewriting of texts, the

---

[3]   St Benet's Hall. This closed in September 2022.

reversal of the normal direction of worship, the smashing of altars, the dismissal of expert choirs, the destruction of whole libraries of liturgical, spiritual, and theological books, the nuns in short skirts, and wearing makeup, and all the rest. These things were the offspring, not of a desire to tinker and improve, but of a sort of infernal zeal, an *animus delendi.*

The house of cards

It is easy, and it is certainly true, to say that the reform process got out of hand, but at the time, and later, very few people with the power to do so took the trouble to restrict or reverse the excesses. What took place had the sanction, not of magisterial texts, but of ecclesiastical authority. It was the result not of theological debate or legal enactment, but, fundamentally, of raw power. The reasons for this were certainly complex, but the result was an objective fact which has shaped the Church since the 1970s.

What this means is that major planks of Catholic life—liturgical, devotional, catechetical, and disciplinary—lack theological or indeed rational justification. Why were references to sacrifice and grace removed from the liturgical texts? Why was Friday abstinence abolished? What happened to the nice old vestments? Why don't we hear Gregorian chant in Mass any more? What has happened to the Church's teaching on the relationship between husband and wife, on usury, or on the death penalty?

There are no satisfactory answers to these questions. In some cases what happened had actually been explicitly forbidden at the Council or afterwards: the reception of Holy Communion in the hand is the most famous example,[4] but there are many others. Even things which did spring from some official initiative, such as the three-year Lectionary, often did so without any roots in the tradition. They simply presented themselves as things which someone, perhaps Pope Paul VI, perhaps his advisors, thought were a good idea. But is this how things should work? Should even the pope, or, for that matter, an ecumenical council, pluck radical

---

[4]   See the Instruction of the Congregation for Divine Worship *Memoriale Domini* (1969).

ideas out of the air and use them to sweep away a millennium or more of the wisdom of the Church?

When I say these things lack *justification*, it may seem like a criticism of the Church, but in a way it is a defence of her. Catholics do not need to defend what does not derive from the Church's traditions and principles. Were an Eastern Orthodox Christian to point out that a one-hour Eucharistic Fast is ludicrously short; were a Quaker to point out that the disappearance of silence from the liturgy deprived it of its most powerful moments of communion in prayer with the Divine; were a Hindu to point out that an archaic, sacred language has irreplaceable value for preserving theological continuity and imbuing liturgical formulae with dignity; we can say: yes, you are correct, the Church agrees and has always done so.

In many cases we could even quote modern magisterial texts to support this. On Latin, for example, the Congregation for Catholic Education declared in 1980:

> The Council is far from having banned the use of the Latin language. Indeed, it did the contrary. Thus the systematic exclusion of Latin is an abuse no less to be condemned than the systematic desire of some people to use it exclusively. Its sudden and total disappearance will not be without serious pastoral consequences.[5]

Bear in mind the ridicule commonly poured on Latin liturgy in seminaries, and the persecution frequently suffered by priests who dared to celebrate even the reformed Mass in Latin. What the Congregation for Catholic Education is telling us is that the liturgical reality of ordinary Catholics since the Council is premised on an abusive disobedience to the Second Vatican Council, as well as to the tradition of the Church. It is not really the Church who has done this to us, but her wayward children.

I could fill this essay with similar quotations, but they had absolutely no effect when they were published, and are today read by no one but the occasional liturgical historian. They remind me of a scene from a TV series on the German prisoner-of-war camp at Colditz. The war is drawing to

---

[5]   Instruction *Ratio fundamentalis institutionis sacerdotalis.*

a close, but the honourable Commandant is powerless to prevent some atrocity by his superiors. He dictates a strongly-worded letter of protest, and says to his secretary: type it up, date it, and . . . put it in the safe.

Even as records of the Church's teaching, these documents are marred by half-hearted concessions to the progressives. (Why should people who want to use Latin exclusively be condemned? On what documents or traditions would such a condemnation be based?) What they do do is to serve to remind us that even basic principles of the postconciliar liturgical landscape, such as the insistence on the use of the vernacular, have no justification. It is a house of cards.

Progressives and conservatives

The project of restoration, then, seemed fragile, because it existed entirely outside the establishment and its well-resourced institutions, whether progressive or conservative, filled with clever people. On the other hand, for the reasons just outlined it was and is both inevitable and unstoppable.

The progressive project simply leads to apostacy: this was clear long ago. There are progressive theologians and prelates who are comfortable in their well-heated and well-carpeted institutions, with their squashy chairs arranged in circles and plenty of biscuits on little plates. But they preside over a conveyor-belt of young Catholics on their way out of the Church: lay people, religious, and priests. As this process has continued, their institutions are quietly closed down or merged. Selling buildings can produce lots of money, and this pays the bills, but we are approaching the final stages of the process. Ten years from now liberal Catholicism in Britain will be insignificant; in twenty years it will be gone. There will be a regretful notice in the last liberal Catholic periodical, comforting the few readers of its final edition with the thought that the faith journey continues, whether nominally Catholic or not. And we will hear from them no more.

The conservative project is intellectually dishonest. It depends upon pretending that the Church's tradition does not exist. An easy way to see this is by looking at the footnotes or bibliography of conservative books and documents. The references almost never go further back in time than the Second Vatican Council, and Pope John XXIII's famous calling of the Council in 1959, with the exception of Pope Leo XIII's *Rerum Novarum* (1891): a document which anticipates the conservative approach by containing very few references to previous magisterial texts.

I was once asked to review a book which collected together texts on education. It was supposedly a conservative introduction to Catholic thinking on the subject. Why, I asked the editor, did it not include the most important document on education produced before Vatican II, Pope Pius XI's 1929 encyclical, *Divini Illius Magistri*? Oh well, he replied, it would have been nice to have had space for that, but somehow there wasn't. Instead, he had filled the book up with anodyne non-magisterial texts, including the writings of non-Catholics such as C.S. Lewis. Pius XI didn't make the cut because he insisted on an education suffused with Christian values, condemned sex education, and warned against the co-education of boys and girls.

Pius XI's views on education are deeply embarrassing to postconciliar conservatives. The same is true of Pope John XXIII's teaching on family life,[6] Pius XII on the liturgy,[7] or Pius X on modernism:[8] and that is not even to stray beyond the twentieth century. For the conservative project to work, these must be ignored: hidden, like Msgr Gilbey's early morning Mass, behind a thick curtain, and not officially referred to.

What this means, of course, is that for practical purposes the conservatives have created their own substitute magisterium, with the bits they don't like left out. As the case of *Rerum Novarum* indicates, this is not primarily a matter of chronology, but of content. They have applied an ideological filter to the teaching of the Church which they were prepared to accept.

It sounds harsh to say this, of those who fought hard for and suffered much for the Church, especially on "life" issues, and I should emphasise that much of this process, for many of those involved, was a matter of *embarrassment* rather than *denial*. My point remains, however, that as

---

[6] See *Ad Petri Cathedram* (1959), §50.
[7] See *Mediator Dei* (1947).
[8] See *Pascendi Dominici Gregis* (1907).

an intellectual project this was never going to work. Conservatives were the first to emphasise that the Church has a long history, and that the force of her teaching derives from the fact that it is unchanging. This is, however, incompatible with the way they themselves approached a long list of theological issues.

Becoming a traditional Catholic is a process of becoming *docile:* of starting to regard the historic teaching of the Church, not with contempt (the progressive attitude), or with a blind eye (the conservative attitude), but with love, attention, and respect. This attitude can and should be applied to the Second Vatican Council too, but the Council looks very different if viewed in a wider context, and not (as Cardinal Ratzinger memorably put it) as a "super-dogma" which cancels out everything else.[9]

The problem I have just outlined is increasingly acknowledged, especially by the younger generation. The conservative project is not going to peter out like the progressive one; the direction of travel, rather, is a merger with the traditional project. In this process one can begin to see a pathway out of the crisis.

The project of restoration

In his later life, having converted to High Anglicanism, the poet T.S. Eliot understood the crisis of modernity, and the demand the crisis makes of us. He wrote a series of poems called "Choruses from The Rock" which express the barrenness of the post-Christian world: the city with no meaning, the street with no end, "noise without speech, food without taste."

This barrenness can be experienced not only in the secular world, but in aspects of the institutional Church, which has been invaded by the world. Before we can seriously address the task of converting society, there

---

[9] "The truth is that this particular council defined no dogma at all, and deliberately chose to remain on a modest level, as a merely pastoral council; and yet so many treat it as though it had made itself into a sort of super-dogma which takes away the importance of all the rest." From the address by Joseph Cardinal Ratzinger to the Chilean bishops, Santiago, July 13, 1988; full text at https://www.ccwatershed.org/2019/11/07/13-july -1988-josef-cardinal-ratzinger.

must be a restoration of the Church as it appears to society: the physical churches, the schools, the people one finds in them, the liturgy celebrated in them, the books used or sold in them: all the things people encounter when spiritual hunger drives them to seek out the Mystical Body of Christ.

This task of restoration is an enormous one. Rather than be daunted by this, I take comfort from it, because it means that there is something for everyone to do: even those of us with a very deficient Catholic education and limited natural gifts. I may not be a second St Thomas Aquinas, but I can teach my children the old catechisms, and help arrange the odd pilgrimage. In these simple tasks I can be confident that I am doing something pleasing to God, and perhaps even irreplaceable in my little corner of the world. As Eliot expressed it:

> Without delay, without haste
> We would build the beginning and the end of this street.
> We build the meaning:
> A Church for all
> And a job for each
> Each man to his work.

2

What Is the Liturgy For?

There seem to me to be three different views of the liturgy doing the rounds in Catholic discussion today.

The first sees the liturgy primarily in terms of sacramental validity. The purpose of the Mass is the confection of the Blessed Sacrament, so the validity of the rite is the focus of attention. Making the ceremonies attractive in various ways is obvious a good thing, but ultimately if Mass is validly celebrated, the key objective has been attained. The same goes for the ceremonies which accompany the other sacraments. This is for practical purposes the view of many, if not all, conservative Catholics, specifically, those of them who have decided that the liturgy is not a hill upon which they are willing to die.

The second sees the liturgy primarily in terms of community. Sunday Mass is the only event which brings Catholics together with the frequency and intimacy necessary to develop and sustain any sense of fellow-feeling and of human community, and it is this aspect of the celebration that is emphasised. This is the view of many more liberal Catholics.

The third sees the liturgy primarily as a privileged opportunity of making contact with God, even if the participant does not receive Holy Communion.

The peculiar nature of our current situation is that the third view is not so much rejected, as simply incomprehensible, to many Catholics. Why should attendance at a formal church service have a greater potential for putting us in touch with God than private prayer, or some do-it-yourself

Address to the Keys, the Catholic Writers' Guild, November 27, 2019.

liturgy which arises out of our personal needs and creativity, or, for that matter, a country walk? Or, alternatively, what can it add to the reception of the Incarnate God, under the species of bread and wine?

And yet it is the third view which is expressed in the teaching of the Church. The liturgy is the perfect prayer of the Church. The connection with the sacraments is not accidental, but it is not essential either. One can receive Communion outside Mass, and one can attend Mass without receiving. And there is a whole world of liturgical services, the Divine Office, which doesn't normally involve the celebration of any sacrament.

Furthermore, against the second view, the liturgy as an expression of the prayer of the Mystical Body of Christ puts the Mass as community celebration in a somewhat different light. The point of it is not that a geographically defined group of people can establish a social connection with each other through the liturgy, although this is of course both possible and desirable, but that each of us, even if celebrating or attending a service alone in a desert, or in a large and anonymous city church, is connected in a special way to that spiritual community which is the Church—not just the living members who happen to be nearby, but every Catholic of the present and the past, the Saints in heaven and the Holy Souls in purgatory included.

It hardly needs to be stressed that the three conceptions of the liturgy will naturally lead to three very different kinds of liturgy. People talk about liturgical "preferences," but that is a misleading expression. It's not a matter of taste, but of theology. If any of you wanted to bring me over to a different liturgical orientation, you would be unlikely to imagine you could do this simply by showing how nice your preferred liturgies can be. You would, I am sure, present me with theological arguments.

The one partial exception to this is with the traditional liturgy. I am grateful to the Catholic Writers' Guild for this opportunity for presenting my ideas in an extended verbal form. Nevertheless, I believe it would be far more effective in getting across what I would like to communicate to you this evening, if I were able, somehow, to get those of you not already familiar with the traditional Mass to attend it, let's say, three times in fairly quick succession. You needn't wonder about doing this the other way around. You would be hard put to find anyone attending the

Extraordinary Form who hasn't been to scores of Ordinary Form Masses, of all kinds of styles.

One of the ironies of the debate is that those who think of the efficacy of the liturgy, not just the sacraments but the liturgy itself, in the most objective terms, are those who feel most confident in the power of the traditional liturgy to say something to a person who has simply wandered in off the street. Those of us who think that it works whether you feel it working or not, nevertheless like to point to testimonials from people who perceive its effects.

I want to lay that paradox on one side for a moment to consider another one. As I noted above, the view of the liturgy, including the whole public prayer of the Church, as a privileged opportunity for approaching the Throne of Grace, because when the Church prays in this way it is Christ praying in her, this view is the official view, the view set out in official presentations of the teaching of the Church. You will find it in the *Catechism of the Catholic Church*, for example, and it is expressed very clearly in Vatican II's Constitution on the Sacred Liturgy, *Sacrosanctum Concilium* (§7), in the preliminary section dealing with general principles:

> From this it follows that every liturgical celebration, because it is an action of Christ the priest and of His Body which is the Church, is a sacred action surpassing all others; no other action of the Church can equal its efficacy by the same title and to the same degree.

And yet, as I have explained, it is far from clear that this is the guiding principle of either what we might call conservative or liberal approaches to the reformed liturgy; it might be said to be the guiding principle, rather, most of all of these who celebrate and attend the ancient liturgy. In this way, as in a number of others, it is liturgy which has not been influenced by *Sacrosanctum Concilium*, which is most faithful to its principles.

The liturgy as a sacred action

I noted above that the view of the liturgy as a privileged way of getting in touch with God is incomprehensible to many Catholics, so I want to spend some times trying to make it comprehensible.

When *Sacrosanctum Concilium* says that the liturgy is a most *efficacious* thing, what *effects* are at issue? The passage immediately preceding the one I just quoted explains:

> Christ indeed always associates the Church with Himself in this great work wherein God is perfectly glorified and men are sanctified. The Church is His beloved Bride who calls to her Lord, and through Him offers worship to the Eternal Father.
>
> Rightly, then, the liturgy is considered as an exercise of the priestly office of Jesus Christ. In the liturgy the sanctification of the man is signified by signs perceptible to the senses, and is effected in a way which corresponds with each of these signs; in the liturgy the whole public worship is performed by the Mystical Body of Jesus Christ, that is, by the Head and His members.

The efficacy of the liturgy is, therefore, the sanctification of the worshipper, in the context of the perfect worship of God. The goal of the sanctification of the individual does not make sense apart from that context, of course, because the liturgy just *is* an action of worship, and it is because it is directed to God as an act of worship, which is to say as a prayer, that it places the individual in contact with God, and unites him with the action of Christ through and in whom the worship is offered.

There can be no question, then, of any tension between the roles of the liturgy as giving glory to God and as sanctifying the individual. It is only because he is caught up in an act of giving glory to God that the individual worshipper is sanctified.

We may, perhaps, find it easier to understand how the sanctification of the individual Christian occurs in the context of private prayer. In private prayer, on the one hand, by praising God and laying the concerns of the moment before Him, we remind ourselves of our dependence on God and learn to submit ourselves to His will more completely. On the other hand, we open ourselves up to the action of God's grace upon us.

It might seem, from this brief description, that private prayer is most effective when it truly personal, the result of personal initiative and effort. In this it contrasts with liturgical prayer which consists at least in large part of listening to various kinds of texts being read or possibly sung by someone else, and even when we do get to say something, we generally have no choice about what it is. This would suggest that collective prayer has less power to sanctify us than private prayer.

But this is not so. In the first of a series of liturgical conferences in Merton College in Oxford, in I think 2006,[10] Archbishop Nichols of Birmingham, as he then was, spoke rather movingly of his experience of visiting Auschwitz. He was rather traumatised by the visit, and found his way to a chapel there, but was unable, he told us, to find the words to pray. He was rescued from this predicament by the Breviary. It was the words of the Church which come to our assistance when our own words fail. Or as St Paul tells us (Romans 8:26–27):

> Likewise the Spirit also helpeth our infirmities: for we know not what we should pray for as we ought: but the Spirit itself maketh intercession for us with groanings which cannot be uttered. And he that searcheth the hearts knoweth what is the mind of the Spirit, because he maketh intercession for the saints according to the will of God.

If the public prayer of the Church is the prayer of Christ, then the fact that the words used are not ours, and the fact that the voice which utters them may not be ours, does not make this prayer less effective at expressing what we need to express, but actually more so. What we need to express is not the clever things we may think up, but the things which the Holy Spirit would rather we said. Our most necessary petitions are offered up more accurately and more fervently by Christ than by us ourselves. What we need to do above all is to unite ourselves to the perfect prayer of Christ offered ceaselessly to God by the Church. We don't need to worry about the content, so much as the unity of intention which we establish with it. The liturgy is not going to transform us so effectively if we are not present at it, or if we are in present in body, but not in mind. It is in uniting ourselves to it that we offer this prayer as our own.

[10] The CIEL Conference. Archbishop Nichols preached at Vespers.

The Liturgy, the Family, and the Crisis of Modernity

Liturgical participation and understanding

This brings us to the question of liturgical participation, which is the most persistent theme of my book *The Case for Liturgical Restoration*.[11] The question of what participation in the liturgy is, and of what aids it and what impedes it, is the central question about the liturgy, not just of the postconciliar era, but of the previous century, and indeed longer.

On the question of participation, we are faced with another paradox. If you were to ask a sample of Catholics attached to the traditional Mass what concrete features of it they find particularly helpful or attractive, you will hear above all about the use of Latin, celebration *ad orientem*, with the priest facing the apse not the nave, the role of silence in the liturgy, and its complex ceremonial. If you were to ask a sample of well-informed Catholics *not* attached to the traditional Mass what features of the preconciliar liturgy most impeded participation, and thus were most usefully changed by the liturgical reform, you would, I suspect, hear mentioned above all the use of Latin, celebration *ad orientem*, silence, and the complex ceremonial. Those features of the Mass which are apparently the most obstructive of worshippers' participation seem to be the very features which worshippers find most helpful to their participation.

Closely related paradoxes abound in the history of the liturgical reform. Pope Paul VI admitted that the loss of Latin and Gregorian chant would be a great sacrifice for Catholics, and yet it was a sacrifice somehow urgently necessary for Catholics to make. Archbishop Bugnini said that the *Dies Iræ* had to go from the Mass for the Dead, because it was not characterised by Christian hope, and therefore pastorally unhelpful, and in the same breath admitted that it was enormously popular, and, one might infer, a great consolation to the bereaved.[12] Liturgical experts then, as ever, seem to have had a knack of giving people what they do not want, claiming that they do really want it.

[11] Joseph Shaw, ed., *The Case for Liturgical Restoration: Una Voce Studies on the Traditional Latin Mass* (Brooklyn: Angelico Press, 2019).
[12] Annibale Bugnini, *The Reform of the Liturgy 1948–1975*, trans. Matthew J. O'Connell (Collegeville, MN: Liturgical Press, 1990), 773.

In the case of Latin, *ad orientem*, silence, and complex ceremonial, the resolution of the paradox is relatively simple. The confusion derives from two different conceptions of liturgical participation. The reformers' conception of participation is based on comprehension. If you can't understand it, they reasoned, you could not participate in it. If you can't see a ceremony because the priest has his back to you, if you can't hear a prayer because it is being said silently, if you can't understand it because it is in a language you do not know, or if you can't grasp the meaning of a ceremony or prayer because it is complex and obscure, then it is impossible for you to participate effectively in what is going on.

This appears so obvious to many people that they do not feel it necessary to give arguments for this view. The reformers themselves were encouraged in this by the fact that it is agreed by everyone that understanding a text or knowing what is going on in a ceremony is a powerful aid to participation, and long ago there developed a whole industry dedicated to translating or paraphrasing and explaining liturgical texts and ceremonies, in order to aid people in their participation at Mass. This wasn't just a product of the Liturgical Movement in the late nineteenth and early twentieth centuries, but can be traced back to the opportunity presented by the invention of the printing press and increasing literacy rates. As soon as there is a market for popular Catholic books, there are popular books explaining the Mass.

However, saying that understanding texts and ceremonies aids participation is not the same as saying that it is necessary for participation. Still less is it to say that participation is aided by changing prayers and ceremonies to make them easier to understand.

We certainly wouldn't make the mistake of thinking that these different things were equivalent in relation to any other work of art. A poem or a painting can engage us powerfully without us knowing very clearly what it is about. An explanation of it may well enhance our participation in it, but we would not be inclined to say, of those who did not have the benefit of such an explanation, that they were incapable of real participation in, say, William Blake's poem *Jerusalem*, or the Wilton Diptych. At any rate, if we did say such a thing, it would be unbearably priggish.

This phenomenon is not limited to classical works of art. Modern art, both high art and popular art, seems to cluster in the borderlands of the comprehensible, even when it doesn't cross over completely to the realm of the unintelligible. If you don't believe me, Google a few pop song lyrics. In many cases, they are tantamount to nonsense verse. It does not follow that they lack power, like the daddy of all nonsense verse, Lewis Carrol's *Jabberwocky*. Alice spoke for many addle-brained music fans when she said that she didn't understand it, and yet it filled her mind with ideas.[13]

Or as another Nichols expressed this, this time the Dominican Fr Aidan: "The notion that the more intelligible the sign, the more effectively it will enter the lives of the faithful is implausible to the sociological imagination. . . . a certain opacity is essential to symbolic action in the sociologists' account."[14]

Why might this be? It's not so difficult to see. An opaque symbol may stick in the memory and stimulate the imagination more than a clear one, and it can more easily bear multiple and profound meanings. A symbol which conveys something too deep for words is not a symbol whose meaning can be explained in a couple of sentences.

These realities were certainly not lost on the authors of Scripture. Here we find a collection of stories, sayings, and other texts which are complex and frequently opaque. If many confusing passages can be clarified with a little exegesis, other passages, which appear reasonably clear at first glance, can on closer inspection reveal unexpected complexity. This is not exactly a problem: it is simply a reflection of the richness of the text. Our participation in God's Word would not be improved by the substitution of a simplified, children's version of the text. Our Lord spoke in parables not to confuse people or limit the impact of his preaching, but to reach the sincere seeker after truth who was prepared to ponder his words. The most baffling of stories, like Jacob wrestling with God,[15] can be the objects of the most powerful religious art and make a home for themselves

---

[13]   Lewis Carroll, *Alice in Wonderland*, first published in 1865.
[14]   Aidan Nichols, *Looking at the Liturgy: A Critical View of Its Contemporary Form* (San Francisco: Ignatius Press, 1996), 61.
[15]   Gen 32:22–32.

in readers' imaginative lives. Some things, again, can be understood by those who cannot articulate their understanding. Other things can rest in our memory before being activated, like an unexploded bomb, perhaps decades later, by some chance event or conversation. We should not expect, or even desire, to recover the full meaning of a passage of Scripture, without leaving anything behind, as we might squeeze a sponge dry. We can rather look forward to seeing another aspect of it when we return to meditate upon it years later.

Liturgical participation and obscurity

I don't expect many people to disagree with what I have said about Scripture and art, but some may well dispute the parallel with the liturgy. If liturgical texts are said in Latin, and silently, or if ceremonies are performed with those involved standing with their backs to the nave, these seem to make things obscure quite unnecessarily. What good is served, one might ask, by deliberately or accidentally hiding a text or a ceremony, which presumably has some meaning and therefore value?

What value, indeed, is there in veiling something? What does it mean to veil the tabernacle, for example? The veiling of the tabernacle, as of the ciborium within it, is a vivid symbolic expression of the holiness of what it contains. The use of a liturgical language distinct from the language of everyday life is an equally powerful symbol of the distinctive, set-apart nature of the liturgy, and this was no doubt why a Latin clearly distinct from that of the street or of political debate was employed for the earliest Latin liturgy. The praying of the central texts of the Mass, the Canon, silently, sets this apart as still more significant and worthy of awe. The performance of ceremonies facing the apse, and not the people, and the saying of the priestly prayers silently, shows us very concretely that these ceremonies and prayers are not being offered to us, in the congregation, but to God.

Earlier I mentioned symbols whose meaning is obscure. One may also talk about the symbol of obscurity, for want of a better word, itself: of silence, of hiddenness, and so on. This is a symbol with a very special power. Any fair-minded person attending the ancient Mass must agree that this particular symbol gets its message across. Latin marks off the time during which the liturgy takes place, the whole is directed towards the Crucifix and the East, and after the Preface and Sanctus the church descends into an extraordinary silence.

> Anyone who has experienced a church united in the silent praying of the Canon will know what a really *filled* silence is. It is at once a loud and penetrating cry to God and a Spirit-filled act of prayer. Here everyone does pray the Canon together, albeit in a bond with the special task of the priestly ministry. Here everyone is united, laid hold of by Christ, and led by the Holy Spirit into that common prayer to the Father which is the true sacrifice—the love that reconciles and unites God and the world.[16]

Thus, Joseph Ratzinger, in *The Spirit of the Liturgy*.

In short, obscurity, as a symbol, *works*. This has been noticed by all sorts of people. I like to quote Pope John Paul II, who noted back in 1980 of the Latin of the Mass that "through its dignified character [it] elicited a profound sense of the Eucharistic Mystery."[17] I could equally quote Pope Francis, who, talking about the liturgies of the Eastern Churches, said that in comparison with them, "we have lost some of the sense of adoration."[18] I don't need to labour the point. When Pope Benedict XVI referred to the "sacrality which attracts many people to the former usage,"[19] he was just stating the obvious. Some people like the traditional Mass, and they like it because it conveys very effectively a sense of the sacred.

Yes, the use of silence, Latin, *ad orientem*, and complex ceremonial conveys with perfect clarity the sacred character of what is being done. It does so, moreover, not as a self-conscious *messenger*, but as a *witness*. You

---

[16] Joseph Ratzinger, *The Spirit of the Liturgy*, trans. John Saward (San Francisco: Ignatius Press, 2000), 215–16.

[17] John Paul II, Apostolic Letter *Dominicae Cenae* (1980), §10.

[18] Apostolic Journey to Rio De Janeiro on the Occasion of the XXVIII World Youth Day: Press Conference of Pope Francis during the return flight, Sunday, July 28, 2013.

[19] Letter *Con Grande Fiducia* (2007), accompanying *Summorum Pontificum*.

could put up a big neon sign above the altar which flashed up the words "This is sacred," and it would *not* convincingly convey the message that this is sacred. Instead, we know that what is going on is sacred in character because we can see that those involved regard the liturgy as something which *merits* the use of a sacred language, complex ceremonial, and silence, and regard it as something which, because it is directed to God, should be done facing East, the direction in which everyone else is facing, and from which we expect Christ to return in glory.

To look at another aspect of the liturgy, many volumes have been filled on the meaning of truly obscure liturgical symbols, such as the addition of a small amount of water to the wine at the Offertory, to use an example also found in the reformed Mass, or the dropping of a small portion of the consecrated host into the chalice before Communion. This kind of thing is, at least to me, very interesting, and I recommend those numerous volumes to those who wish to deepen their appreciation of the liturgy. Evidently, however, it is not the meaning of the ceremonies at that granular level of detail which convinces the onlooker that something stupendous is taking place. It is rather the higher-level fact that this is a rite with many complex and intriguing details. That latter fact is obvious even to a first-time participant, and its meaning is not obscure, it is clear. It gives witness to the *seriousness*, the *solemnity*, the *richness*, and the *profundity* of what is going on.

It is interesting that those particular examples were maintained in the *Novus Ordo Missæ*, while so many other little ceremonies were removed: the canonical fingers, the double genuflection at the consecration, multiple signs of the cross made over the gifts, the ringing of the bell at various points, the ritualized Kiss of Peace, and so on. These, for my money, are considerably easier to understand than the first two examples, which were presumably kept primarily because of their antiquity. What they all contribute to, however, is the richness of the rite. The more you look into it, the more there is to see, and the more there is to discover about what you do see. It is, in fact, an inexhaustible field of study. The ancient liturgy possesses irreducible complexity: a complexity which does not disappear once you get to a certain level of detail.

Liturgical comprehensibility

For all that I have said, the question of intelligibility, it may be said, remains. Shouldn't we agree with St Paul, and not "rather speak five words with my understanding, that I may instruct others also, than ten thousand words in a tongue" (1 Cor 14:19)? Having said that liturgical prayer is prayer in the Spirit, the comparison may seem apt. The liturgical texts of the ancient missal and other books contain many things in them which would instruct and edify the faithful. The truth of this is particularly obvious with relation to the Scripture readings, but it covers everything. If the texts were delivered aloud, and in the congregation's mother tongue, the people would gain more from them, more directly, than hearing them in Latin, or simply being present when they are recited inaudibly.

This may seem obvious, despite what I have said up to now. And yet the difficulties with this in practice are so numerous, I am going to have to give you a numbered list, in order to keep track of them.

First, whose mother tongue? Not everyone, alas, has the privilege of English as a native language. It is not just a few Catholics who cannot regularly access the liturgy of the Western Church in their mother tongue, but tens of millions. Instead, they are most often obliged to hear Mass celebrated in the language of a former or actual colonial power, be that English, French, Spanish, or modernised Mandarin Chinese. For many, including many Cantonese speakers, this is no more comprehensible than Latin. For all, the use of such languages can give the liturgy a very unfortunate political colouring.

Second, how good is the translation, and how often should it be revised? For some languages—I was reading recently about the case of Scottish Gaelic—the tiny group of people capable of producing a translation are also the only ones who would be capable of giving a translation considered criticism. This isn't true only of tiny language-groups, it's true of any language which does not have a well-developed educated Catholic elite. But these linguistic communities may be fortunate, compared with speakers of major European languages, who have to endure interminable arguments about how *orate fratres*, *ineffabile*, or *pro multis* are best rendered in their languages.

Third, many liturgical texts need to be sung. Sometimes this works out decently with translations, and sometimes it does not. No one who appreciates the Gregorian chant tradition, however, would view with indifference the disappearance of the tradition of singing the original texts to the original melodies. Certain Pope Paul VI did not. He warned religious superiors who wished, in the mid-sixties, to have the Office in the vernacular:

> In present conditions, what words or melodies could replace the forms of Catholic devotion which you have used until now? You should reflect and carefully consider whether things would not be worse, should this fine inheritance be discarded. It is to be feared that the choral office would turn into a mere bland recitation, suffering from poverty and begetting weariness, as you yourselves would perhaps be the first to experience.[20]

Fourth, in the Extraordinary Form the Roman Canon is said silently (except for a couple of phrases), and all in Latin. In the Ordinary Form this forms the longest of the Eucharistic Prayers, which must be said aloud. If said in Latin, its length and complexity is particularly noticeable, and there is an option to shorten it by leaving out a substantial section. The designers of the Ordinary Form thought that it was impractical to use the Roman Canon in the Ordinary Form, because of its length and complexity, and it was retained only at the insistence of Paul VI.[21] One can see the reformers' point. The Roman Canon works, in the Extraordinary Form, because it is not experienced by the congregation as a long and dense block of text, but as a period of silence.

The point here is that one cannot simply say that a given rite ought to be said out loud and in the vernacular. In order to have a liturgy which is out loud and in the vernacular, and which actually works, texts must not only be translated, but may have to be adapted in all sorts of ways.

These difficulties with the vernacular liturgy can also be expressed as advantages of the ancient Latin liturgy. It is, on my first point, no one's

---

[20] Letter *Sacrificium Laudis* (1966).
[21] Bugnini, *Reform of the Liturgy*, 450.

mother tongue, and the tongue of no modern colonial power, but in Pope John XXIII's phrase, "equally friendly to all."[22] On the second and third points, it expresses universality and continuity, not only with the immediate past, but with the Church of the age of the Fathers. On the third point, it can be sung to the ancient chant melodies, including those of the Epistle and Gospel, which are themselves works of art.

This is not to deny the advantages of a vernacular liturgy. What I am doing here is simply pointing out that these advantages do not come without a cost. This is not the moment in the history of the liturgy where we are obliged to choose between a vernacular liturgy—at least, one in English—and a Latin liturgy. This is the moment, rather, for me to try to make once more comprehensible the value of the ancient Latin liturgy experienced by Catholics for fifteen or so centuries, when this value is far from clear to many.

It is clear enough that there are advantages to being able to understand the Mass without a special mental effort. This argument should not, however, be exaggerated. If someone wants to understand the traditional Mass, there is no shortage of books, leaflets, and smart-phone apps to make this possible. What, exactly, is the barrier to understanding presented by a liturgy in Latin? It exists, but it is low. No one who really wants to know what is being said is going to find it difficult to find out.

Conclusion

I have my views about the future of the Catholic liturgy, but to reiterate the point I have just made, I don't expect everyone to agree with me, and I certainly don't have the power to impose my views on anyone else. What we are beginning to see, particularly in England and Wales, but increasingly in the United States and in other countries, is a recognition that the traditional Mass is here to stay, that it has a contribution to make to the life of the Church, but that, equally, it draws only a tiny fraction of Catholic Mass-goers.

---

[22] John XXIII, Apostolic Constitution *Verterum Sapientia* (1962).

Its very existence annoys some people—those of the older generation, perhaps, who staked their careers and theological self-understanding on the claim that the old stuff was all nonsense. It turns out, at the fiftieth anniversary of the worldwide celebration of Pope Paul's *Novus Ordo Missæ*, that things are a bit more complicated than they seemed back in the 1960s. This is so in the Church, as it is in many aspects of life.

3

Understanding the History of the Liturgy

In this presentation I would like to offer some reflections on the concept of tradition, in the context of the liturgy.

In the Introduction (part 1), I will explain the notion of the "givenness" of the liturgy, as set out in Pope Benedict's *The Spirit of the Liturgy*, and then examine the objection that the reality of liturgical change undermines the idea that we are called on to be faithful to an objective liturgy.

For the bulk of this presentation, I will be engaged in explaining how liturgical changes can come about even when those involved believe themselves to be bound to pass on the liturgy as they found it faithfully. I will start this discussion (in part 2) by establishing the necessity of respect for tradition, and continue (in part 3) with an examination of how changes can occur. I will follow this with a brief response to an objection based on the liturgical developments of the earliest centuries (part 4).

This will be followed (in part 5) by a consideration of whether Vatican II's Constitution on the Sacred Liturgy, *Sacrosanctum Concilium*, can be said to uphold, or to undermine, the principle of respect for liturgical tradition, and in what sense.

The concept of tradition, and its authority, is an enormous one, and closely related debates are today taking place in the liturgy, in theology, and in canon law: it is, indeed, one of the fundamental problems of our day. In this context I should emphasise the modesty of my project in this chapter, which is just to point to some resources, specific to the history

Presented to the Paix Liturgique Conference, Rome, October 23, 2020, under the title "The Concept of Tradition."

of the liturgy, which can help us untangle a specific problem in the debate about the liturgy. This may or not be helpful in the wider debate, but it certainly doesn't settle the wider question.

1. *Introduction*

The notion of respect for tradition was taken up by Joseph Ratzinger, before his election as Pope Benedict XVI, in his discussion of the "givenness" of the liturgy, or rather, of how the liturgy *ought* to have the character of something given, handed on to us and carefully preserved, and not the character of something manufactured by us and for us.

In the opening chapter of *The Spirit of the Liturgy*[23] Ratzinger draws attention to the request of Moses to Pharaoh in the Book of Exodus. This is not that the Hebrews be given a fairer deal over their brick-making work, nor that they be allowed to emigrate—these possibilities are not even mentioned. What Moses asks Pharaoh is that the Hebrews be allowed to go into the desert to worship God, in the way that God will reveal to them.[24] And in the end this is what happens. God reveals in great detail how they are to worship him, and they carry these instructions out to the letter.

Before this is completed, however, there is also an experiment in a spontaneous liturgy that comes from the community. It does not end well. As Ratzinger wrote:

> The worship of the golden calf is a self-generated cult. . . . Worship becomes a feast that the community gives itself, a festival of self-af-firmation. Instead of being worship of God, it becomes a circle closed in on itself: eating, drinking, and making merry. The dance around the golden calf is an image of this self-seeking worship. It is a kind of banal self-gratification. The narrative of the golden calf is an image of this self-initiated and self-seeking worship. Ultimately, it is no longer concerned with God but giving oneself a nice little alternative world, manufactured from one's own resources. Then liturgy really becomes

[23] Ratzinger, *Spirit of the Liturgy*, 13–23.
[24] Ratzinger, 15.

pointless, just fooling around. Or still worse it becomes an apostasy from the living God, an apostasy in sacral disguise.[25]

The puzzle which I want to address today is this. We may talk about the "given," the "objective tradition," in the liturgy, but we know that the liturgy has developed over the centuries. It was not given to us whole and entire from a mountain wreathed in smoke, as the Book of Exodus describes the giving of the liturgy of ancient Israel. It was, instead, created piece by piece by human beings, with the exception of a modest core of dominical institution. That core is not what is in dispute when we talk about liturgical reform. Almost every element of the liturgy which *is* in dispute, which has been affected by the 1960s reform, which the traditional movement clings to, and which the "reform of the reform" people perhaps would like to restore, has a date attached to it. The ancient Sunday Gospel cycle was present in the seventh century, but other aspects of the ancient Lectionary continued to develop until the ninth century. The traditional method of receiving Holy Communion was enforced universally in the Latin Church in the ninth century. The Roman Canon seems to date from the fourth century. Other important developments took place in the twelfth century. Any history of the liturgy will furnish many more examples.

This grounds an objection to the attitude of supporters of the traditional liturgy, and to the Ratzingerian argument just noted, as follows. We traditionalists want to treat the missal of 1960, or possibly an earlier edition, as representing this *something* which is given to us: the objective tradition, as it has been handed down to us. However, the objector will point out that these missals are nothing more than iterations of a constantly evolving body of rites. Surely, the objector will continue, the 1960s generation had as much a right to adapt these rites to the needs of their own day as earlier liturgical innovators such as St Francis of Assisi, Pope St Gregory the Great, or the popes of the fourth century did? After all, it is of the nature of liturgical tradition to develop over time.

[25] Ratzinger, 23.

In response to this objection there are some arguments which, I believe, are not going to be adequate to the task in hand.

Thus, we could point out that the reforms of the 1960s were unprecedented in a number of ways. This is certainly true, but it needs to be explained why this particular kind of reform was problematic, if it was, and why.

One way of specifying exactly what the problem is would be to say it is a matter of degree: the degree to which things changed in a short period of time. Now it is true that the *pace of change* is important in ways which liturgical progressives tend to ignore, because of the psychological significance of habits of devotion. I do not want to say, however, that if the 1960s reform was a rupture in the tradition, the same reform would not have been a rupture if had taken place in slow-motion. The gap between the liturgical and theological principles underlying the old and new liturgies would still be problematic.

So the second way of specifying the problem would be to focus on those principles. Let us imagine, then, a possible reform of the 1960 missal more to our taste: if the reformers, led by someone perhaps like Fr Louis Bouyer, had been cleverer, more sensitive, and more learned, and if the historical, psychological, and sociological scholarship of that era was not about to be overtaken so completely by new discoveries and intellectual fashions. Certainly, such a reform would have been less open to criticism, even if the changes had been equally extensive.

If it had been, however, *equally extensive*, then this reform would still have destroyed the sense of the liturgy as a given. Supposing that the principles underlying it were indeed preserved, it is surely the case that the same principles could be manifested in more than one liturgical rite. With a wide-ranging change, a Bouyer-type reform would have changed the liturgy, if not in its principles, then *as liturgy*. If you take the liturgy of your fathers and grandfathers and re-write it comprehensively, then you are not treating it as a given. This failure to treat it as a given will then, even with a much better reform, lead to many of the problems which we have seen with the Bugnini reform. If the pope doesn't treat the liturgy as a given, you can't expect priests charged with its celebration, or the faithful in the pews, to respect it as a given, either.

The Liturgy, the Family, and the Crisis of Modernity

To put the problem another way, imagine a proposal to pass on to our children a version of the Bible which contains only the best bits of the canon of Scripture, as selected by a panel of theologians, a really excellent panel of theologians. This would be wrong—we would all agree—because the Bible is a source of revelation. Putting the theologians in charge of the Bible is putting the cart before the horse: it is the Bible which should be in charge of the theologians. In a lesser, but still analogous way, the liturgy, while not inspired, is a theological source. It is not for the liturgical theologians, even the best ones available, to sit in judgement upon it. What *they* do not understand or appreciate, our children or grandchildren may find helpful, and indeed may one day find more helpful than things which excited a set of long-dead experts.

The idea of the liturgy as a theological source is closely connected with the Ratzingerian argument about the liturgy as a given, and as something which, having developed under the hand of providence, conveys to us God's will about how He wishes to be worshipped. None of these ideas is really compatible with a large-scale, planned reform.

I would add that it also seems dangerous to try to defend the idea of the givenness of the liturgy as a matter of *degree*: if we were to say that we are allowed to change, for example, up to 5 percent of the liturgy every twenty years, and still say we are treating it as a given. If our predecessors in the Faith had taken some such view as that, every line of text and every rubric could have been replaced every 400 years, and over the very long periods of time which are the currency of the history of the Church, it would not so much be a liturgical tradition at all, but something more like a game of Chinese whispers.

And yet, objectors will say, the liturgy *has* changed: we have the manuscript evidence to prove it. This being so, our predecessors in the Faith cannot have had such a strict idea of what fidelity to the tradition meant, and neither should we. This, indeed, is the puzzle I want to address in the rest of this chapter.

To resolve this puzzle it will be necessary to consider not what has been going on over the last century, but what was going on in the centuries before that. We need to come to appreciate, and indeed to assimilate, *a pre-modern understanding of what adhering to a tradition means.* To come to see this, allow me to take a short detour.

2. *The preservation of an oral tradition*

As a father of children, I take a keen interest in folk tales, and I have come to make a sharp distinction between stories which emerged from the genuine folk tradition, and those which merely ape it: the latter category comprising the fairy stories of Hans Christian Anderson, Oscar Wilde, and the like, which are mere pastiche imitations of the genuine folk tradition.

Now, we may ask, were the folk storytellers more creative, or did they have greater psychological insight, than the likes of Hans Anderson? Not at all. They were not the authors of these stories, but merely passed them on. Indeed, this reality deeply impressed itself on the collectors of these stories, such as the famous Brothers Grimm in Germany. The traditional story-tellers were extremely anxious to get all the details right, and to correct any errors as they went along. The keynote of the folk tale tradition is not *creativity*, but *fidelity*.

But, of course, by the time they came to be written down, these stories had *evolved over time.* We know this because different versions of what are clearly the same story were recorded by modern folklorists in different places, and some of them bear a striking resemblance to stories which made their way into written form in twelfth century Scandinavia, or even to stories from ancient Greece. This tells us two things: first, that the fidelity to tradition of these storytellers was sufficient to maintain these similarities over the course, not just of a few generations, but over *millennia*; and, secondly, that this fidelity was not absolutely successful in resisting change.

It is only the first of these facts which should surprise us. Of course variations, different emphases, and subtle updatings, will creep into a story which is passed from story-teller to story-teller over vast periods of time. How could they not? But it is only possible to talk of a *story* being passed on, a single, recognisable *story*, if each link in the chain is doing his utmost to preserve it. If the folk story-tellers had decided at some point that, well, evolution of their stories is inevitable, and come to that no bad thing, and why not make a few changes to make it more meaningful for the present generation?; or if they had adopted the practice of the ancient Greek dramatists and many others over the centuries, who freely improvised on themes from the folk tradition; then there simply would have been no folk tradition. These venerable stories, which speak to us from the very roots of European culture, would simply not have been passed on.

The point of this little detour is to emphasise three things. First, the pre-modern concept of fidelity to tradition, in the sense that one is not, really, free to change even in small ways what has been passed on to one, is a perfectly familiar idea, and indeed a fundamental aspect of pre-modern culture. Second, this attitude does not in actual fact prevent all change, because that would be impossible. Third, this attitude nevertheless successfully maintains the continuity of a tradition, even over immense periods of time.

We may usefully contrast the pre-modern conception of tradition with a modern one. Liturgists who regard themselves as conservatives, as well as progressives, often say, in effect: I will pass on to the future those parts of what I have been given *which I choose.* After a few generations of such choices, subject to changing intellectual fashions, continuity will have worn extremely thin. The pre-modern conception is: I will pass on to the future the whole of what I have been given, insofar as it is in my power to do so: both what I understand and appreciate, and also things I do not understand fully, things which offend the aesthetic fashions of my time, and things which touch painfully the favourite sins of my generation.

Shifting the focus back to the case of the Latin liturgical tradition, only persistent fidelity makes it possible, over the very long term, for successive generations of Catholics to be able to say: we worship as our predecessors in the Faith worshiped, in an unbroken tradition going back to the apostles. It is this, in turn, which gives plausibility to the linked ideas: that the liturgical tradition is a means by which God communicates to us His will about how He should be worshipped; that it is a theological source; and that it is objective, a "given."

3. *Change and preservation in the liturgy*

What I have just said needs important qualification. The liturgical tradition is vastly more complex than an oral storytelling tradition, and changes at different levels do not all have the same significance. Most obviously, changes to the sanctoral cycle are not an anomaly within this tradition, but a normal process, and one might say the same about feasts of devotion. On the other hand, with a written tradition, fidelity can be more punctilious, and recovery from mere errors is possible, by comparing liturgical books preserved in different places.

What I hope I have, nevertheless, begun to suggest, is that the idea of strict fidelity to tradition is not simply a paranoid reaction by a small group of modern Catholics unable to cope with modernity; nor is it a special feature of the embattled Church of the Tridentine era, following the more free-wheeling Middle Ages. Both of these claims are commonly made by liturgical progressives, and they are mistaken because they involve the very problem, of naïve anachronism, of which they accuse their opponents: they project back into the pre-modern past a modern conception of what respect for tradition entails. A pre-modern conception is in fact the necessary condition for a tradition of this kind.

Now, even if I have given this conception of tradition some plausibility, it faces a considerable challenge, namely, the changes which the liturgical tradition has evidently undergone from antiquity to the time of Trent, when, we are to suppose, this traditional attitude of fidelity to tradition was to be found in its full vigour. To address this challenge, you will be relieved to know that I do not propose to go in detail through the entire history of the liturgy. I am just going to make some observations about the nature of historical liturgical changes in order to give some general idea of how this objection might be addressed.

The key issue is: How did changes to the liturgy come about in the pre-modern era, and what drove them? We can distinguish a number of different kinds of, or motives for, change. To keep things simple, I will address four kinds of change: elaborating changes, changes which respond to new needs, borrowing changes, and abbreviating changes.

3.1. *Elaborating changes*

There are many examples of liturgical developments which tend to expand, elaborate, and lengthen the rites. One would be the multiple coped cantors of the Gallican rites. Another is the story told by chant historians, that the extemporising of singers made the Alleluia *jubilus* of such great length that in time the happy thought occurred to someone that a suitable psalm verse could be sung to the melody thus created. Sequences were also added on certain days to follow the Alleluia. The point of such developments is evidently to maximise the solemnity of the liturgy, to give it the greatest possible glory, especially when liturgical resources such as time and expert singers are relatively plentiful.

The significance of these changes for the liturgical experience of the faithful is real enough. In some cases, such as of the coped cantors, when the tide of liturgical resources begins to ebb, they disappear again, but in other cases, such as the Alleluia verse, they remain.

My question is whether such developments constitute an innovation or a rupture in the liturgical tradition. The answer is "no." Those behind these developments were merely taking advantage of the freedom which was at the time understood to exist for adding such things. Just as today we can field two torch-bearers or four in a *Missa Solemnis*, and we can sing a suitable motet after the Offertory antiphon, so, at the critical juncture in the past, adding, subtracting, or developing the number of coped cantors or psalm verses after the Alleluia was one of the things one could do, and only after the consistent and prolonged use of a certain practice did it come to be regarded as normative, and found its way into the missal text.

What I have just described is the development of custom, a process extremely familiar to medieval historians. Customs with normative force, such as the right to hold a market in a certain village on a certain day, the right to receive a certain rent for a certain field, or the right to appeal to a certain judge in a certain kind of legal case, develop out of repeated and accepted practice over time. Such phenomena are not indications that customary practices were not regarded as binding, but the very opposite.

This is something which critics of the traditionalist position in today's debates sometimes appear not to understand. A regular practice is not regarded as a binding custom at first, but eventually it is. At no point need there be error or deception about the origin of the practice, nor is there any make-believe about the nature of customary obligation. The notion of customary obligation retains a serious role today, in international law:

it's not a concept restricted to illiterate medieval peasants. One can reject the idea that custom makes law, but no one is entitled to claim that the idea is not well understood and widely accepted.

In the context of the history of the liturgy, it is essential to understand that Catholics came to feel themselves under an obligation to continue to do what had become the regular practice, *even though* their predecessors had not felt themselves under such an obligation. Above all, we must accept the fact that both the later and the earlier generation's assessment of the situation made perfect sense, without appealing to anyone labouring under historical misunderstandings. That is simply how customary obligations come into being.

Consider some other examples. The exorcisms preliminary to baptism, and the Preparatory Prayers at Mass, are still sometimes described as not part of "baptism proper" or "Mass proper." They are, indeed, preliminaries. Liturgical historians tell us that in origin they were separated from the main rite in time or place: the exorcisms took place at the Scrutinies which prepared candidates for Baptism, and the Preparatory Prayers were said in the Sacristy before Mass, or during the procession to the altar. For a period of time they did not enjoy customary force; then perhaps they did, but their being joined to the main rite itself was just a matter of convenience, as a priest today might say the Angelus before a Mass celebrated at noon. Eventually, the original rite and these preliminaries came to be seen as a single unit, because they had been in practice treated as such for a long period of time, and for this reason it came to be understood that to discard the preliminary rites would be contrary to a proper fidelity to the liturgical tradition.

To summarise my argument at this point, as illustrated by the process I have just described: first, there is nothing remotely mysterious about this as a historical process; second, at no point did anyone contravene the obligation of fidelity to tradition; and third, at no point was anyone guided by any kind of error. I'm not saying that infidelities and historical misunderstandings never took place in the history of the liturgy: it would be surprising if they did not. I am just saying that the development of the liturgy does not depend upon them.

What this means is that a liturgical rite could develop considerably over a period of, say, ten generations, without a single one of those generations being unfaithful to tradition. It seems a paradox: the thing changes without anyone changing it. But actually it is a perfectly simple and familiar historical process.

3.2. *New liturgical needs*

A major example of new liturgical needs would be the rise of the European monarchies, who needed a suitable ceremony of installation. Although these have almost completely disappeared from use today, the coronation liturgies which developed in the Middle Ages are extremely impressive, and their appearance on the liturgical scene does look at first glance like a pre-modern precedent for the deliberate creation, and not the mere passing on, of liturgy.

However, even here we do not really get away from the givenness of the tradition, because these ceremonies were not created from whole cloth. They took their start from secular ceremonies which had from time immemorial been practiced among the peoples at issue, which were brought into church and began to be presided over, to a greater or lesser extent, by the clergy. Added to these tribal ceremonies were elements derived from the Old Testament, above all the concept of anointing kings, as Saul and David were anointed by the prophet Samuel, a tradition which had been preserved in the anointings used in sacramental rites.

We must look at this, once again, from the point of view of the people involved at the time. St Columba of Iona, according to his biographer,[26] anointed the King of the Scots. What that means is that he was summoned to take part in a traditional ceremony of some kind, to add to it his own approbation and blessing. He did so in the appropriate form indicated in the Old Testament, which had its parallel in a number of well-established liturgical rites in use in his own day. We may say that this was an innovation, but it was a deeply traditional one. It did not merely respect tradition, but actually obeyed it.

[26] Adamnan, *The Life of St Columba.*

Another reason why St Columba cannot be accused of engaging in liturgical innovation is that only in the most attenuated sense was he engaging in liturgy at all. He was just giving a blessing, in a way which seemed appropriate to the occasion. Only with the passing of the centuries would the practices surrounding the coronation of monarchs begin to be regarded as normative, and set out in liturgical books, as I explained in the preceding section.

Indeed, we should free ourselves from our clear-cut distinctions between what is strictly liturgical and what is not, if we wish to enter into the thinking of our pre-modern predecessors in the Faith. A less cut and dried categorisation of the rites makes it easier to understand how what looks like a plainly non-liturgical event, such as the proclamation of a new king, or, come to that, an early medieval wedding ceremony, can over time simply segue into a liturgical rite, taking place in church and under the auspices of the clergy. In the last century we can something similar happening, as indeed Jungmann himself notes, with the Leonine Prayers coming to be seen as a liturgical rite which continues Low Mass,[27] though modern liturgists will no doubt long continue to insist that these constitute a mere paraliturgical appendage to the liturgy properly so-called.

3.3. *Borrowing from other traditions*

A third category of changes are cases of one liturgical tradition borrowing from another. This happened for more than one reason.

In the early ninth century the Frankish Church under Charlemagne adopted much of the Roman rite because the Frankish books were thought to have been corrupted by errors. In the following century the Roman liturgy received a dose of non-Roman material from a non-Roman source because, this time, it was the Roman books which were, as it was thought, in need of correction.

---

[27] Josef Jungmann, *The Mass of the Roman Rite: Its Origins and Development ("Missarum Sollemnia")*, trans. Francis A. Brunner (Notre Dame, IN: Christian Classics, 2012), 2:459.

Sufficient justification for borrowing specific ceremonies or texts could be found, moreover, not only in deficiencies of the existing books, but in the excellence and prestige of what is being borrowed. Jungmann tells us that the Kyrie was adopted from Eastern rites into the Roman liturgy in the fifth century.[28] The four Sequences which found their way into the Roman rite from Gallican sources did so, one might say, on their merits. Again, a tradition can borrow from itself, as when the Gloria, originally specific to Christmas, spread to other parts of the Church's year.

The most comprehensive cases of borrowing arise, naturally enough, when the borrower is starting with a blank slate. This doesn't happen very often, but one such occasion was when St Augustine of Canterbury had to decide what liturgical forms to use in the mission-field of England at the end of the sixth century. Pope Gregory the Great's famous advice was to select whatever he thought best from what he had seen.[29] In this case, St Augustine is not being advised to compose a new liturgy, but to borrow one, from the best available sources.

Similarly, the *Hadrianum Sacramentary*'s journey from Rome to the court of Charlemagne, and the *Romano-Germanic Pontifical*'s later voyage from Metz to Rome, referred to above, were historically momentous for the development of the liturgy, but were not intended to be instruments of *change as such* by the people involved at the time. They were being as faithful as possible to the tradition: to their own, local tradition, where they could, and failing that, to the tradition with the greatest possible antiquity and prestige available to them.

What of smaller-scale borrowings? Adding the Christmas Gloria to other Sundays, adding the Gallican Sequence of Corpus Christi to the Roman missal, or adding the Eastern feast of the Transfiguration to the Roman calendar: does this kind of thing indicate a liturgical attitude which is relaxed about change? Adopting the custom of the next diocese, or some more distant but prestigious tradition, can sometimes be destructive of a

---

[28] Jungmann, *Mass of the Roman Rite*, 1:333.
[29] Quoted in Alcuin Reid, *The Organic Development of the Liturgy*, 2nd ed. (San Francisco: Ignatius Press, 2005), 20ff.

local tradition, and on this basis was sometimes fiercely resisted, as with attempts to impose the Roman rite on Milan. What is important for present purposes is that the competition between local customs, when one custom, or aspects of it, triumphs over another, is determined by reference to categories *internal to the concept of tradition*: the antiquity of the traditions at issue, the prestige of the dioceses to which they are attached, the beauty, piety, and fittingness of a rite or text, and so on. These developments cannot be pointed to, by the liturgical historian, as showing that the Catholics of the past did not respect tradition.

3.4. *Abbreviating changes*

Another kind of liturgical development is one driven by the scarcity of time, space, singers, or sacred ministers: that of abbreviating and compressing rites. A good example of this is the appearance of Low Mass in the ninth century; the appearance of the *Missa Cantata* is a parallel development in modern times. The initial motivation for Low Mass seems to have been to enable priests in religious communities to celebrate a daily Mass. The significance of this development is considerable, since what started as an adaptation for a specific need later became a major or even a dominant feature of many Catholics' liturgical experience.

Does this kind of liturgical development form a counter-example to my claim that those who handed on the liturgical tradition felt a strong obligation not to change it? The answer is "no."

Compare the priests who celebrated Mass in prison, under Nazi or Communist persecution, using a thimble for a chalice, a raisin soaked in water for the wine, without a server, reciting the texts from memory, and so on. They were obliged to leave out certain aspects of the liturgy. In a sense we might say that they were liturgical innovators, but in the most important sense of course they were nothing of the kind, because they did not intend their innovations to be passed on to the next generation. To say the same thing in a different way, if we think of the liturgical tradition as something which extends across the generations, they were not tampering with it, because they were not leaving their mark on it. They were in fact being *as faithful* to tradition as was possible *in their circumstances*.

Low Mass *was*, of course, passed on, and remains with us today, a millennium later. But it was not intended to replace the *Missa Solemnis*, and it has not done so. Low Mass represents the maximum fidelity to tradition possible if twenty Masses are to be celebrated before breakfast in miniature chapels in a monastery, while still preserving the full celebration of the *Missa Solemnis* as a daily reality. In this way, those who developed Low Mass might have said that the liturgical tradition as a whole was not compromised by the arrival of Low Mass. On the contrary, we might say that the appearance of Low Mass carried the liturgical tradition into situations where it could not otherwise go: into those side-chapels, for example, and as later history was to reveal, into mission stations, battle-fields, and prisons. This was not so much a change *to* the tradition as it was a new product *of* the tradition.

Of course we are not obliged to endorse what they did: one can take the view that the custodians of the Eastern rites were more correct to insist that the Mass always be celebrated with solemnity. The question is an open one: Does fidelity to tradition require the fullness of the ceremonies, or allow, under certain conditions, that they be abbreviated? I will only say, as a Latin-rite Catholic, that I understand and appreciate the force of the argument—not indeed for axing venerable rites for the sake of convenience, but for preserving them in vestigial form on account of necessity.

For that is how the creators of Low Mass went about it. Ceremonies which could not, under certain conditions, be celebrated in full, were maintained in a symbolic, compressed form, which maintains the full symbolic value of the original, longer, rite. An example is the carrying of the missal from the south to the north end of the altar by the acolyte, a compressed form of the Gospel procession with lights and incense at a *Missa Solemnis*. Another example is the tucking of the paten under the corporal, a "poor man's" equivalent of the veiling of the paten by the sub-deacon.[30] This process can also be seen with other abbreviating developments: the few lines of Psalm 25, *Lavabo inter innocentes* etc., stand in for the whole Psalm, once recited at the celebrant's washing of his hands. This

---

[30] I am indebted to Peter Kwasniewski for this example.

is one of the things which gives the ancient Mass as celebrated today its tremendous richness: the density of its symbolic and textual references.

4. *The liturgy of the early Church*

Liturgists who want to maintain the idea that pre-modern Catholics were unconcerned about liturgical innovations will appeal to other cases which will have to be examined one by one, and I cannot anticipate all the possible arguments here; nor would I be qualified to do so. I will consider one major objection, however, to what I have said, namely that in its origins the liturgy must have had a greater degree of freedom to change and adapt. The creation of a Latin liturgy in the first place, the objector may say, is surely an example of an upheaval of tradition.

Against this objection I will make two observations. One is that supposing this is true, Catholics of the earliest Christian centuries were not in the same position as Catholics in the eighth or later centuries. As already noted in passing, the antiquity of a tradition is a key element in determining the respect due to it. Related to this, it should be noted that a lot of the force of the idea that the Latin liturgy must have represented a break with tradition is dissipated when one recognises that the early Latin liturgical texts do not appear to be translations of earlier Greek texts, but on the contrary are as old, or older, than the earliest Greek liturgical texts which have come down to us.

My other observation is that we have very little idea how these very early liturgical developments happened. In Josef Jungmann's memorable phrase, "the beginnings of the Latin Mass in Rome are wrapped in almost total darkness."[31] Mere speculation about the attitudes of those, like Pope St Damasus or others of his era,[32] who were presumably involved in the development of the early Latin liturgy, is no basis for a serious argument.

If we are going to ask the question, what attitude to tradition is indicated by the development of the Latin liturgy, we should at least keep in mind

---

[31] Jungmann, *Mass of the Roman Rite*, 1:49.

[32] "The framework of the Roman Mass ... must therefore have been essentially determined by the turn of the fifth century" (Jungmann, 1:58).

that the early Christians of Rome, like their successors who developed the coronation ceremonies discussed earlier, had much traditional material to draw on, including the liturgy of the Temple and the Synagogue, the Last Supper, and the civic and religious ceremonies of their own societies. St Basil the Great emphasises yet another source: "We are not confined to the things the apostle or the gospel record [i.e., the content of the New Testament], but both before and after, we say things that have a great importance for the mystery, things from the unwritten teaching."[33]

In general, Mediterranean society in late antiquity was a melting-pot of traditions and cultural influences, and yet still a highly traditional society where the present was justified in terms of the past, and complex, archaic, and partially incomprehensible rituals were regarded as conferring divine favour, legitimacy, and prestige. Christianity emerged from one of the most traditional societies of this world, that of Judaism, and the Western Church made its home in another one of the most traditional societies of this world, that of ancient Rome. There is a vast difference between these two cultures, to be sure, but a reverence for tradition on a level entirely beyond the comprehension of many people today is something they had in common. As an example, I recommend to the reader's attention the Roman marriage ceremony, as used among the aristocracy, whose ceremonies can be read about today in all their archaic obscurity.

The idea that somehow, in between the religious culture of the Book of Leviticus in the Jerusalem of Herod's Temple, and the religious culture of Ovid's *Fasti* in the Rome of the Caesars, the early Christians somehow broke free from their bondage to tradition and enjoyed an interlude of living by post-Enlightenment conceptions of personal freedom, spontaneity, and self-definition, lacks plausibility, to put it mildly.

5. *Respect for tradition in* Sacrosanctum Concilium

5.1. *Restoration vs. reform*

In the final part of this chapter I would like to address the question of whether the attitude to tradition I have been talking about is still normative

---

[33]   Basil of Caesarea, *De Spiritu Sancto*, 27.66 (PG 32:188).

for Catholics today, even in light of the Second Vatican Council. In short, does the Council's Constitution on the Sacred Liturgy, *Sacrosanctum Concilium*, teach us that we need no longer regard liturgical tradition as a guiding principle for liturgical renewal?

This question is thrown into sharper focus by the contrast which is sometimes drawn between restoration and reform. Those making this distinction sometimes appear be using "restoration" as shorthand for the promotion of the ancient liturgy, and "reform" as code for the specific liturgical reform carried out after Vatican II. Nevertheless we should hold them to the meaning of these words, and demand to know what exactly is being distinguished.

In order to answer this question, we must attend very carefully to the language of *Sacrosanctum Concilium*. We find early in it an important passage describing what it sets out to do. The translation on the Vatican website gives us the following:

> Lastly, in faithful obedience to tradition, the sacred Council de-clares that holy Mother Church holds all lawfully acknowledged rites to be of equal right and dignity; that she wishes to preserve them in the future and to foster them in every way. The Council also desires that, where necessary, the rites be revised carefully in the light of sound tradition, and that they be given new vigour to meet the circumstances and needs of modern times.

The key clause here is the penultimate one, which reads in Latin: "caute ex integro ad mentem sanæ traditionis recognoscantur."

This, the fourth paragraph of the Preface, sets the terminological tone of the rest of the document. The key verb just noted, *recognosco*, appears nineteen times in the document as a whole; between them, the noun and its cognate verb, *instauratio* and *instauro*, appears twenty-one times; another closely related term used in the document is *restituo*, which is used seven times. All of these terms appear to be used more or less interchangeably: the action of the verbs *recognosco*, *instauro*, and *restituo* is to be applied to the Mass, the Office, the rite of adult baptism, the liturgical books, the liturgy in general, and so on, and the result will be an *instauratio* or a *recognitio*, just as happened, according to *Sacrosanctum Concilium*, when Pius X restored the books of Gregorian chant (§116), or when Cardinal Bea produced his new Latin translation of the Psalter (§91).

What, then, do these words mean? The English translation on the Vatican website gives "revise" for *recognosco*, "restore" for *restituo*, but on *instauro* and *instauratio* it wavers between "revise," "restore," and "reform." In actual fact, any Latin dictionary will tell you that *instauro, instauratio*, and *restituo*, all mean "restore": *instauro* is what the Kings Hezekiah and Josiah do to the Temple in the Vulgate of 2 Chronicles.[34] *Recognosco* carries a technical meaning in the Church's Latin of checking something over for accuracy. In the above passage, to say that the rites must *recognoscantur*, be checked for accuracy, according to the *mens*, the mind, of sound tradition, is to say that they must be restored.

In English, and of course in other languages, there is a real distinction between restoration and reform. During the time of Tony Blair as the UK's Prime Minister, we were often told that things needed to be "reformed," and if institutions or constitutional arrangements were of long standing, this on its own seemed to be an argument for change. To reform generally meant to change something into an entirely novel shape, with little or no precedent, and with still less thought about the consequences that would follow.

Restoration, by contrast, means putting something back into an older form, and the word has become associated with the work of conservationists. They will restore buildings and artifacts to the form they had at some specific moment in the past, destroying if necessary later features and additions, as if they had the power to transport things back in time.

However, neither concept is what is intended by *Sacrosanctum Concilium*, and we can be grateful that, translations aside, the document makes its meaning quite clear. If we improve the translation of the already quoted passage slightly, we get: "The Council desires that, where necessary, the rites be restored carefully according to the mind of sound tradition, and that they be given new vigour to meet the circumstances and needs of

[34] 2 Chron 29:3; 34:8, 10; 35:20.

today." Restoration and renewed vigour are not competing aspirations: the new vigour is to be imparted by the restoration. The document is not content to state this idea just once; it says it again later, in paragraph 50: "Elements which have suffered injury through accidents of history are now to be restored to the vigour which they had in the days of the holy Fathers, as may seem useful or necessary." Again, "vigour" is to be imparted to the rites by "restoration."

What may seem particularly remarkable is the confidence of the Council Fathers that what is needed, in order to meet the rapidly evolving challenges of modernity, is a set of liturgical rites which have been *restored according to the mind of sound tradition*. For this is the founding principle of the traditional movement.

Of course, this idea as expressed here has a back story. Certain members of the Liturgical Movement believed that the primitive liturgy had the very characteristics which are needed to appeal to modern people, above all simplicity. This idea made possible a coalition between liturgical scholars who hoped for the kind of radical restoration of ancient forms of worship which Pope Pius XII had called "exaggerated and senseless antiquarianism,"[35] on the one side, and pastoral-minded liturgical reformers who cared little about the past, on the other. This fragile alliance did not last long when the actual process of reform got going.

However, such debates on the fringes of the Council do not control the meaning of the text for us. What it says, in the context of the tradition of the Church and the use of the key terms in documents over the centuries, is that tradition is *normative*, a properly guiding principle, when it comes to liturgical renewal. It says this prominently, emphatically, more than once, and without subordinating respect for tradition to other considerations.

5.2. *Examples of restoration*

Now it must be faced that, while the guiding principle of *Sacrosanctum Concilium* seems clear enough, the examples of *instauratio* it gives are less so, and fit into a pattern between 1955 and 1970 which is troubling.

---

[35]   Pius XII, *Mediator Dei*, §64.

The new Holy Week rites of 1955 are called the *Ordo Instauratus* in the document promulgating them,[36] and we often see them referred to in the following decades as "the restored Holy Week rites." In what sense the changes made to Holy Week in 1955 can be described as a "restoration" is, however, problematic. Rather than opening that can of worms, consider other examples. Although *Sacrosanctum Concilium* gives few concrete proposals for reform, one it does put forward is that of a multi-year lectionary (§51), something for which there is no precedent in the history of the Catholic liturgy. It does not explicitly describe this as an example of *instauratio*, but on the documents' own principles it should be one.

The apotheosis of this problem occurs later, in the promulgation of the reformed missal itself by means of the Apostolic Constitution *Missale Romanum* of 1970. There Pope Paul VI uses the remarkable phrase *præcipua instaurationis novitas*, referring to the Eucharistic Prayer—a phrase translated artlessly, on the Vatican website, as "the major innovation," but literally meaning "the particular novelty of the restoration." There is a restoration going on, in other words, and it involves novelties. At this point it is clear that there is something rather strange going on.

An apologist for this document might say that the notion of *instauratio* here is primarily one of restoring something to vigour, flourishing, or better functioning. If that involves bringing in novelties, so be it. This understanding of *instauratio*, which with hindsight seems to have been in the air in 1955, is, however, itself a novelty. It implies a rejection of the respect for tradition I have been discussing throughout this paper. This is what we would expect, of course, since only in the context of such a rejection could the liturgical reform have been carried out in the way it was carried out.

It is characteristic of the documents of that era, and since, that the perennial and fundamental principle, which guided the Catholic attitude to the liturgy over so many centuries, is not explicitly rejected. On the contrary, as I have explained, *Sacrosanctum Concilium* gives it a very clear

---

[36] Sacred Congregation for Rites, Decree *Maxima Redemptionis Nostrae Mysteria* (1955).

expression. At the level of theological principles, the answer to my earlier question—Does Vatican II teach us that tradition is not a normative liturgical principle?—remains "no." At the level of practice, the matter becomes more complicated. The tension between what *Sacrosanctum Concilium* says should be the ultimate guiding principle, and the actual changes which it and popes before it and after it endorsed, is a problem. However, it is a problem for those seeking to defend those changes, not for the movement dedicated to the restoration of the ancient liturgy.

Conclusion

The conception of tradition which I have defended in this chapter may be criticised as an extreme one, but my desire has been simply the accurate identification of the long-standing Catholic attitude. This was the attitude of ancient and medieval Catholics, which corresponds to a wider attitude found in pre-modern societies, and it was the attitude of the Catholics of the post-Tridentine period, who in the context of an increasingly uncomprehending elite secular culture fought so hard, and ultimately successfully, against the liturgical innovations of Protestants, Jansenists, and Josephists. It is the attitude encapsulated by the famous verse of St Paul: *ego enim accepi a Domino quod et tradidi vobis:* "for I have passed on to you what I received from the Lord."[37] And it is the attitude which is implied by the Ratzingerian conception of the liturgy as given to us, not invented by us. In the end, if we change the liturgy, it is not a given.

How this attitude is compatible with the development of the liturgy in the course of late antiquity and the Middle Ages is the central problem I have tried to address. The answer I have given is that what look like changes to the historian, were not changes to the tradition at the time: they were changes to things not yet incorporated into the inner, unchangeable core of the liturgy, which were drawn into that core by constant practice. This draws attention to the aspects of the liturgy which we can today use in particular ways to meet the needs of our time, which future generations

---

[37] 1 Cor 11:23.

may even see as developments of the liturgy, insofar as they become so firmly established as customs that they come to be seen as normative.

Finally, I have argued that this attitude is not at odds with the reforming orientation of the Second Vatican Council, since the very word which is rendered as "reform" in English in the text of *Sacrosanctum Concilium*, *instauratio*, actually means "restoration," and the same document spells out a reverence for tradition, together with a trust in the power of tradition, as the fundamental principle of liturgical renewal.

4

Understanding Liturgical Participation

The liturgical crisis of the twentieth century has been largely a conflict about liturgical participation. Not to the exclusion of other factors: the reform of the liturgy was an opportunity to express, through the new texts, a distinctive theological vision, and this possibility was no doubt welcomed by many of the reform's architects. Nevertheless, the justification for the reform, in prospect and in retrospect, was and is most often couched in terms of participation. We read, in official documents as well as in theological commentaries and informal remarks, that the new liturgy made participation better, easier, or, simply, possible, and the primary focus of such remarks is generally the use of the vernacular.

Thus, Pope John Paul II wrote, of the lessons and psalms in the Mass: "The fact that these texts are read and sung in the vernacular enables everyone to participate with fuller understanding."[38] What, might we ask, was going on during the many centuries in which the liturgy was celebrated in a language not readily understood by the great majority of the people? The Congregation for Divine Worship tells us: this time, during which the patrimony of sacred music was composed, was "a period when the active participation of the faithful was not emphasized as the

---

This is a slightly developed version of my contribution to *Fidem servavi. Escritos en homenaje al Prof. Julio Retamal Favereau*, ed. Jaime Alcalde (Valencia: Tirant lo Blanch, 2023).

[38] John Paul II, *Dominicae Cenae*, §10.

source of the authentic Christian spirit."[39] In other words, it was a time when the authentic Christian spirit was not fostered by the liturgy as it should have been.

This justification for vernacularisation can be summarised as what I shall call the "Participation Thesis": "Adequate participation in the liturgy depends on understanding the words it uses; this is impeded, except for those with a highly unusual command of Latin, by the use of Latin instead of the vernacular."

At first glance it would appear that if the Participation Thesis is true, then the argument for vernacularisation is overwhelming. In this paper I shall argue, first, that even if it is true the case for vernacularisation is not straightforward; and second, that the Participation Thesis is false.

The issue of participation was not new in the twentieth century: it was central to the liturgical battles of the Jansenists, expressed most clearly in the would-be reforms of the Council of Pistoia of 1786. Further back in history, the Protestant liturgical reforms of the sixteenth century, while carrying more explicit doctrinal freight, were, and are still, typically defended in terms of participation. Throughout this five-century debate, liturgical traditionalists have not found it easy to articulate the cases against the Participation Thesis, and their writings often seem to focus on other issues only tangentially related to participation, such as the universality of Latin, the antiquity of the texts, or the beauty of the music to which they have been set.

This chapter proceeds from a consideration of the limited answer given by Trent to Protestant demands for vernacularisation, and, on the other hand, the practical difficulties which vernacularisation faced (part 1). I turn to the Liturgical Movement's embrace of the Participation Thesis (part 2), and of the Holy See's attitude to Latin before the Council (part 3). It was immediately following the Council that a response to the Participation Thesis was finally expressed, in terms of the sacred character of Latin, by Pope Paul VI (part 4), but this was immediately discounted

---

[39]   Congregation for Divine Worship, Instruction on Concerts in Churches (1987).

because of a misguided argument about elitism (part 5). This will lead to a consideration of the sociology of liturgical participation (part 6), the problem of a rejection of tradition by an educational elite (part 7), and a more detailed analysis of liturgical participation (part 8).

1. *Trent on the Participation Thesis*

One illustration of the extent to which traditionalists—defenders of traditional liturgical forms—have been on the back foot on the question of participation is offered by the decrees of the Council of Trent. The Council defends both the ceremonies of the liturgy and the use of Latin, but does not do so in the same terms. On ceremonies, the Council explains as follows:

> And whereas such is the nature of man, that, without external helps, he cannot easily be raised to the meditation of divine things; therefore has holy Mother Church instituted certain rites, to wit that certain things be pronounced in the Mass in a low, and others in a louder, tone. She has likewise employed ceremonies, such as mystic benedictions, lights, incense, vestments, and many other things of this kind, derived from an apostolical discipline and tradition, whereby both the majesty of so great a sacrifice might be recommended, and the minds of the faithful be excited, by those visible signs of religion and piety, to the contemplation of those most sublime things which are hidden in this sacrifice.[40]

The leading idea here is that the ceremonies aid participation: they affirm and make visible the "majesty" of the rite, and draw our attention to God. The Council's defence of Latin, however, seems less robust.

> Although the Mass contains great instruction for the faithful people, nevertheless, it has not seemed expedient to the Fathers that it should be everywhere celebrated in the vulgar tongue. Wherefore, the ancient usage of each church, and the rite approved of by the

---

[40] Council of Trent, Session 22 (1562), Chapter V.

holy Roman Church, the mother and mistress of all churches, being in each place retained; and, that the sheep of Christ may not suffer hunger, nor the little ones ask for bread, and there be none to break it unto them, the holy Synod charges pastors, and all who have the cure of souls, that they frequently, during the celebration of Mass, expound either by themselves, or by others, some portion of those things which are read at Mass, and that, amongst the rest, they explain some mystery of this most holy sacrifice, especially on the Lord's days and festivals.

It would seem that the Participation Thesis is not denied, but that in practice its force is outweighed by "ancient usage," which itself comes down to "expedience." We might say that the Council Fathers replied to the Thesis: "Yes, but . . ."

The argument from "expedience" may seem particularly weak today, in light of the stress laid by the reformist party on how the liturgy was translated *into* Latin to aid the comprehension of the faithful, and how it has been translated into a number of other languages by the churches of the East. This argument, familiar as it is, is misleading. We do not have any records of the reasoning behind the composition of the Latin liturgy, but the kind of Latin used suggests that popular comprehension was not the overriding consideration, in contrast to the importance of appropriating the tradition of solemn and sacred Latin for the use of the Church at a moment when Paganism was no longer a threat.[41] I shall return to this point below.

Again, with regard to the Oriental Churches, it curious that they should have been motivated by considerations of popular comprehension of the liturgy on those rarely occurring occasions when the liturgy has been rendered in a new language for a newly evangelised cultural and linguistic group, and, at least until very recently, not at all motivated by that consideration the rest of the time, during which these churches' liturgical languages gradually became incomprehensible to anyone without

[41]   On this see Christine Mohrmann, *Liturgical Latin: Its Origins and Character* (London: Burns & Oates, 1959), 46, 59–61, 66–68.

a specialist education. It may be that the real reason for the use of Church Slavonic, Ge'ez, and other such languages is, as I have just suggested about Latin, the appropriation of culturally important traditions of the sacred register of a prestigious local language, a form of inculturation which is actually emphasised all the more, rather than undermined, when this sacred register becomes so divorced from popular speech as to be incomprehensible without a special education in it. However, further exploration of the Eastern practice goes beyond the scope of this chapter.

Leaving these alleged precedents for vernacularisation on one side, therefore, Trent's reference to expedience is most easily filled out by reference to practicability, and this is indeed a powerful argument. Neither in earlier centuries, nor at the time of Trent, was it practical to translate the liturgy into all the vernacular languages spoken by members of the Latin Church. The problems of the stability of these languages, their multiplicity, and the fact that a good many did not have well-established written forms at that time, let alone in earlier centuries, were insuperable obstacles, as the experience of the Protestant reformers was, in fact, to confirm.

To illustrate these difficulties, it is notable that Thomas Cranmer was obliged to create a new and highly idiosyncratic register of English for his *Book of Common Prayer*, endowing the dialect used in Kent and London, which by his day had become established as the language of the English Court, with due solemnity. To do this he adopted a number of linguistic peculiarities, such as archaisms, which make the language of the *Book of Common Prayer* distinct from that, for example, of Shakespeare, and which were in turn influential in the creation of the King James Bible. How easily this strange new language was understood around the country is a complex question, but from Cumberland to Cornwall many ordinary folk of the western edges of the Kingdom did not speak English at all, to say nothing of Ireland and Scotland, and it would certainly have sounded very foreign in northern England.

The influence of the *Book of Common Prayer* and the King James Bible on the development of the English language has been immense, and indeed we may say that to an important extent they created, over the centuries, the linguistic reality which was supposedly their justification.

The same can be said of Martin Luther's use of High German. Only in the twentieth century was the victory of a standard German, greatly influenced by the High German universalized by Luther, complete. What the sixteenth-century peasantry made of Luther's services and Bible we can only imagine, though no doubt it varied considerably from region to region.

One wonders, in fact, how much Luther and Cranmer, having scored their debating points about the importance of a truly comprehensible liturgy and Bible, cared about how much their services could really be understood in the further reaches of their respective countries.

Such difficulties, of course, have not gone away. In Africa and China, and indeed in multilingual parishes in the West, the Church today offers a supposedly vernacular liturgy to tens of millions of Catholics for whom it is, at best, a second or third language, and at worst entirely incomprehensible. Even for native-English speakers the attempt to provide an easily comprehensible language has inevitable pitfalls. The sociologist Anthony Archer comments, of the *Novus Ordo*: "Its very language was that of a particular class. People had listened to it before in the courtroom and the classroom. . . . In English, the new Mass could no longer conceal the class commitment that lay behind its neutrality, a commitment that inevitably jarred with the new talk of community."[42] One is reminded of G.K. Chesterton's observation:

> We hear men speaking for us of new laws strong and sweet,
> Yet is there no man speaketh as we speak in the street.[43]

2. *The Liturgical Movement*

Trent's argument from "expediency" was not, then, as weak as one might assume. All the same, the *status quæstionis* after Trent invited attempts to

---

[42]   Anthony Archer, *The Two Catholic Churches: A Study in Oppression* (London: SCM Press, 1986), 142.

[43]   G.K. Chesterton, from his poem "The Secret People," www.gkc.org.uk/ gkc/books/secret-people.html.

overcome, in one way or another, the problem, supposedly exacerbated by Latin, of participation. A dissatisfaction with the level of popular participation led to the destruction of almost all Europe's rood screens, and acres of stained glass, not by Protestant or atheist revolutionary fanatics, but by Catholics wishing to enable the faithful to see the ceremonies more clearly.

Most pertinent to the twentieth-century liturgical reform was the Liturgical Movement, which if broadly defined can be said to have started with Dom Prosper Guéranger in the mid-nineteenth century. In his monumental work, *The Liturgical Year*, he explains: "Liturgical prayer would soon become powerless were the faithful not to take a real share in it, or, at least, not to associate themselves to it in heart. It can heal the world, but only on the condition that it be understood."[44]

The first thing which should astonish the reader is Guéranger's having forgotten—one can only assume, both inadvertently and momentarily—the objective efficacy for the living and the dead of a Mass even if celebrated by a priest entirely on his own, for example in prison.

From this troubling starting point, Guéranger is concerned that the faithful take a *real share* in the liturgy, which seems to mean *understanding* it, as opposed to merely *associating oneself with it in heart*, the latter possibility being presented as a second-best. Does Guéranger really mean that a merely intellectual comprehension is preferable to heartfelt interior association? Surely not, but the seed of the idea that *comprehension, as opposed to interior association*, is necessary for genuine participation, is certainly present in this passage.

Guéranger's work was followed by a long series of attempts to get the faithful to take part in the liturgy in the way the Liturgical Movement desired. The liturgical guidebooks of Guéranger himself, Cardinal Ildephonso Schuster, and Fr Pius Parsch are the outstanding positive achievements of these attempts. The movement promoting the "Dialogue Mass" in the early twentieth century attempted in a different way

---

[44] Dom Prosper Guéranger, *The Liturgical Year* (Great Falls, MT: St Bonaventure Publications, 2000), vol. I: *Advent*, 6–7.

to involve the people more thoroughly with the texts of the Mass. In the meantime, handbooks for the laity for use in Mass, which had a history going back to the earliest days of printing, underwent a transformation, from a series of appropriate meditations and prayers to a record of the complete liturgical texts, perhaps with a little commentary.

It is interesting to note in this regard that the printing of the Canon in translation for the laity was actually forbidden by the Holy See as late as the mid-nineteenth century. A similarly hesitant response from Rome was forthcoming in reaction to the "dialogue Masses" in the first half of the twentieth century: the final capitulation to the idea that leaving the dialogue to the servers was a less "perfect" form of participation for the faithful came only in *De Musica Sacra* in 1958.[45]

The success of these developments fell short of their promoters' hopes, however, and their frustration found expression in frank condemnations of the kind of participation most Western Catholics had been engaged in for many centuries, and too many still were. Pope Pius XI himself used the notorious phrase "dumb spectators" (*muti spectatores*)[46] as a description of Catholics who weren't singing the chants in accordance with Pope Pius X's recommendations in *Tra le Sollecitudini* a quarter of a century earlier. In 1958 the liturgical scholar Josef Jungmann contrasted an imagined golden age of liturgical participation with a later epoch: "Something like a fog curtain settled between and separated Liturgy and people, through which the faithful could only dimly recognize what was happening at the altar . . ."[47] The use of Latin was not the whole of the problem, but it was inevitably seen as a major factor.

A dramatic, one might even say hyperbolic expression of this point of view may be found in a letter Annibale Bugnini addressed to the distinguished church historian Hubert Jedin, in response to an article penned by the latter in the January 15, 1969 edition of *L'Osservatore Romano* in which Jedin had lamented the almost total loss of liturgical Latin. We

---

[45] See "The *Missa Lecta*," in Shaw, *The Case for Liturgical Restoration*, 37–44.

[46] Pius XI, Apostolic Constitution *Divini Cultus Sanctitatem* (1928), §9.

[47] From Jungmann's "The Pastoral Idea in the History of the Liturgy," quoted in Reid, *Organic Development*, 166.

know what Bugnini said in this letter because he helpfully quotes it in his post-reform apologia, *The Reform of the Liturgy*:

> As a good historian who knows how to weigh both sides and reach a balanced judgment, why did you not mention the millions and hundreds of millions of the faithful who have at last achieved worship in spirit and in truth? Who can at last pray to God in their own languages and not in meaningless sounds, and are happy that henceforth they know what they are saying? Are they not "the Church"? As for [Latin as] the "bond of unity": Do you believe the Church has no other ways of securing unity? Do you believe there is a deep and heartfelt unity amid lack of understanding, ignorance, and the "dark night" of a worship that lacks a face and light, at least for those out in the nave? Do you not think that a priestly pastor must seek and foster the unity of his flock—and thereby of the universal flock—through a living faith that is fed by the rites and finds expression in song, in communion of minds, in love that animates the Eucharist, in conscious participation, and in entrance into the mystery? Unity of language is superficial and fictitious; the other kind of unity is vital and profound. . . . Here in the Consilium we are not working for museums and archives, but for the spiritual life of the people of God.[48]

Back in 1947, to rein in the excesses of the Liturgical Movement, Pope Pius XII had rejected the view that the only fruitful way to participate in the Mass was by means of word-for-word comprehension:

> Many of the faithful are unable to use the Roman missal even though it is written in the vernacular; nor are all capable of understanding correctly the liturgical rites and formulas. So varied and diverse are men's talents and characters that it is impossible for all to be moved and attracted to the same extent by community prayers, hymns, and liturgical services. Moreover, the needs and

---

[48]   Bugnini, *Reform of the Liturgy*, 283.

inclinations of all are not the same, nor are they always constant in the same individual. Who, then, would say, on account of such a prejudice, that all these Christians cannot participate in the Mass nor share its fruits? On the contrary, they can adopt some other method which proves easier for certain people; for instance, they can lovingly meditate on the mysteries of Jesus Christ or perform other exercises of piety or recite prayers which, though they differ from the sacred rites, are still essentially in harmony with them.[49]

It was not the assisting of the faithful towards an intellectual understanding of the rites which drew Pope Pius's ire, naturally, but the criticism of the quality of the participation enjoyed by those who did not have a high level of intellectual understanding. The idea that they are not participating fruitfully is, in the end, absurd. They are doing what they forefathers did, and this not only sustained them spiritually throughout their lives and under persecution, but brought forth saints.

The Holy See's defence of Latin over this period is our next concern.

3. *The Holy See on Latin up to Vatican II*

As noted, the impression from the Council of Trent that the use of Latin is, at least from the point of view of participation, *regrettable*, is a very striking one. Nor do we find anything very substantive, by way of argument, in Pope Pius VI's condemnation of the "novelties" of the Council of Pistoia, however forcefully expressed:

The proposition of the synod by which it shows itself eager to remove the cause through which, in part, there has been induced a forgetfulness of the principles relating to the order of the liturgy, "by recalling it (the liturgy) to a greater simplicity of rites, by expressing it in the vernacular language, by uttering it in a loud voice"; as if the present order of the liturgy, received and approved by the Church, had emanated in some part from the forgetfulness

[49] Pius XII, *Mediator Dei*, §108.

of the principles by which it should be regulated,— rash, offensive to pious ears, insulting to the Church, favourable to the charges of heretics against it.[50]

Pius XII's *Mediator Dei* similarly condemns the use of the vernacular as an "innovation" (§59), but again does so without explaining what, exactly, is wrong with the idea.

John XXIII defended Latin in his Apostolic Constitution *Veterum Sapientia* (1962), but the oft-quoted phrases of this document praising Latin—"universal," "dignified," "unchanging," "equally friendly" to speakers of all languages, and so on—were not, in fact, written with the liturgy in view. Pope John's concern was that:

> For these reasons the Apostolic See has always been at pains to preserve Latin, deeming it worthy of being used in the exercise of her teaching authority "as the splendid vesture of her heavenly doctrine and sacred laws." She further requires her sacred ministers to use it, for by so doing they are the better able, wherever they may be, to acquaint themselves with the mind of the Holy See on any matter, and communicate the more easily with Rome and with one another.

In short, the use of Latin by priests—presumably, in the Mass and the Office—is a way of ensuring that they have enough familiarity with the Church's language of administration and teaching that they can read official documents and maintain a common language with their fellow clergy.

The same emphasis is found in the very numerous Church documents, both before and after *Veterum Sapientia*, exhorting seminaries to teach Latin. The FIUV Position Paper on teaching Latin in seminaries[51] lists these—perhaps not exhaustively—and in addition to *Veterum Sapientia* no fewer than six were promulgated in the course of the

---

[50] Pius VI, Bull *Auctorem Fidei* (1794).
[51] Subsequently published in Shaw, *The Case for Liturgical Restoration*, 161–68.

1960s alone.[52] The series was continued under Pope John Paul II, Pope Benedict XVI, and Pope Francis, and no doubt there will be more such documents in the future. What is striking about these documents is the concern for Latin education with, for the most part, only glancing reference to the liturgical use of the language, and sometimes no such reference at all.

The same attitude is found in Pope Paul VI's well-known General Audience address introducing the *Novus Ordo Missæ* in November 1969, which expresses his acceptance of the Participation Thesis. Having said that the Mass would be in the vernacular, he continued:

> But, let us bear this well in mind, for our counsel and our comfort: the Latin language will not thereby disappear. It will continue to be the noble language of the Holy See's official acts; it will remain as the means of teaching in ecclesiastical studies and as the key to the patrimony of our religious, historical, and human culture. If possible, it will reflourish in splendour.

The wisdom of *Veterum Sapientia*, contrary to Pope Paul, that a Latin liturgy was an indispensable bulwark for the use of Latin for studies and communication, seems to have been confirmed by events: despite the urgent tone of the documents on Latin in the 1960s, of the *Ratio funda-mentalis institutionis sacerdotalis* of 1970 (§66), and of later documents, the loss of Latin from the liturgy was indeed accompanied by its downgrading or complete disappearance from seminaries.

In the meantime, the Participation Thesis, never explicitly opposed in the magisterium, was increasingly being pressed by members of the Liturgical Movement, and was openly admitted in Vatican II's Decree on the Liturgy, *Sacrosanctum Concilium* (1962) §36:

---

[52] Congregation for Seminaries *Sacrum Latinae Linguae Depositum* (1962); Paul VI, Apostolic Letter *Summi Dei Verbum* (1963); Paul VI, Apostolic Letter *Studia Latinitatis* (1964); Instruction *In Edicendis* (1965); the Second Vatican Council's Decree on Priestly Training *Optatum Totius* (1965); Paul VI, Apostolic Letter *Sacrificium Laudis* (1966).

1. Particular law remaining in force, the use of the Latin language is to be preserved in the Latin rites.
2. But since the use of the mother tongue, whether in the Mass, the administration of the sacraments, or other parts of the liturgy, frequently may be of great advantage to the people, the limits of its employment may be extended.

However, it is precisely at this historical moment that arguments against the Participation Thesis begin to emerge in magisterial documents, and I turn to these next.

4. *The beginnings of a defence of Latin*

Two of the most telling defences of Latin come from the man supremely responsible for the attack against it: Pope Paul VI. One is in his remarkable 1966 Apostolic Letter *Sacrificium Laudis*; the other is the 1969 General Audience address which I have already quoted.

Sacrificium Laudis is an impassioned plea for the retention of the Latin Office by religious. He describes the Latin Office as "an abundant well-spring of Christian civilisation and a very rich treasure-trove of devotion." He urges religious superiors "to ponder what they wish to give up, and not to let that spring run dry from which, until the present, they have themselves drunk deep." Three years later, the General Audience address makes the astonishing assertion:

> The introduction of the vernacular will certainly be a great sacrifice for those who know the beauty, the power, and the expressive sacrality of Latin. We are parting with the speech of the Christian centuries; we are becoming like profane intruders in the literary preserve of sacred utterance.

Again, he refers to "that language of the angels," "the divine Latin language."

Pope Paul's point in *Sacrificium Laudis*, which is echoed in the General Audience address, is that the use of Latin is supremely valuable from an artistic and spiritual point of view, because the two aspects of the liturgy—artistic and spiritual—are inseparable. It must be admitted by all that the

Latin Psalms and antiphons, with their chant settings, are supremely important cultural artifacts. This is of central interest to the Church because what they are *about*, as art, is spiritual, and their *artistic expression* of spiritual realities is irreplaceable, if not absolutely indispensable, in the devotional life.

This argument applies equally to other kinds of sacred and devotional art. Truly great sacred art in the form of painting, architecture, and so on, does not simply *express* spiritual realities in a uniquely effective way, but is part of a *meditation* upon them which extends, expounds, and illustrates their meaning. The glimpse of these spiritual realities in liturgical art may not always shock the viewer into making an intellectual assent to a truth of Faith—though that can occasionally happen—but they seep into a regular viewer who comes to them with an attitude of openness and reverence, as a kind of spiritual nourishment: in Pope Paul's metaphor, as reviving and sustaining water. They act, in fact, very much as do regular use of the sacraments, prayer, hearing sermons, and the reading of the Scriptures and spiritual books, all working on a Catholic with the right dispositions, to sustain and direct his spiritual growth over many years.

Bad art, by the same token, will have the opposite effect, distorting and misleading, in subtle ways, a Catholic's spiritual development. As Dietrich von Hildebrand expressed it:

> Mawkish prayers and hymns distort the religious ethos of the faithful; appealing to centres in man that are far removed from the religious one, they draw him into an atmosphere which obscures and blurs the face of Christ. Sacred beauty, therefore, is of great importance for the formation of the true ethos of the faithful.[53]

Bad religious art at once robs sacred things of their dignity and fosters inappropriate, superficial, and inauthentic emotional responses in the viewer or listener.

The value of the liturgy as a mediation, commentary, and illustration of the Faith is greater than that of any other art form, of course, because of the

---

[53]   Dietrich von Hildebrand, *Trojan Horse in the City of God* (Manchester, NH: Sophia Institute Press, 1996), 236.

centrality of the liturgy to the spiritual life, and because it is a "theological source," a *locus theologicus*. As *Sacrosanctum Concilium* expresses it, "it is the primary and indispensable source from which the faithful are to derive the true Christian spirit." It has incalculably more authority, therefore, than such important monuments of religious art as, say, the paintings of the Catacombs of Priscilla in Rome, Chartres Cathedral, or the musical works of the Renaissance masters.

Pope Paul's General Audience address develops the point in a more general way. It is not just a matter of the artistic value of this or that sublime chant antiphon: the entirety of a Latin liturgical event is given power, expressiveness, and sacrality by the Latin language. We can observe that Latin's association both with scriptural translations of great antiquity and with a great body of Patristic and later theology means that its liturgical formulae can incorporate theological and scriptural references with an ease not available to any other language. The advantages, for the liturgy, of its stability over time, and its universality, are too obvious to labour. Above all, however, the nature of the Latin register used in the liturgy, and the long association between this kind of Latin and the Church's worship, lend traditional Latin liturgies *dignity*, by which we mean gravity, weight, force, importance, sacrality, and authority. It is this association, anticipated by the long-noted significance of the use of Latin on the *titulus* of the Cross on Mount Calvary,[54] which justifies Pope Paul in calling Latin "divine."

It is necessary to disagree, on this point, with the words put into the mouth of St Thomas More by the playwright Robert Bolt in *A Man for All Seasons*. Signor Chapuys, the Imperial Ambassador (a character cut from the film version) refers to Latin as a "holy language." More improbably

---

[54] See, for example, St Thomas Aquinas, *In IV Sent.*, dist. 8, *expositio textus*: "Let it be known that in the celebration of the Mass, where the Passion is re-presented, certain Greek words are used ... certain Hebrew ones ... and certain Latin ones ... for the title of Christ's Cross was written in these three languages." For other examples and commentary, see Uwe Michael Lang, *The Voice of the Church at Prayer: Reflections on Liturgy and Language* (San Francisco: Ignatius Press, 2012), 48–50, 143–44.

responds: "'Tisn't 'holy,' Your Excellency; just old."[55] This remark could stand for the typical response made by liturgical progressives to the kind of argument just outlined. The liturgy was translated into Latin, they tell us, for the same "banal, prosaic" reason, to use Pope Paul's phrase, for which it was translated into modern languages: that people should be able to understand. Latin has no special vocation as a liturgical language: 'tisn't holy, just old.

In a similar vein, the late Fr Reginald Foster, the well-known Vatican Latinist, remarked in an interview: "Latin is a language. It didn't come down in a golden box from Heaven. You don't have to be clever to speak it. In ancient Rome it was spoken by poor people, prostitutes and bums."[56] Fr Foster was primarily making the point that Latin is not accessible only to linguistic geniuses, but his words have often been quoted to support the idea that it is not a sacred language.

I have already begun to address this thought above. The Roman Canon would have been at least as incomprehensible to fourth-century prostitutes and bums as Cicero's convoluted orations would have been to their predecessors. In such cases the style, vocabulary, and in general the register is not designed for immediate and universal comprehension. In the case of the Roman Canon, we find archaisms, neologisms, Hebraisms and other foreign loan words, and echoes of the unnatural syntax of sacred and legal language.[57] In any case, from an early date, and quite possibly from the start, it was said silently, by a celebrant hidden from the congregation in the nave by curtains. If verbal comprehension was the object of the Latin liturgy's composition, Pope Damasus (if it was he) and his collaborators went about their task in a most surprising way.

As a matter of fact, the prostitutes and bums of ancient Rome would not have expected to hear and understand the sacred formulae from pagan

---

[55] Robert Bolt, *A Man for All Seasons: A Play of Sir Thomas More* (London: Methuen, 1995), Act 2, p. 53. The play was first published in 1960.

[56] Quoted on the website of the BBC: www.bbc.co.uk/news/magazine -21412604.

[57] This is discussed at length by Mohrmann, *Liturgical Latin*, 53–80.

priests, who frequently disappeared from view into temples to perform their rites, leaving the crowd outside, just as the Jewish high priest disappeared into the Holy of Holies. What they expected, and what they got, was a liturgical act clothed in words of the utmost *dignitas*, conveying to them the holiness and importance, the distinctiveness from ordinary life and everyday things, of what was being enacted.

5. *The argument of elitism*

Pope Paul's argument, however, did not save the Latin liturgy, even from the actions of Pope Paul himself. He was in no danger of agreeing with Fr Foster's vulgar remarks. His own thinking, expressed in his General Audience address, seems to have been that the "beauty, the power, and the expressive sacrality of Latin" was, though perfectly real, something which could be appreciated only by an elite few. For he goes on to wonder whether (but, most curiously, not actually to assert that) "the divine Latin language kept us apart from children, from youth, from the world of labour and of affairs, . . . [it being] a dark screen, not a clear window . . ."

The suggestion that only an educational elite can get anything from the beauty and expressive sacrality of Latin is, however, a mistake. It is perfectly evident to those who attend the traditional Mass today, as it was to earlier generations of Catholics, that the ancient liturgy is not limited in its appeal to the more highly educated. Indeed, Fr Bryan Houghton noted "the undeniable phenomenon that the people who know Latin least are usually those who most lament its departure."[58] A hint in this direction may be gleaned from another pope not especially friendly to the traditional liturgy, Pope John Paul II. I have already quoted his early apostolic letter, *Dominicæ Cenæ* (1980), asserting the value of vernacularisation for comprehension. Immediately after this comes an acknowledgment of the existence of those who felt that something has been lost:

> Nevertheless, there are also those people who, having been educated on the basis of the old liturgy in Latin, experience the lack of this

---

[58]   Bryan Houghton, *Unwanted Priest: Autobiography of a Latin Mass Exile* (Brooklyn: Angelico Press, 2022), 74.

"one language," which in all the world was an expression of the unity of the Church and through its dignified character elicited a profound sense of the Eucharistic Mystery.

One does not get the impression that the people to whom he refers are members of some kind of elite, savouring the niceties of Latin poetry. What they used to experience was simply that the liturgy was in a mysterious, otherworldly language, which led them to an appreciation of the holy and mysterious nature of the Eucharist: "plena altum sensum Mysterii eucharistici."

Twenty years later, his point was developed by the Instruction *Liturgiam Authenticam*, which encouraged vernacular translations in "a sacred style that will come to be recognised as proper to liturgical language."[59] Archaisms contribute to such a style, as do "inelegant expressions" deriving from attempts to stick closely to the Latin. While the Instruction says that expressions which "hinder comprehension" should be avoided, it is obvious that the recommended features are going to do exactly that, as critics of the Instruction have been quick to point out. The Instruction must be proposing a trade-off between comprehensibility and a recognisably hieratic register, presumably because the latter has some value, for the faithful, distinct from the value of understanding the texts word by word. The Instruction's principles eventually resulted in the revised English translation of the *Novus Ordo* published in 2011.

Another casualty of the belated realisation that a liturgical text which is somewhat opaque might make a deeper impression on the worshipper is the theory that making the liturgy *everyday* in its language allows it to enter the *everyday world*: the "world of labour and of affairs," as Pope Paul VI put it. Similarly, the Instruction of the Congregation for Divine Worship, *Inæstimabile Donum* (1980), praised "successful efforts to close the gap between life and worship."[60] The notion of "closing the gap," which

---

[59] Congregation for Divine Worship and the Discipline of the Sacraments, Instruction *Liturgiam Authenticam* (2001), §27.

[60] Sacred Congregation for Sacraments and Divine Worship, *Inaestimabile Donum* (1980), Foreword.

has been pled in justification for all kinds of liturgical abuses, from pottery chalices to using illicit and invalid matter, is at right-angles to the whole of the Catholic liturgical tradition, with which *Liturgiam Authenticam* attempted to re-engage.

6. *The testimony of anthropology and sociology*

At this point we may appeal to sociology and anthropology to assist us. What we want to ask these disciplines is this: in considering religious rites in general, and those of the Latin Catholic Church in particular, do people without a high level of modern education (whether of a classical kind or not) appreciate more highly, or less, mysterious rituals which are not easy to understand, in languages or forms of language removed somewhat or wholly from the language of everyday speech?

It isn't difficult to gauge their response. The use of archaic, special-ized, and obscure language naturally accompanies the employment of complex and mysterious ceremonies, and it is towards rituals character-ized by both that human religions seem powerfully drawn all over the world, presumably because such rites seem to have greater dignity and power. Fr Aidan Nichols summarises the point, as we noted in chapter 2: "The notion that the more intelligible the sign, the more effectively it will enter the lives of the faithful is implausible to the sociological imagination. . . . A certain opacity is essential to symbolic action in the sociologists' account."[61]

When bearing in mind the mysterious rites of African paganism, for example, one realises that far from it being the case that devotees must have a high level of education in order to participate in them in a pro-found way, the habits of mind usually inculcated by modern education can be precisely those most unfriendly to losing oneself in religious ecstasy. The Catholic anthropologist Mary Douglas, to whose theory I will turn shortly, noted that it was the less educated Catholic laity who were most sorely deprived by the liturgical reform and the abolition of rules such as that of Friday abstinence. She excoriates the superficial and patronizing

---

[61] Nichols, *Looking at the Liturgy*, 61.

attitudes of the reformers, noting: "it is as if the liturgical signal boxes were manned by colour-blind signalmen."[62]

More evidence is provided by the sociologist Anthony Archer, who interviewed elderly working-class Catholics in Newcastle in the early 1980s. I will quote Archer at a little length:

> If the old mass most noticeably provided a break from the mundane, it was also able to bear a great deal more than the new mass. No doubt this was partly due to the half-understood mutterings and gestures and silences—and its familiar shape for as long as anyone could remember:
>
> "Whether it was the very fact that I couldn't understand it, but it was much nicer. As I say you couldn't see much of what was going on while the priest has his back to you, you couldn't understand, but you somehow still enjoyed it. . . .
>
> "I couldn't understand three parts of it, but I used to love to hear it. I could sit and listen to it and me mind was far way. I could imagine all these things when I was listening to the mass.". . .
>
> "If I went back I'd rather it'd been in Latin. Them just gabbing off in English now—there's no feeling in the mass now. I liked to listen to the priest saying it and follow it in me old mass book rather than everyone together yapping away. It's just killed the mass off. They've killed the feeling of the mass off. You could be anywhere—right in the middle of Land's End."
>
> In this way the mass came to press in on the individual. Not only had it become in itself much less of a means of solemn withdrawal from the world. It no longer permitted individual withdrawal.[63]

Archer, therefore, like Douglas, tells us that the liturgical reform was most pleasing precisely to the educated middle classes, and disastrous for the

---

62 Mary Douglas, *Natural Symbols: Explorations in Cosmology*, 2nd ed. (Abingdon: Routledge, 1996), 44. It was first published in 1970.

63 Archer, *Two Catholic Churches*, 138–40.

less educated working classes. This of course is the reverse of what Pope Paul assumed would be the case.

The focus by Douglas and Archer on social class reflects, of course, the concerns of their professions at the time of their writing. The writer Fr Bryan Houghton expressed a similar contrast between the Church's educational elite and its foot-soldiers, in terms of the dissonance between the clergy, especially the higher clergy, and the laity. Others have investigated the contrast between men and women, women being more at ease with verbal communication and "horizontal," inter-personal relationships, and men with hierarchy, transcendence, and ritual.

These different approaches are not necessarily mutually exclusive, though none offers a complete explanation. The truth at the bottom of them all can be expressed in this way: the assumption that word-by-word comprehension is the indispensable key to meaningful engagement with the liturgy is something most attractive to people who are, for whatever reason, themselves personally focused on verbal communication. Such people are apt to ignore or downplay non-verbal communication, which may play a much more important role in the lives of others than it does in their own. Non-verbal communication includes the feeling of comradeship in a football crowd; the place of the *paterfamilias* at the head of the dinner table; natural expressions of affection by small children; and those ideas and feelings transcending words which are elicited by songs, great buildings, powerful works of art, the natural world, and the liturgy.

The problem at the time of the reform was, above all, a lack of both empathy and self-knowledge on the part of those who focus on verbal communication. Pope Paul did not say that he himself could not engage fruitfully in the Latin liturgy: on the contrary, he imagined that it was *only* he, and a small elite of which he was a member, who could engage with it. The ancient Latin liturgy, indeed, munificently rewards those focused on verbal communication, who make the effort to engage with it at the verbal level. To them is opened the riches of style, poetry, and scriptural allusion which make the ancient texts such masterpieces of literature: in this, perhaps, it offers a contrast with the religious rites of pagan Africa. What Pope Paul (and a large part of the Liturgical Movement) failed to understand is that those *not* focused on verbal communication, who therefore do not fully, or at all, appreciate the stylistic grandeur and beauty of the ancient Collects or the Roman Canon, can and do nevertheless derive something of immense spiritual significance from the liturgy, at a non-verbal level. The fact that the liturgy is in a sacred language, set apart from profane use, communicates grandeur and beauty even to those who do not understand that language.

7. *The anti-traditional elite*

As one of the old men quoted by Archer suggests, it might seem, indeed, that the liturgy communicates this supernatural reality even more powerfully to those who cannot understand Latin, than to certain ones who, like Fr Foster, understand Latin so fluently that the Latin of the Mass seems prosaic.

Latin has been the West's working language of scholarship for longer than it has been the language of the Catholic Church. The Latin of the liturgy, as noted above, has a sacred character because of its highly distinctive register. This distinctiveness ought to be the more acutely appreciated the more highly developed one's skill in Latin is. Neither knowledge of Latin, nor ignorance of Latin, therefore, is necessary for a profound appreciation of the Latin liturgy, and knowledge is naturally preferable to ignorance.

Something more should be said, however, of the phenomenon of the anti-traditional elite, which has been visible in the Church at least since Erasmus and others made fun of the beliefs and practices of the simple faithful. For one thing, we should avoid swapping Pope Paul's stereotype of traditionalists as high-browed classical scholars, for another stereotype, that of Mary Douglas's pagans going into religious ecstasies. To explore this I should say a little more about Douglas's theory.

A key distinction in Douglas's classic work *Natural Symbols*[64] is between two different kinds of traditional society, or, better, two ends of a spectrum. On the one hand, there are the more highly hierarchical societies, which tend to have more ritualized religious practices. On the other, there are the more loosely structured societies, which tend to have

---

[64] Douglas, *Natural Symbols*, 57–71.

less ritualized religious practices. Douglas notes that the anthropologists of colonial times described the second group as more "primitive" than the first. The example Douglas cites is the Pygmies, who are nomadic or semi-nomadic hunter-gatherers. Their social structure and religion contrasts with that of the settled farmers living in the same area, who have a hierarchical society and a ritualized religion.

Anthropological generalisations are, of course, hazardous. Many hunter-gatherer societies, like the Inuit, have at least part-time Shamans of considerable social and religious importance. Some Aboriginal Australian groups have highly developed religious ceremonial.[65] Perhaps the Pygmies are not simply a well-chosen example of what Douglas is talking about, but practically the only one. Nevertheless it seems fair to say that complex ritual is correlated with some stratification of society, if only because it will require specialised practitioners, and if it is taken seriously, it will give those practitioners some social importance. Again, the intensity of religious experience is likely to be correlated to the use of elaborate ritual, since, to speak loosely, it is the function of the ritual to intensify religious experience: they are supposed to be impressive.

Douglas enjoys the irony of classifying progressive, educated, middle class Westerners with the Pygmies, but it is perfectly true that progressive family structures and workplaces tend to be less structured and hierarchical than traditional ones, and their products are less interested in ritual, whether civic, familial, or religious. In the West, the most hierarchical family structures, and the people with most interest in ritual, are, or were at the time of Douglas's writing, to be found among the traditional working classes, and, she notes, in the aristocracy. When Africans are exposed to a progressive education, we may expect a diminution of their sympathy for ritual. Insofar as this education takes hold, the complex social structures found in many traditional societies (though not among the Pygmies) will tend to break down, just as they have in the West.

---

[65] For a brief introduction to these and other groups, see Harold Barclay, *People without Government: An Anthropology of Anarchy* (Seattle, WA: Left Bank Books, 1990), 39–54.

On the other hand, Africans exposed to a traditional education in their own culture will not for that reason become estranged from their own religious traditions, or seek to establish less formal and hierarchical families or other associations, any more than highly educated European medieval scholars and aristocrats were *ipso facto* estranged from the traditions of the Christian West.

The problem is not education, but the type of education, and the social, cultural, and economic factors which reinforce or counteract it. The progressive outlook, which rejects hierarchy and prizes spontaneity over symbol and ritual, has indeed become an ideology which can come apart from the sociological conditions most favourable to it, and in its social implications can go far beyond the still highly structured conditions of even the most easy-going corners of the developed world. The result is not a society of happy-go-lucky Pygmies, but a good many young people whose upbringing has not equipped them with the habits of mind and social skills necessary to negotiate normal adult life. Fr Aidan Nichols follows Douglas in generalising that a family background lacking in ritual and hierarchy leads to an incomprehension of religious ritual and symbolism in later life.[66] This must, however, be qualified by the observation that many people of this background acutely feel the lack of ritual and symbolism in their lives, and seek it out in some form: a phenomenon exemplified by the continuing attraction of the occult, the New Age Movement, the much-studied movement towards more conservative religious denominations in North America,[67] and the youthful nature of the movement for the restoration of the ancient Catholic liturgy.

To draw this aspect of the discussion to a conclusion, the traditional education which, at least in part, formed Pope Paul and various conservative bishops and priests of the 1960s gave them an appreciation of the Latin liturgy of a type which, they correctly realised, was not available to

---

[66] Nichols, *Looking at the Liturgy*, 74.

[67] See, e.g., Dave Shifflet, *Exodus: Why Americans Are Fleeing Liberal Churches for Conservative Christianity* (New York: Penguin, 2005); Colleen Carroll, *The New Faithful: Why Young Adults are Embracing Christian Orthodoxy* (Chicago: Loyola Press, 2002).

everyone. An education more influenced by a bourgeois, individualistic culture, and the progressive ideology most at home in such a milieu, perhaps undermined the appeal of the traditional liturgy for other Catholic intellectuals of the same generation. What both groups failed to appreciate is the intense religious engagement which could be felt by those, perhaps with a limited education, who have an instinctive affinity for religious mystery and ritual: it is this which is brought out by Douglas and Archer. What no one, perhaps, at that time could have anticipated was that the stripping away of ritual and hierarchy from the lives of more and more families would lead to many of the victims of this process, not feeling contempt for ritual, but feeling an aching need for it: this is the implication of many more recent studies.

8. *Appreciation and participation*

At this point we should note that what is being asserted here is that we can say of the use of Latin what Trent said about the ceremonies, candles, bells, and so forth: as I quoted the Council above, they are all things "whereby both the majesty of so great a sacrifice might be recommended, and the minds of the faithful be excited, by those visible signs of religion and piety, to the contemplation of those most sublime things which are hidden in this sacrifice." Liturgical Latin is, in fact, a "visible sign of religion and piety."

The connection between the richness of the ceremonies and what Pope Paul called (in his General Audience address) the "silken garments" of the language being used while the ceremonies are proceeding is, indeed, a very natural one, and it seems surprising that this point was not more emphasised in the past. The explanation, perhaps, is that authorities in the Church, at Trent, in response to Pistoia, and in response to the murmurings of the Liturgical Movement about the barrier presented by Latin, did not wish to deny that learning Latin would enable Catholics to achieve a *higher* appreciation of the liturgy. Indeed, the teaching of Latin to as many Catholics as possible was a major objective of Catholic education. The Participation Thesis contains this grain of truth: the *fullest* appreciation of the liturgy is indeed reserved for those who can understand it at a verbal level.

The Liturgy, the Family, and the Crisis of Modernity

What needed saying, therefore, was not that the use of Latin presents no barrier at all to those who do not understand it, but rather that vernacularisation would not open participation to all but instead would destroy that thing in which its proponents wanted to participate. On the one hand, the liturgy would no longer have the stylistic and referential features which make the Roman Canon, the ancient Collects, and so on, such great works of sacred art, as appreciated by the highly educated. On the other hand, the use of the vernacular would rob the entire liturgy of the dignity and sacred character which is lent to it by the use of an ancient sacred language, as appreciated, potentially, by everyone.

What is left, after vernacularisation, are sacramental forms precisely *without* that atmosphere of *dignitas* which allows the individual to lose himself in the rite, to transcend his own thoughts and concerns. For this reason, meaningful participation is harder after vernacularistion, for everyone.

I have said that an education in Latin assists the individual to *appreciate* the literary qualities of the liturgy. I do not wish to say that a person without such an education will not be able to *participate* as fully, however, and this should be explained. Degrees of participation in the liturgy are a matter of degrees of the intensity of our spiritual engagement with it. Spiritual engagement is (other things being equal) assisted by the beauty of the liturgy, including the beautiful literary qualities glimpsed only by Latinists. Without saying that ignorance is preferable to knowledge of Latin, it remains true that those ignorant of Latin may well participate more fully than those expert in it, because despite this disadvantage they may be holier individuals. Fr Bryan Houghton, who I mentioned earlier, a particular champion of the preconciliar laity, points out that for all their simplicity they can be open to the grace of supernatural prayer. If this is happening, we should not be so bold as to belittle their level of liturgical participation. Houghton writes:

> Human activity is reduced to its minimum. Then the miracle occurs. At the fine apex of their souls, imperceptible even to themselves, the Holy Ghost starts making little shrieks of "Abba, Father" or,

after the consecration, soft groans of the Holy Name, "Jesu, Jesu." They adore: or rather, to be more accurate, the Holy Ghost adores within them.[68]

Again:

> It was also at Mass that the simple faithful practice prayer throughout their lives. They may have known little theology but they prayed as theologians often do not. Moreover, the simplest of them attained to heights of prayer and sanctity far beyond me.[69]

Reflecting on Fr Houghton's words, it is clear enough, in fact, that this *does* happen.

It is interesting, in this regard, to see that the *Catechism of the Catholic Church* regards non-verbal, contemplative prayer as a model for liturgical participation (§2711):

> Entering into contemplative prayer is like entering into the Eucharistic liturgy: we "gather up" the heart, recollect our whole being under the prompting of the Holy Spirit, abide in the dwelling place of the Lord which we are, awaken our faith in order to enter into the presence of him who awaits us.

Conclusion

I hope, in this chapter, I have gone some way to explaining both why the liturgical value of Latin was not more clearly articulated before the 1960s, and also why the Latin liturgy was deliberately destroyed by those who, in many cases, genuinely loved it. The idea that the old liturgy was appreciated by *them* but could not possibly be appreciated by the great mass of less educated Catholics was, I am convinced, both sincerely held and fairly widespread among ecclesiastical authorities in the 1960s and 1970s.

---

[68] Bryan Houghton, *Mitre and Crook* (Brooklyn: Angelico Press, 2019), 44. Originally published in 1979.
[69] Houghton, 169.

In support of this perhaps surprising claim, we may consider the response of generally conservative bishops and superiors to the grief of their subordinates over the liturgical reform. This could take two characteristic forms.

First, they would often assume that lay objectors had not, in fact, a real appreciation of the liturgy at all. If the new liturgy shook them up, that was not a bad thing. Fr Houghton explains:

> The new reforms in general and the liturgical reforms in particular were based on the assumption that the Catholic laity were a set of ignorant fools. They practiced out of tribal custom; their veneration of the Cross and the Mass was a totem worship; they were motivated by nothing more than the fear of Hell; their piety was superstition and their loyalty habit. But the most monstrous falsehood was that most Catholics had a Sunday religion which in no way affected their weekday behaviour.[70]

The second response, to those—perhaps the more highly educated laymen, or fellow clergy—to whom they allowed a genuine liturgical piety, was to say that the reforms had to be accepted as a *sacrifice*, as Pope Paul himself put it, for the good of others. These "others" would be the more simple folk among the faithful, children, or, if these examples did not ring true, the missions. What *we* appreciate, they would say, is a barrier to great masses of *other* people. In this way, those seeking to attend or celebrate the traditional Mass can be regarded as, of all things, *selfish*, lacking in charity: seeking to preserve something which will keep others, if not themselves, away from God. Both responses can still be encountered today.

I would like to end by noting that, on the argument of this chapter, we should not regard preconciliar liturgical practice, even that not much influenced by the Liturgical Movement, as a pastoral failure. One of the most intriguing questions of recent religious history is to what extent the Church in the 1950s was "hollowed out": a mere façade of success which

---

[70] Bryan Houghton, *Judith's Marriage* (Brooklyn: Angelico Press, 2020), 7. Originally published in 1987.

would crumble at the slightest provocation, in light of the astonishing speed of the collapse in vocations, conversions, and so on, in the course of the 1960s and 1970s. There is much to say about the causes of this collapse, and the weaknesses of the Church at the eve of the crisis which allowed it to happen, some of which I address in the next chapters. What I conclude from the forgoing discussion, nonetheless, is that, for all the imperfections of its celebration, and of the those attending it, the preconciliar liturgy did not fail to speak to the ordinary faithful.

5

Traditions and the Narcissism
of Consumer Capitalism

Byung-Chul Han's *The Disappearance of Rituals: A Topology of the Present*, a short book of about one hundred pages, could be described as a post-modern critique of the forces that are destroying both traditional societies and the remaining traditional elements of Western civilisation. It is not unique in this project, but it is a representative example of a kind of book that has become more common in recent years, and the arguments it contains are worthy of serious consideration by conservatives approaching the issues from a rather different perspective.

I am not an expert on Han's sources—Gadamer, Foucault, Baudrillard, Barthes, and others—so I take Han's arguments simply as presented in this work. They display some of the characteristics of post-modernism which make it such a frustrating area to work in: sweeping generalisa-tions, simplistic contrasts, dubious historical claims, and inconsistencies. To give an extreme example, Han appears to believe that ancient warfare did not involve projectiles (arrows and so on),[71] which I think would have been a surprise to anyone living at the time. To some extent, one has to go along with him and see if a sound argument can be constructed out of the impassioned and intriguing elements he presents.

This review appeared as "A Post-Modern Defense of Ritual," *The European Conservative* online, March 6, 2022. *The Disappearance of Rituals* was first published in German as *Vom Verschwinden der Rituale: Eine Topologie der Gegenwart* (Berlin: Ullstein, 2019). Its English translation was published by Polity Press of London in 2020.

71 Han, *Disappearance of Rituals*, 69.

Han's primary contrast is between a ritual society and a non-ritual one. The latter is what we have in the developed world, emerging out of the former. The rituals Han has primarily in view are social—etiquette, playing one's conventional role in society, and so on—but he includes religion as well. Han explains the erosion of ritual not only in terms of the Enlightenment, but also in terms of capitalism and, more recently, social media.

In order to be "authentic" in the sense popularised by Romanticism, we cannot simply be what we are made by our social role: a carpenter, a husband, or a father, for example, all things understood in a particular way in a ritual society. To allow ourselves to be formed by those roles would be inauthentic; it would not be a genuine reflection of one's true inner identity. Instead, we must carve out our own identity.

The apotheosis of this process is the carefully curated social media image, created out of nothing by the individual, a product which Han places in the context of capitalist production. For these images are products for others to consume and that are to be sold by the social media platforms, indirectly, to their advertisers. We are play-acting ourselves, out of necessity rather than playfulness, and not for our benefit, as slaves of liberal capitalism.

The anti-traditionalist may insist at this point that it is the individual in the ritual society who is play-acting, by conforming to a social role which has not sprung up from within himself: this implies a conflict between one's inner reality and outward behaviour. Han observes that self-constructed modern people with their artificial public social media images are actually the ones whose external appearance is most at odds with how they really feel and who they really are. This is a telling point, but with an insight which I think is worth the cover price of the book, Han goes beyond this. He writes:

As a form of ritual, politeness is without heart and without desire, without wish. It is more art than morality. It exhausts itself in the pure exchange of ritual gestures. Within the topology of Japanese politeness as a ritual form, there is no inside, no heart that would render the politeness a merely external etiquette. It cannot be described using the opposition of inside and outside. It does not dwell in an outside that, a pure semblance, could be juxtaposed with the inside. Rather, one is fully form, fully outside.[72]

Han is saying that in a ritual society it does not make sense to contrast the internal and the external in the way Romanticism encourages us to do. It does not make sense to ask, when an individual expresses welcome, friendship, or gratitude, through the appropriate ritual gestures, "Is this genuine? Does it come from the heart, from inside?" These questions do not make sense because there *is* no *inside* to be at odds with the outside. The individual is completely identified with the meaning of the ritual.

Han writes of the Japanese tea ceremony:

> The proper movements of the hands and body have a *graphic clarity,* and there is no uncertainty about them deriving from the influence of the mind or soul. The actors immerse *themselves* in ritual gestures, and these gestures create an *absence,* a *forgetfulness of self.*[73]

The Enlightenment accusation, against traditional societies, is that their members' behaviour, because set by custom, is not authentic, because it has been set by custom. Han responds that the outward appearance is *all there is,* because the individual has identified with it. There is no conflicting inner self struggling to be free.

This may sound as though Han thinks that rituals are performed by slaves or machines, but he suggests the reverse is the case. The forgetfulness of self he refers to frees us from the narcissism characteristic of non-ritual society and makes *play* and *art* possible. Indeed, for Han, ritual *is* both play and art: it is the playful addition of unnecessary, decorous features to otherwise bare human actions and artefacts: and, indeed, to the naked human body.

It would have been helpful if Han had further developed the implication that identification with ritual does not destroy creativity but on the

[72] Han, 67.
[73] Han, 64.

contrary makes it possible. Indeed, the whole world of art is a convention, a form of ritual in a wide sense. The boor who says "art is bunk" is the ultimate convention breaker, and in breaking the fundamental convention of art, by breaking the spell, he would make art impossible.

Again, Han identifies ritual with the possibility of freedom, the sovereign freedom of the warrior, for example, who is willing to give his life for a ritual construct such as honour or community. The self-made product of capitalism is too selfish for such a sacrifice: he could not see the point of it. All he has left is the production and consumption of things directed at his basic desires. For Han, this makes him the true slave.

Three difficulties occurred to me as I read this book. One is that Han repeatedly contrasts ritual with communication. But in an obvious sense, ritual communicates a great deal: the important difference, for example, between welcome and hostility. In fact, Han's contrast is between the elaborate packaging of a Japanese present, of an elegant but trifling witticism, or of a ceremonious seduction, with the undecorated, un-signified world of goods, data, and pornography. Han tells us that in a ritual, the packaging is more important than the contents. By contrast, modernity demands content with the minimum of packaging: the facts, without the ceremony. One can see Han's point, but to limit the term "communication" to the passing on of bare data is unhelpful.

A second problem is that contrary to Han's arguments, traditional societies can be very concerned with the contrast between inner and outer: with sincerity, the heart. In the biblical tradition, we often hear the complaint made by Isaiah and quoted by Christ: "This people honours me with their lips, but their hearts are far from me" (Isa 29:13; Matt 15:8). In general, the people of traditional societies care deeply about disloyalty, betrayal, lies, ingratitude, and oath-breaking, crimes which they regarded with horror.

Han seems to be making his point, however, by reference to the ideal: in the ideal knight, for example, wholly taken up in his role, there is no contrast between inside and outside. When someone falls short of this ideal, he has held something back, like a corrupt judge who holds back from complete identification with justice, to keep a space for venality.

A third difficulty is Han's contrast of ritual with "morality." Morality, a concern for "souls," he tells us, has taken over from politeness the following of rules:

> Forms of politeness are disappearing, disregarded by the cult of authenticity. Beautiful forms of conduct are becoming ever rarer. . . . Apparently, the ascendancy of morality is compatible with the barbarization of society. Morality is formless. Moral inwardness dispenses with form.[74]

Han seems to have identified morality with a Kantian focus on the inward self as a source of guidance, in which sincerity and consistency are prized above forms of life specific to a community. (Han's idiolect here is reminiscent of Kierkegaard's.) In the normal sense of "morality," the customs and obligations of each community must find their context in a system of universal principles of justice: as Aquinas said of human (positive) law, it can add to the obligations of natural law, but not contradict it.[75] Han does not appear to accept the notion of a universal law of nature, or anything equivalent to it.

As far as Han's conclusions are concerned, there is no doubt that he is correct to see a conflict between the post-Enlightenment obsession with self-creation and community. A community can exist only to the extent to which a group of individuals have something in common, and if a household, village, or nation is to have the character of a community, its members must allow themselves to identify with values and ways of life which they have inherited, and not created for themselves. The internet provides spaces where people can come together who have by mere coincidence created similar identities for themselves, but these identities are not *commitments*, and such groupings last only until their members re-create themselves in a new way.

Given this, it is difficult to reject Han's association of the rejection of ritual with isolation, loneliness, and narcissism. What is left to us, when

---

[74] Han, 68.
[75] Thomas Aquinas, *Summa theologiae* Ia-IIae, Q. 95, art. 3.

community and indeed relationships are removed, is, as Han suggests, *work,* something encouraged by what Han calls "the neoliberal regime." The focus on work as what gives meaning to life is opposed to contemplation, whether religious or artistic, which depends on our ability to use words and indeed ourselves not in the most literal and prosaic way, but playfully, lingering in a festival or in a village's central gathering space, disconnected, at least for a time, from utility.

Han announces in a "Preliminary Remark" that "the present essay is not animated by a desire to return to ritual. . . . Avoiding nostalgia, I sketch a genealogy of their disappearance, a disappearance which, however, I do not interpret as an emancipatory process."[76] This, however, is not true. Throughout the book, the imperative for restoration is implicit, and occasionally Han makes it explicit. "We might thus expect *a re-enchantment of the world* to create a healing power that could counteract collective narcissism."[77] "What must be won back is contemplative rest."[78] "Against this formless morality, we must defend an *ethics of beautiful forms.*"[79]

Han, a Korean by birth and German by adoption, represents something interesting and relatively new in this debate: an articulation of the case for ritual by someone highly educated in Western ideas but whose cultural heritage is in the ritual societies of the Far East. We do not have to agree with everything he says to appreciate the importance of his perspective. At the least, Han draws attention to the value of things which have been the subject of neglect and indeed vilification for three hundred years in the West: inherited loyalties, roles, and customs. He does so, moreover, from a cultural and political direction which may make his arguments harder for the opponents of tradition on the political Left to dismiss.

[76] Han, *Disappearance of Rituals*, vi.
[77] Han, 26.
[78] Han, 46.
[79] Han, 64.

6

Tradition, Liberation, and Meaning

I wish to place a recent development in the Catholic Church into the context of the wider cultural and political debate. The development is the publication, on July 16, 2021, of a document called *Traditionis Custodes*, and an accompanying Letter to Bishops, by Pope Francis. These documents seek to restrict, and ultimately abolish, the celebration of the Church's older form of liturgy.

This may look like an obscure internal dispute, but the Catholic Church, today and in terms of her place in history, is large enough to be the arena for an important conflict. For the Church is not simply old: in a certain way it preserves the past. It is a feature of the Catholic worldview to take seriously, within certain limitations, her own past practices and to regard them as action-guiding, normative, for the present and the future. This has long been ridiculed by the Church's opponents as a matter of doing the same thing as has always been done simply for the sake of it, even when the reasons for the original practice are no longer applicable or have been forgotten. Both the practice of treating tradition as normative, and the criticism of this as obscurantism, are very clearly on display in the history of the Catholic liturgy, though the Church's legal system, theology, and many other aspects of her governance and culture could also provide examples.

Liturgical development and interpretation

To give an example, there is a tradition in the Catholic liturgy that the priest, when saying the holiest prayers of the Mass, the Canon, inaudibly

Published in *The European Conservative* online, October 31, 2021.

at the altar, breaks the silence to say aloud a single phrase of the text he is reading: "nobis quoque peccatoribus" ("to us sinners, also"). In his 1949 *The Mass of the Roman Rite*, we are informed by the great liturgical historian Fr Josef Jungmann SJ, who was also an advocate of reform, that in some century distant from our own this custom was established as a signal for some other liturgical functionaries to do something. Developments since that time have been such, however, that this signal is no longer necessary.[80]

Jungmann's proposal is in itself perfectly plausible. The question is whether it debunks the meaning of this custom as understood by the worshippers of later generations. Thus, St Albert the Great points out that the priest's raising of his voice serves to draw attention to his act of confession: a confession of unworthiness, on the part of the clergy, which is frequently underlined in this liturgical tradition. St Peter Damian connected it also to the exclamation of guilt by the crowd at the crucifixion, the Sacrifice of Christ which the Mass re-presents. Amalarius of Metz associated it with the confession of Christ's divinity by the Centurion, which followed Christ's death on the cross. And so, the tradition of interpretation of the ritual goes on.[81]

The idea that a ritual is capable of bearing only the meaning given it by the person who created it is a mistake, parallel to the idea that a word can mean only what its etymology implies. Recovering the forgotten origins of a rite from the old manuscripts can certainly add to our historical knowledge and appreciation, but it does not cancel the significance a ritual may have acquired since that origin.

An anthropologist would say that this is a fact of life about culture: meanings commonly become attached to practices, not the other way round. A Christian could attribute this kind of development to Divine Providence. In neither case is this a matter of an infinitely malleable meaning: the context sets limits to what makes sense, and later ways of understanding it build upon earlier ones. The more this development goes

---

[80] Jungmann, *Mass of the Roman Rite*, 2:258.

[81] Jungmann, 2:259, and also Fr Thomas Crean, *The Mass and the Saints* (San Francisco: Ignatius Press, 2009), 156–58.

on, the more meaning there is for the worshipper to discover, and also the more detailed context there is for later commentators. They cannot take a radical new turn in interpreting the ritual without overturning the heavier and heavier weight of tradition. This implies, of course, that developments which fail to respect the earlier tradition are recognised as such and rejected.

This, then, is the paradox of the development of tradition. The richer the tradition, the more there is to contemplate, to inspire art, music, and poetry: and all this can be taken in different directions. At the same time the tradition binds us, and the central meaning, reiterated in a hundred ways by generations of commentators, is rendered the more emphatic.

The view of Jungmann and other critics of the tradition since the sixteenth century is that the elaboration of tradition—"accretions" is a favourite word of this school of thought—serves to obscure the original and authentic meaning of the liturgy. For those on the inside of a community of belief, however, unless they think that neither Providence nor the Church officials charged with weeding out heterodox developments had any effectiveness, this is a puzzling claim. Those developments, rather, must be understood as building upon, commenting on, elaborating and clarifying the authentic meaning: even, of constituting the "authentic" meaning in cases where there is no useful "original" meaning, as perhaps is the case of using an elevated voice for the phrase "nobis quoque peccatoribus."

Jungmann and others are correct, nevertheless, that this liturgical tradition is a kind of burden. It limits our options. The recent action of Pope Francis, in expressing his desire to wipe from the face of the earth the Church's more ancient liturgical forms, is the latest attempt to free the Church from having anything to do with it. Even something only celebrated by a tiny number of priests and attended by a tiny number of lay Catholics was, in a telling phrase from his 2021 Letter to Bishops, deemed something which threatened to "block her path." For when his predecessor, Pope Benedict XVI, declared in his Letter to Bishops in 2007 that "what earlier generations held as sacred, remains sacred and great for us too," he was declaring the validity of something that claims the authority to bind us, to condition future developments, to rule out certain things.

A version of this conflict lies at the heart of the post-Enlightenment debate about politics and culture. There are those who view the institutions and forms of life that have grown up organically in human society over time as not only offering us, as individuals, basic protection, but also as giving us meaning, making possible complex life-projects, beauty, and understanding. This can be so even if these institutions and forms of life, usually lacking the guarantee of a revealed religion, are imperfect and in need of reform, and even if a wide range of non-conforming lifestyles are in practice tolerated. Those on this side of the divide will nevertheless want to preserve these institutions and forms of life, to improve them if possible, and to pass them on to future generations.

On the other side, there are those who think that all such institutions are oppressive. Detailed argument about specifics need not detain us, as human freedom is impeded, on this view, whenever our understanding of the world or our set of life-options is decisively influenced by pre-existing cultural norms. On such a view, loosening such norms is progress, but abolishing them altogether is the ultimate goal. Only when there are no cultural expectations, no categories, and no conventions will we be truly free and truly able to express ourselves and develop authentically, because only then will the full range of possibilities be open to us without impediment.

To illustrate, legislation to permit divorce under certain circumstances is presented as increasing the freedom, the options, of married persons. These options are still further increased if divorce is made easier, and easier, and easier. Sooner or later, in the implementation of such reforms, we arrive at the point when there is no longer any difference, legally, between being married and not being married. This is the situation, for the liberal, of ultimate freedom, but it is also the point at which marriage ceases to exist for practical purposes.

The conservative points out that this process has not increased freedom at all. When marriage is abolished, it is removed as an option: people can no longer marry. They can only do what they could have done anyway, namely engage in some form of open-ended cohabitation. Not only that, but the option represented by marriage is an extraordinarily rich and interesting one, since the lifelong, socially recognised, sexually exclusive commitment makes for an especially fulfilling kind of relationship, and opens up possibilities for relationships within and between families which are not otherwise possible.

A society in which the idea of lifelong commitment is absent, where there is no legal or social norm which allows a couple to be publicly recognised as committed to each other, is obviously a society in which one cannot seek fulfilment through married life. It is one in which the goods offered by marriage as traditionally conceived are not available. It is poorer not only from the point of view of the welfare of children, but for the life-options of adults as well.

Just as certain liturgical liberals within the Catholic Church will not be happy until the ancient forms of the liturgy are completely obliterated, so those who regard traditional marriage as oppressive will not rest until no one is permitted to marry. It is not enough that some people, with varying degrees of legal toleration, may live lives which conflict with established norms. The norms themselves must cease to exist, lest they even *influence* people's life choices. As Simone de Beauvoir famously said in a 1975 interview about the vocation of the housewife: "Women should not have that choice, precisely because if there is such a choice, too many women will make that one."[82]

The process of loosening, trivializing, and ultimately abolishing all the cultural institutions, expectations, and shared meanings of Western culture is the great project of Enlightenment liberalism. It is not, ultimately, a coherent project, because it is impossible to live without anything resembling these things.

The paradox of Duckspeak

To take a fundamental example, language itself is a set of conventions, expectations, categories, and shared meanings. It is not surprising to see

---

[82] "Sex, Society, and the Female Dilemma," interview with Betty Friedan, *The Saturday Review*, June 14, 1975, pp. 12–21, at p. 18.

radicals today rebelling against language, and trying to overthrow conventions which embody, symbolize, or simply can be used to refer to values and realities which they oppose.

Thus, by imposing "Simplified Chinese" on schoolchildren, the Chinese Communist Party has made the younger generation incapable of reading the classics of Chinese literature as originally written. In a different way, the erasure of the language of biological sex, for example in English courts of law, makes it impossible to articulate what is objectionable about a biological male being present in an all-female space, such as a shelter for victims of domestic abuse.

George Orwell anticipated such manipulation of language in his dystopian novel *1984*. In the story the totalitarian Party is preparing a radically simplified language, Duckspeak, which will cut the population off from the written records of the past and make it as difficult as possible to formulate a critique of the regime, since the new language lacks the necessary concepts and distinctions.[83]

Even Duckspeak contains some linguistic concepts and grammatical rules, however, otherwise it would be useless as a form of even the most basic communication. An even more radical idea has been doing the rounds since the 1960s, that teaching the rules of spelling and grammar is *itself* an act of oppression. No doubt those making this argument assume, in a vague way, that even if no one is taught the rules, they will linger on with sufficient strength for us to be able to use language to buy the groceries we want, and not the ones we don't want. However, it would be inconsistent to permit society as a whole to maintain an oppressive system, having stopped school teachers doing so. On the other hand, we really do need a widely-understood way to distinguish carrots from courgettes.

The radicals are not wrong in thinking that language is value-laden, and of course the values implicit in any given language are imperfect. The same is true for the rules that constitute the social conventions of art, of

---

[83] In Orwell's dystopia, where the totalitarian government has endeavored to replace Oldspeak with Newspeak, the final iteration of the process of the destruction of language is called Duckspeak.

politics, and of religion. The conventions nevertheless give us the means to say and do things which would otherwise be, literally, inconceivable, and any long-established and complex system will contain the resources necessary to critique its own values.

In the name of freeing us from the oppression represented by these values, the post-Enlightenment project constantly narrows our cultural resources: of what we can do, say, or imagine. Its complete victory is impossible, so in practice, after each liberal victory, society tends to coalesce around reformed or simplified versions of the various institutions, or else reacts against the process with new forms of allegiance and solidarity, often taking ugly forms. What is possible, nevertheless, is what liberals are pleased to call "progress": the weakening of one institution or norm after another, or their replacement with artificial substitutes, which offer less restraint, and less meaning, and may even be, as Orwell warned, the tools of new forms of oppression.

Conclusion

Liberalism's victims are soon forgotten; so too are its opponents. We may hope for a reaction, and indeed some degree of reaction is inevitable. Unless conservatives win the fundamental argument about the role of cultural norms in giving us worthwhile options, however, in the long term this will turn out be only another temporary pause for the liberal juggernaut.

At the same time, we must devote ourselves in practical ways to the preservation and restoration of the traditions which give life meaning. In this context, the battle over the liturgy of the Catholic Church is not something which outsiders can afford to ignore.

Part II

Crisis

7

What Vatican II Did to the Church

In 2013 I led a small research project for the Latin Mass Society, with the help of some volunteers, extracting statistics from old copies of the *Catholic Directory for England and Wales*.[84] At that time the *Directory* published tables of figures from all the dioceses of England and Wales, giving the number of baptisms, receptions of adults into the Church, marriages, and the number of priests. Since these are based on properly-maintained parish and diocesan records, they seem a secure foundation for an overview of Catholic practice. The estimates of the Catholic population by diocese were likely to be less precise. Most of the figures go back to 1913, but the number of clergy went back further. The *Directory* also listed the priests being ordained each year, though these we had to count, laboriously. Not long after we did this, the *Catholic Directory* ceased publication; when revived, this information was no longer provided.

It seems surprising that no one had done this work before, at least no one we could find, but perhaps this was because the results were so depressing. I summarised them in a press release as follows.

Marriages: The number of marriages collapsed by a third between 1968 and 1978 (from 47,417 to 31,534), and has continued a rapid decline since then, now standing at less than 10,000 a year, a quarter of the 1968 level in absolute terms, and even less in relation to the

---

[84] The fruits of our labours may be downloaded from https://lms.org.uk/statistics.

estimated Catholic population (from 12 per thousand in 1968 to 2½ per thousand in 2010).

Conversions fell off a cliff in the 1960s. From a peak of 15,794 in 1959, it fell to 5,117 in 1972; in relation to the Catholic population, it fell by more than 70 percent between those two years. It has not recovered.

Baptisms halved between 1964 and 1977 (137,673 in 1964 to 68,351 in 1977), and are even lower today (oscillating around the 60,000 mark). This is not just the effect of the end of the "baby boom": considered in relation to total live births for England and Wales (using data from the Office for National Statistics), the first half of the twentieth century saw steady growth, with Catholic baptisms peaking at nearly 16 percent of all live births in 1963. This was followed by a decline of a third between the mid-1960s and the mid-1970s. A more gentle decline has continued to the present: today fewer than 10 percent of babies born alive in England and Wales are being baptised in the Catholic Church.

Ordinations fell by more than 56 percent between 1965 and 1977 (from 233 to 101), and the decline has continued. Even on the more optimistic figures supplied by the National Office of Vocations (compared to the *Catholic Directory*) for the current year, showing an increase in recent years, numbers are at scarcely 30 percent of their 1964 level. (Counting only ordinations to the diocesan clergy, there were 134 in 1964; the NOV predicts 41 this year.)

A similar story is told by the statistics of other countries in the developed world. Although the precise peak year varies a little, the numbers tell of a spectacular collapse in the ten or fifteen years from the early 1960s, and a steady decline thereafter. It is something in need of explanation.

Just how complex this explanation is going to be is indicated by statistics from the wider world. In a classic work of sociology, *Bowling Alone*,[85]

---

[85]   Robert Putnam, *Bowling Alone: The Collapse and Revival of American Community* (New York: Simon & Schuster, 2001).

Robert Putnam examines what happened to American society in the course of the twentieth century. Measures of religious belief, membership in political, religious, social, community, and volunteering groups, the number of people going to dinner parties and poker-playing circles, and a whole lot of other things, display an uncannily similar pattern. With dips for the two world wars, they went up in the first half of the century, and from about 1965 or 1970 they went into steep decline.

The process Putnam describes for the United States, which has parallels in other developed countries, is extremely worrying. People no longer know their neighbours; the level of trust among the members of neighbourhoods has declined; people feel isolated and depressed. He describes this process as the loss of "social capital." What it amounts to is a decline of all kinds of communities, along with the sense of belonging and the mutual support which they provide.

Putnam considers several different hypotheses to explain this process. The central fact which seems to need explaining is that people no longer have the time and inclination they used to have to attend meetings or parties or any of the kinds of things that used to put them into contact with the people in their geographical area. It seems likely that there is a combination of causes at work. Chief among Putnam's favoured factors are lengthening commuting times, and television, because they both reduce the free time people have available to go out of the house to meet people.

Putnam would be the first to agree that there are lot of other things going on in this vast, long-term, and apparently unstoppable process. Nevertheless, the shift of millions of people from dense city-centre living to diffuse suburban living, made possible by the increasing affordability of cars, and the extraordinary take-up of television ownership (from almost no one to almost everyone) in the course of the 1950s, fit the time-scale quite neatly, and I don't doubt they had an important effect.

Putnam himself did not think that these two factors explained the full effect, and he attributes an important part in the process to something he expresses only in general terms: the change of values between generations. He is able to show that younger people don't behave in the same way as earlier generations, even under the same external conditions. Chief among the changes of attitude between generations was the sexual revolution of the 1960s, which was itself connected with a number of factors: the disruption to existing communities caused, first, by the war, and then by suburbanisation, and finally by the new prosperity of the young, giving them unprecedented freedom and the apparently undivided attention of the advertising industry. The sexual revolution also fed on and reinforced increasing individualism and was rapidly validated by medical technology (the contraceptive pill) and legislation (on abortion and divorce).

Religion and social network effects

More recent work, focused on religious affiliation and practice, has been able to build up a more detailed picture of this process. In *Mass Exodus*,[86] Stephen Bullivant, a professor of the sociology of religion, focuses on the role of communities in the transmission and maintenance of values, including religious beliefs and practices: something called by sociologists "social network effects." Catholics who inhabit a community where Catholic belief and practice are normal are much more likely to maintain that belief and practice than if they live in a social context in which it is abnormal or frowned upon. This should be obvious. Equally obvious, and confirmed by empirical study, is the fact that the years following the Second World War were characterised by a number of things which undermined the influence of communities on their members, and even the existence of the communities themselves.

The war itself had this effect, not only by physically dislocating populations (as happened on a massive scale in central Europe, and to a lesser extent in England), but by exposing men enlisted to fight, and women drafted into factories and farms, to new influences and new friendship groups. War damage, slum clearance, and the building of social housing and suburbs in the following decades disrupted communities still more. Tight-knit Catholic Irish communities in Britain, and many ethnic and religiously-based communities in the USA, were dispersed in this process.

---

[86]   Stephen Bullivant, *Mass Exodus: Catholic Disaffiliation in Britain and America since Vatican II* (Oxford: Oxford University Press, 2019).

At the same time, the radio, and then, much more powerfully, television, brought different values and assumptions into the heart of the home, and a vast expansion of higher education took increasing numbers of young people out of their home communities and exposed them to a different set of influences.

Bullivant argues that a critical factor for religious affiliation and practice is the degree to which members of a religious group are influenced by fellow-believers, or by outsiders. It is inevitable that disaffiliation—lapsation—will increase as cultural influences hostile or indifferent to the religion at issue become more dominant in a person's life. It follows that the set of circumstances which pertained in the decades after the Second World War in the developed world would inevitably see an increase in religious disaffiliation.

Looking back at Putnam's wider concerns, the same factors had their effect on communities we might think of as quite secular. More people will lose interest in the values and practices of their local community if they are continuously soaked in a quite different set of values and practices, especially if these are packaged in a highly attractive way by the entertainment industry or in the prestigious context of higher education. Even things like inviting the neighbours over for dinner looks less attractive compared to the entertaining and exciting ideas coming out of the mass media or picked up from university.

Attention to social network effects and how these tended to fall away in the post-war period allows us to add to Putnam's thesis. He identified the lack of *time* people had for community-building activities from the 1960s, and noted the younger generation's changed values. This change of values can now be explained in terms of the weaker social network effects caused by migration and suburbanisation, television, increased higher education, and so on. These fed into a self-reinforcing process: communities had less influence over members to attend community-building events, which weakened the network still further.

It should be noted that while it is conventional to lament the loss of social capital, an important constituency of people would rather dance on the grave of mid-century social networks than see them preserved or revived. It is said that some British town planners saw the end of close-knit Irish Catholic neighbourhoods and the like not as a matter of regret but as a happy result of their work, because they disagreed with the values these communities inculcated: they regarded them as regressive and dull, and characteristic of uneducated social inferiors. While composing this chapter, the well-known left-wing British journalist George Monbiot tweeted: "I was brought up in a village that was almost exclusively white and Christian. It was the most boring and stifling place I've ever known."[87]

Experience should have demonstrated by now that it is easier to destroy communities with values you don't like than to build up communities with values you prefer, but the lesson is lost on much of the West's cultural elite, who tend to share Monbiot's negative attitude towards the vigorous communities of the recent past. For present purposes, the Monbiot attitude indicates one reason why the destruction of social capital has been so difficult to counter, in either society as a whole or in the Church. Policies which could have been, and still could be, adopted to reinforce community ties would be seen as strengthening socially conservative attitudes, which most policy-makers reject.

To conclude this section, a higher than usual degree of lapsation was inevitable in the post-war era, and we can see this effect on a wide range of religious groups in the developed world. This process is paralleled by what happened to the non-religious cultural practices which are also part of community life. It is essential to understand this process if we are to understand the crisis in the Church.

The Church, in the meantime, was not inert. At the very moment that the social crisis of the twentieth century was gaining momentum, the Church decided to change itself.

Vatican II and its effects

For many years, the boilerplate response by the more progressive end of the Catholic establishment, to talk about collapsing numbers at Mass and other measures of decline, has been to blame "sociological factors."

---

[87] November 29, 2022.

As indicated above, these factors are certainly real. The next question is whether the policies the Church adopted in this period made things better or worse. The boilerplate response goes on that things would have been even worse if the Church had not changed.

More radical progressives take this response a step further, saying that the Church's decline is the result of failing to change *more*. If the Church began to ordain women, or bless same-sex unions, and do all the other things on the progressive shopping-list, then, they suggest, the decline could even be reversed.

On the other hand, conservative and traditionally-minded Catholics tend to say the opposite: that the decline of the Church was made worse by the changes made by or after the Council, or by many of these, and perhaps could be reversed if different policies were adopted.

This debate has been a fairly sterile one over the decades, but it need not be so. The question is an empirical one and can be approached in three ways. First, we can ask those who have stopped practicing the Faith what they think. Second, the performance of the Catholic Church can be compared with that of roughly comparable religious organisations which have changed more, or less, in roughly comparable ways. Third, the nature of the changes made in the 1960s and thereafter can be examined in light of the destructive sociological forces at work in this era, with a view to assessing whether they exacerbated or counteracted those forces.

The first approach has been taken by Stephen Bullivant in another work, a survey of lapsed Catholics undertaken for the Diocese of Portsmouth in southern England: *Why Catholics Leave*.[88] It reveals no clear pattern of people saying that they lapsed because the Church's teaching was too conservative, let alone that they would return if it changed. On the contrary, many participants had been deeply demoralised by the failure of their local parish to engage with difficult teaching, and complained about parish catechists rubbishing the Church's official positions. One respondent remarked:

[88] Stephen Bullivant, *Why Catholics Leave, What They Miss, and How They Might Return* (Mahwah, NJ: Paulist Press, 2019).

Education and faith building at the parish level is usually weak and sometimes those doing it probably shouldn't be. It always amazes me that people who don't agree with certain things can push [their agenda] in such contexts and get away with it. The Church really is punitive in this regard. If it were a business, some of these parish leaders would really be brand killers. (male, 23)

Another complained that "people who undermine what the Church teaches are given positions within parishes" (female, 20).

It is hardly surprising that this situation, which is all too familiar, should have undermined the Church's credibility. "If the Church looks confused, seems to change when the pressure mounts, or fudges on difficult issues, then it's not attractive to anyone" (female, 23).

What did surprise me from the survey was the result that 10 percent of respondents agreed or "strongly agreed" with the statement: "I prefer the Latin Mass but there is none in my area."

The second approach, comparing the performance of the Catholic Church with that of other religious groups, reveals quite a strong pattern. Roughly speaking, the more liberal a denomination or religion, or the more it has liberalised, the worse it has fared in the modern West. The Amish in the USA, at the conservative end of the spectrum, and Islam and Eastern Orthodox churches (in the West), have outperformed the Catholic Church and weathered the storm quite well. The Anglican church in England, and English non-conformist (Protestant) churches, and what are called in America "mainline Protestant" churches, have done many or all of the things Catholic progressives propose, and they have done much worse than the Catholic Church. Many of these are by now approaching a total collapse in congregation sizes.

The third approach, an examination of the changes made, should help to explain why things have worked out as they have. Fundamental to the process, as explained in the last section, is the decline of the influence of community. As already indicated, the influence a community has over its members reflects the number and importance of interactions members have with fellow community-members compared with non-members.

To exist at all, members must be distinguishable in some way from non-members. If membership of a particular community is to be attractive, members must be able to see the values and practices of the community being taken seriously by fellow members. In other words, a community must be inward-looking, to some extent; it must have markers of identity; and its practices must involve affirmations of the importance of its values which are costly to those making them. Bullivant calls the last of these things "Credibility Enhancing Displays," or "CREDs": examples in the Catholic context would be people taking part in a rota of watching before the Blessed Sacrament overnight, going on a long walking pilgrimage, and fasting. The ultimate CRED is martyrdom.

The set of attitudes, policies, and initiatives which have dominated the Church since the Council—the conciliar "orientation," as it is called—is typified, in contrast, by the idea that Catholics should look beyond the community, talk more (and more open-mindedly) to members of other faiths, and not worry about markers of Catholic identity or the kinds of practices which enhance the credibility of the community's values.

Catholic churches have been made to look much less distinctive. Those aspects of Catholic worship and the devotional life most unlike other denominations have been dismantled, and the Catholic martyrs have been downplayed. Many of the largely jettisoned devotions—Exposition of the Blessed Sacrament and walking pilgrimages among them—were the very things which had provided opportunities for CREDs. And enduring CREDs of the past, from the cult of the English martyrs to fine church furnishings provided by the pennies of the poor, were downplayed or actually destroyed.

Another aspect of the conciliar and postconciliar era is the simple fact of *change*. Any kind of change is potentially disruptive to a community, as it affects how people interact and their felt connection with the community going back into the past. Even changes for the better, or what seems to be the better, need to justify themselves in this context, and even changes that are unavoidable should be made while keeping this problem in mind. Will members feel the same affection and loyalty to the new parish priest, the new church building, the new liturgy, or the new style of preaching?

The Liturgy, the Family, and the Crisis of Modernity

The Catholic Church went through a process of change of an unprecedented scale between the 1950s and the 1980s, with the most rapid and wrenching taking place from the mid-1960s to the early 1970s. Did this process have a negative effect on how connected Catholics felt to the Church? It could not have failed to do so.

Those leading these changes thought of themselves as being "with it," because younger Catholics, like young people of their generation throughout society, were more open-minded, less ghettoised, less enamoured of traditional Catholic aesthetics, and, being less committed to the faith, less inclined to undertake CREDs or to be impressed by them. For all the reasons already mentioned, this generation was being pulled away from the Catholic community, and this process would naturally manifest itself as an increased reluctance to engage in community-building activities. They would complain about having to go to Church for lots of feast days, or having to fast; they would be disinclined to attend devotions and go on pilgrimages; and so on. Faced with this reluctance, one quite natural response was to ease up on what the Church demanded, as if this was a negotiation: if the Church asks less of people reluctant to give as much as before, perhaps a compromise could be reached.

But of course this was not a negotiation: it was a process of alienation. What was driving the process was young Catholics having diminishing contact with and influence from their community, in terms of meeting its members and in terms of seeing displays of Catholic markers of identity and values. By telling them they need not come to church as much, that they need not fast, that they need not worry about avoiding non-Catholic books or finding a Catholic spouse, and by depriving them, even, of the sight of distinctive Catholic architecture and devotional art, or things which reminded them of the continuity of the Catholic community through time, progressive priests and bishops were actually *accelerating* the process of weakening community influence on these young Catholics, and so accelerating their alienation.

Failing to see the downside to this process of community disintegration, the Church's leadership pushed it on faster and further, at a moment when it would have been wiser to look for ways to counter the effects of unavoidable social changes. In this very simple way, the postconciliar orientation made things worse. The 1960s was a time when the Church needed, not to open the windows, but to raise the drawbridge.[89]

And then, starting in the 1980s but rising in importance over time, came the counter-CREDs of the clerical abuse crisis. As Bullivant shows, this has not been a decisive factor in Catholic disaffiliation, but it is a measurable one.

The Liturgy

I have not said much about the liturgy up to now, but it should be clear what place it has in this story. Up until the liturgical reform, the Catholic Mass was an important marker of identity for the Catholic community, a point recognised even by the reformers themselves. The architect of the reform, Archbishop Annibale Bugnini, wrote:

> The point needs to be made that in the United States and especially in England, and more generally in countries with a strong Protestant majority, the introduction of the vernacular into the liturgy meant to many the loss of one distinction between Catholics and Protestants and of a sign of their attachment to Rome in the face of Protestantism. For these people, the psychological effects of the reform were quite serious. For some, the reform meant the collapse of a world and the practical acceptance of views until then regarded as heretical.[90]

What Bugnini is describing is not the gradual disappearance of an important marker of community identity, but its rapid destruction accompanied by semi-official vilification with the rhetoric of "dumb spectators," "mumbo-jumbo," and the like. As he acknowledged, the effect was profound, and negative.

But it was not just felt in countries with a "strong Protestant majority." Catholics all over the world were shocked, since the Mass was everywhere

---

[89] This is essentially Bullivant's conclusion: see *Mass Exodus*, 253–63.
[90] Bugnini, *Reform of the Liturgy*, 280.

central to Catholic identity. Nor was it as if other markers of identity were strengthened to compensate. Cardinal Ratzinger expressed it even more strongly than Bugnini, in a passage I will have occasion to quote again in this volume:

> A community is calling its very being into question when it suddenly declares that what until now was its holiest and highest possession is strictly forbidden, and when it makes the longing for it seem downright indecent. Can it be trusted any more about anything else? Won't it proscribe tomorrow what it prescribes today?[91]

The policy response

For Ratzinger this was perhaps hard-won wisdom. For the auto-demolition of the Church, of which Pope Paul VI famously complained, was not an accident. It was a deliberate policy. It is described, with approval, by the young Fr Joseph Ratzinger:

> The fact is, as Hans Urs von Balthasar pointed out as early as 1952, . . . she [the Church] must relinquish many of the things that have hitherto spelled security for her and that she has taken for granted. She must demolish longstanding bastions and trust solely the shield of faith.[92]

The idea was that the Church would have more impact on the world as whole, if it was less distinctive *vis-à-vis* the world, and that without the barriers, non-Catholics would be drawn in to the Church more easily. A moment's thought should have revealed that it would also be easier for Catholics to leave, which is what actually happened. But there are two other ways in which this policy was naïve.

---

[91] Joseph Ratzinger, *Salt of the Earth: The Church at the End of the Millennium*, trans. Adrian Walker (San Francisco: Ignatius Press, 1997), 176.

[92] Joseph Ratzinger, *Principles of Catholic Theology: Building Stones for a Fundamental Theology*, trans. Sr Mary Frances McCarthy (San Francisco: Ignatius Press, 1987), 391.

First, if you want to draw people in, there must be something to draw them in *to*. There must be something distinctive which can attract their attention in the first place, and there must be a community waiting to welcome them and give them a home. If the community is undermined, so is the Church's capacity to draw people in and sustain their spiritual lives.

Second, the social "walls" around the Catholic community before the 1960s were already crumbling, for the reasons already noted. If Vatican II had never happened, or if in some sense it could be reversed (whatever that might mean), the dense urban and rural communities of the mid-twentieth century would still have been opened up by the factors already mentioned: suburbanization, expanded universities, television, and so on. Those who say these communities were stifling, and characterized by prejudice against outsiders, can relax. They were doomed anyway. The only question was the degree of dis-integration which was going to take place. If Bugnini, Balthasar, the liberal young Ratzinger, and other Vatican II zealots wanted to see what would happen if the Church was weakened as a social network, all they need have done is wait and see. They didn't need to take a sledgehammer to help the process along.

The quotation illustrates the extent to which there was an ideological element to the process of community-destruction; even today this makes a rational assessment of the situation, and response to it, difficult. From the very beginning, influential voices were sounding the alarm, but the leadership of the Church was dominated by people who had been brought up on the idea that the "demolition of bastions" was a spiritual necessity. They are the equivalent within the Church of the view of George Monbiot, which looks at the community as it existed in the past with disdain.

As noted in passing above, part of this disdain is that of a cultural elite towards the less sophisticated. Members of the progressive elite in secular society and in the Church alike talk loudly about their affection for and solidarity with "working people" and "communities," but their attitudes and policy preferences suggest that they have little understanding of what sustains them.

With the assistance of the Catholic anthropologist Mary Douglas, the sociologist Anthony Archer, and the writer Fr Bryan Houghton, I argued in chapter 4 that the Church's leadership had, and continues to have, little sympathy with how the "simple faithful" participate in the liturgy, since they themselves participate in a somewhat different way, with much greater emphasis on intellectual engagement. I say they lack "sympathy," and not just "understanding," because if confronted with evidence that working-class Catholics participated in the liturgy in a different way, I think members of the progressive elite would typically respond by saying that it must, then, be an inferior form of participation, and that they should be forced to change. This is precisely the patronising attitude condemned by Pope Pius XII in *Mediator Dei*, referring to those who don't follow Mass word-by-word in hand-missals: "Who, then, would say, on account of such a prejudice, that all these Christians cannot participate in the Mass nor share its fruits?"[93]

In the same way, the progressive elite derive their sense of belonging and their network of moral and practical support from somewhat different sources than everyone else. They are far less concerned with geographical proximity and shared cultural practices: they feel cosy and warm not in a familiar neighbourhood populated with childhood friends and second cousins, but wrapped up in the sense of superiority granted by fashionable clothes and smart opinions. If in trouble, they are sustained by a social network constituted, not by neighbours and family, but old university and work chums inhabiting other continents. When it is pointed out to them that social or economic policies they favour are destroying the fabric of working class communities and leading to unprecedented numbers of deaths of despair (a concept combining suicide with drug overdoses and the like), part of what hinders them from taking the problem seriously is that they do not think the way of life which once did sustain those communities was a good one. Its destruction is not something they can bring themselves to regret. They themselves don't need these things that are disappearing. Why can't those working class people just be more like them?

Within the Church we find a progressive elite which does not derive its sense of self from continuity, familiarity, or visible markers of Catholic

---

[93]   Pius XII, *Mediator Dei*, §108.

identity, and are impatient with those who do—or who used to. They don't see a community based on those things as a good thing; they think, without necessarily articulating this clearly to themselves, that it would be better for everyone else to be more like them, and identify with the Church in a more purely intellectual way, or by having some special role in it, paid or not.

The problem, of course, is that the rest of society is not just unwilling to re-define themselves in the way the elite does, but actually unable to do so. Not only does it require a level of education inaccessible to most people, but part of the self-understanding of the progressive elite is precisely as being an *elite:* of not being like everyone else. This is not a class which could, even in theory, open itself up to encompass the whole of society. When they do find their markers of identity, whether fashionable opinions or clothes fashion labels, adopted by more and more people, they are obliged to find new ones.

Conclusion

I have attempted to establish a series of claims in this chapter.

First, that there was a social crisis in the 1960s and 1970s which was independent of the Church, which would have caused higher levels of disaffiliation from the Church than usual regardless of what the Church had done about it.

Second, that the unprecedented changes of the conciliar and postconciliar era amplified the problems Catholic communities were already facing, and made the degree of lapsation worse than it would otherwise have been.

Third, that those responsible for these changes lacked sympathy with the *way* most Catholics had been, up to then, connected with the Church: their sources of loyalty and affection. They thought and still think that this kind of faith is inferior to their own, and are not motivated to defend or repair the highly-networked, "tribal" affiliation to the Church which had served as the Church's sociological basis for the previous two millennia.

I have already noted that for most Catholics, adopting the kind of attachment to the Church enjoyed by the progressive elite is simply not possible. The progressive agenda of permanent revolution in the Church implies, therefore, the permanent loss of the vast majority of the flock.

This, indeed, is a sacrifice some members of the elite are willing to make. To quote the young Ratzinger once again:

> The church will become small and will have to start afresh more or less from the beginning. She will no longer be able to inhabit many of the edifices she built in prosperity. As the number of her adherents diminishes . . . she will lose many of her social privileges. . . . As a small society, [the Church] will make much bigger demands on the initiative of her individual members.[94]

The idea here is that the Church will lose the lukewarm and retain the hardcore, the real believers, what Ratzinger calls "the Church of Faith." When that process is complete, Ratzinger goes on, "she will enjoy a fresh blossoming."

However, this is not how things are working out. The connection with the Church enjoyed by the elite, comprising intellectual assent, institutional connections, and a sense of superiority, is not strong, but rather weak, and members of this group are prone to disaffiliation, particularly as the winds of elite secular fashion begin to blow more coldly on the Faith.

On the other hand, it is a misunderstanding to regard the faith of the Catholic working class of old as something superficial and not worth preserving, just because it was not articulated by them in a highly intellectual way. This attitude towards the simple faithful is nicely expressed by Fr Bryan Houghton, who attributes it to the Catholic hierarchy of the period of the liturgical reform:

> They practiced out of tribal custom; their veneration of the Cross and the Mass was totem worship; they were motivated by nothing more than fear of Hell; their piety was superstition and their loyalty habit.[95]

It is telling that the faith-practice of the simple is often dismissed as "tribal." Tribes, in tribal societies, are central to individuals' self-understanding and represent their personal support network. At its most developed, to leave

---

[94] Joseph Ratzinger, "The Church Will Become Small," in his *Faith and the Future* (San Francisco: Ignatius Press, 2009); the piece was first published in 1969.

[95] Houghton, *Judith's Marriage*, 7.

or be ejected from a tribe is regarded as a disaster. There is nothing superficial about tribal loyalty: it goes into the very bones. Tribes are things people are prepared to die for.

Central to the so-called "tribal identity" of these so-called "tribal Catholics" were the beliefs and practices of the faith: daily prayer, devotion to the Sacred Heart, Mass-going, reverence for the Blessed Sacrament, or however precisely it manifested itself in one time and place or another. Considered in sociological terms, these beliefs and practices were markers of identity, things in which Catholics found a sense of solidarity with each other, and in this way they encouraged each other to maintain them. As Houghton emphasises, it does not follow that their practice was for this reason *insincere* or *superficial*, any more than the loyalty of any tribe-member to a tribe is necessarily insincere or superficial. Much more so, in the case of Catholic devotions and the use of the sacraments, these are things with a supernatural aspect as well, capable of transforming the individual and making him fit for heaven.

Something neglected by the progressives of the mid-twentieth century, and by their followers today, is the use made by God of secondary causation, in creating and sustaining the Church. The primary cause is always God's creation of the universe, but in creating it He created substances with genuine causal powers of their own. When they bring about some effect, this can be described as "secondary" causation. In the case of the Church: as well as being a supernatural reality, the Church is a human institution and a human community. This human community, when it is functioning well, has real causal powers, and we notice the difference when these cease to operate.

To illustrate, generally speaking, God does not simply infuse the minds of children with the truths of faith: this is done by human agency. God only rarely converts people by a direct revelation: the normal way is by the intervention of a human evangelist. The Catholic community, as a human phenomenon, is the normal means, developed precisely for this purpose by God, for Catholics to be educated and sustained in the Faith. Undermine its efficacy as a human community, and God will in general not step in to do the work directly, by a miracle. He will instead let us learn the hard lesson of our presumption.

I wish to leave the last word to Blessed Humphrey Prichard, a Welshman who died for the Catholic Faith in Oxford in 1589, and an example of an uneducated but faithful Catholic. He was employed in an inn, the Catherine Wheel, which during the persecution of the Church was used by Catholics. When it was raided, Prichard impeded the entry of the government agents—the "pursuivants"—in order to give others time to conceal incriminating objects such as vestments. He was arrested along with two priests found there, and a local gentleman who had been their guide.

Like the other three, Prichard was interrogated in London under torture, but brought back to Oxford for execution. His companions were not allowed to speak before being executed, but since he was uneducated, he was. An eyewitness account, soon after printed in Italy, describes the dialogue that followed.

> [Prichard], being on the last rung of the ladder,[96] spoke in this fashion: "Masters who are here present, I beg for you to bear me witness in this world, and on the day of judgement, that I die for being a Catholic and faithful Christian of Holy Church." On hearing this some lout of a Minister said to him: "Poor man, how say you that you die a Catholic, when your ignorance does not allow you to know what being a Catholic means?" To which he answered, "Although I cannot explain in words which the name Catholic means, all the same God knows my heart, and He knows that I believe all the Holy Roman Church believes, and what I cannot explain by mouth, I am ready and prepared to explain and testify to you at the cost of my blood."[97]

---

[96] Condemned men were obliged to climb a ladder up to the noose, with their hands tied. The noose was then placed round their neck, and the ladder turned so they fell off it. Prichard's speech implies a delay by the executioner in turning the ladder.

[97] From the *Brief Discourse of a Notable Martyrdom of Two Priests and of Two Laymen, Befallen the Year 1589 at Oxford University in England*, reproduced in Christine Kelly, *Blessed Thomas Belson, His Life and Times 1563–1589* (Gerrards Cross, Bucks: Colin Smythe, 1986), 89–100, at 100.

8

Liturgy and Orthodoxy

In this chapter I want to address the relationship between the traditional Mass and doctrinal orthodoxy. One might think that a form of the liturgy accepted—indeed, consistently praised to the skies—by the Fathers, Doctors, saints, and popes for more than a thousand years, would be safe from criticism, but this is not so. Those who support this liturgy are criticised for "rejecting" the reformed Mass, and for their "ecclesiology," for example.

On the other hand, it is evident that the adherence to orthodoxy by theologians, office-holders, and ordinary Catholics, for which the Church was once famous, has collapsed since the introduction of the reformed Mass. This can be seen in relation to postconciliar expressions of orthodoxy, such as the 1992 *Catechism of the Catholic Church*, leaving aside the question of how these modern expressions might differ from earlier ones. This collapse is most evident among those least friendly to the traditional Mass, and it is clear that those who actually attend the old Mass cleave far more closely to the Church's official position on issues such as contraception, abortion, divorce, the Real Presence of Christ in the Blessed Sacrament, and the like, than typical congregations.

I want therefore to consider the relationship between the old liturgy and orthodoxy from both a negative and a positive perspective: the claims that there is something theologically dubious about the old Mass or about those who attend it; and the contrasting idea that this Mass is a bulwark of orthodoxy.

I shall start with arguments against the orthodoxy of Catholics attached to the traditional Mass.

Criticisms of the traditional movement

The "theological exactitude" of the new missal

The first world-wide permission, or "indult," for the 1962 missal, after the liturgical reform, issued by Pope John Paul II (under the signature of Bishop, soon to be Cardinal, Augustin Mayer) in 1984, *Quattuor Abhinc Annos*, allowed bishops to give permission for celebrations under certain conditions. One condition was expressed this way: "That it be made publicly clear beyond all ambiguity that such priests and their respective faithful in no way share the positions of those who call in question the legitimacy and doctrinal exactitude of the Roman missal promulgated by Pope Paul VI in 1970"—the implication being that some significant number of the "groups" attached to the older Mass were critical of the reformed missal in a way that demanded a quasi-canonical penalty: they were little short of heretics.

The double standards involved in this condition are evident. Not only is no kind of test of orthodoxy required for attendance at the reformed Mass, but the suggestion that there might be would be laughable. Are only Catholics who meet a certain standard of theological correctness to be admitted to the sacraments? But perhaps the idea was that being allowed to attend the ancient Mass would encourage them in their errors: that the Mass itself is prone to lead people astray, and only those firmly rooted in their orthodoxy should be allowed near it.

A slightly more charitable reading of the phrase is, however, possible. It is reminiscent of the language of Cardinal Gaetano Cicognani, Prefect of the Congregation for Rites (as it was called then), who opened a liturgical conference in Assisi shortly after the reform of Holy Week in 1955. He told participants:

> We have come together not to study problems or propose reforms, but to put into relief, in their vast and many-sided frame, the laws and ordinances emanating from Pope Pius XII in his untiring activity as father and master. And when the armed forces pass in

review, there are salutes and applause, especially when they are wonderfully equipped, as in the present case.[98]

Rome has presented us with a new liturgical book: it is for Catholics, even liturgical scholars, simply to salute and applaud.

That is not, however, how the intellectual life works. Only by raising difficulties, and considering responses, can scholars advance their subject, in any intellectual discipline. Even Cardinal Cicognani had to peddle back on his strange assertion as his address continued: "This does not exclude the possibility," he admitted, of the discussion of "various problems connected with the sacred liturgy."[99]

So what does did Cicognani's first statement mean? It is understandable, at one level, that he should prefer applause to criticism of a reform just completed, and he goes on to emphasise the authority of the Holy See in liturgical matters. Given the liturgical indiscipline which continued to mar the Church after 1970, it is similarly natural enough in that era as well that the official line should be that everyone should stop talking about what is wrong with the liturgy and just get on with it. But the process of reform itself, starting earlier but moving into high gear in 1955, created a situation in which liturgical debate is necessary not just for deepening our spiritual appreciation of the liturgy and perfecting liturgical practice, but to establish the intellectual basis for the next reform. Because once you start on liturgical reform, it is difficult to stop.

Thus the 1955 reform, for good or ill, was the fruit of criticisms of the preceding tradition, and the reform of the 1960s was as well. Discussion did not end there, and successive editions of the reformed missal have been honed and tweaked in response to criticisms. The first edition, in 1970, was rather rushed, and a new edition was published as early as 1974 making all sorts of corrections. A third edition, the product of a rather longer process of debate and reflection, was published in 2002, and made

[98] Gaetano Card. Cicognani, "Opening Address," *The Assisi Papers: Proceedings of the First International Congress of Pastoral Liturgy, Assisi-Rome, September 18–22, 1956*, Supplement to *Worship* 1957, pp. 1–18, at p. 7.
[99] Ibid.

many concessions to critiques of the reform made from conservative and traditionalist perspectives. Many of the orations were re-edited to make them closer to the original versions found in the liturgical tradition, and the Vigil of Epiphany was restored, at least insofar as vigils exist in the reformed missal. This vigil had been abolished in 1955. Even the 2002 edition, however, had to be corrected in a reprint in 2008, which also contained innovations of its own.

Sometimes the public studying of problems and proposing of reforms is sponsored by the Holy See itself. The Synod of Bishops that met in Rome in 2007 studied the question of the reformed Sign of Peace, regarded by many as a disruptive element in the Mass. One proposed solution was to move it to a different point in the liturgy. In the end Pope Benedict XVI decided not to make a change. Nevertheless, the bishops taking part in this discussion, at his invitation, were certainly not wrong to do so, nor were the scholars, liturgists, and assorted commentators who had raised the problem over the preceding years, bringing it to the point at which a serious discussion of it in Rome was regarded as a useful exercise.

Did Pope John Paul II intend that all those taking part in the discussions which eventually bore fruit in new editions of the reformed missal should be forbidden to attend the traditional Mass? Or was it, instead, a matter of preventing people who attend the traditional Mass from contributing to such discussions? Or, again, should these Catholics be forbidden, for example, to study liturgy at a Pontifical University, or indeed anywhere else, which would inevitably involve contact with criticisms of the reformed liturgy?

The answer, I hope, is obvious. The idea that Catholics attached to the traditional Mass should not be allowed to criticise the reformed Mass is simply absurd, and the idea underlying it, that no criticisms of the reformed Mass are possible, or perhaps, that it is somehow contrary to a proper Catholic spirit to voice such criticisms, is even more absurd. Remarks to this effect, even in official documents, need to be read simply as expressions of exasperation with a debate that officials cannot control.

This is not to say that criticising the reformed Mass, for those attached to the old Mass, should be undertaken without due charity and respect for persons, or indeed that it is necessarily a useful exercise at all. Personally, I prefer to leave the debate about how the *Novus Ordo* might be improved to those who habitually attend it; it is not as if there is any lack of such debate. Comparing and contrasting the two missals, on the other hand, at least implicitly, is almost impossible to avoid if one is to say anything about the traditional Mass. Can one prefer one Lectionary or Offertory or indeed the whole Mass to another? Of course. Why ever not?

Cardinal Cicognani's instinct also found a slightly different expression, which sought to attach opprobrium to traditionalists not for criticising the reformed Mass, but simply for attending the ancient one—or even for desiring to do so.

"Defective ecclesiology"

Over many decades, supporters of the traditional Mass have been told that they have a defective "ecclesiology," that is, a defective theology of the Church. The idea that the Church's ancient liturgy is associated somehow with an ecclesiology which is not the one taught by the Second Vatican Council, or after it by the official organs of the Church's magisterium, is, however, two-edged. It suggests that the theological principles of ecclesiology have changed in some important way in or after the Council. If traditional Catholics are being criticised for clinging to the old one, then what we have is two mutually incompatible theologies: one taught, implicitly or explicitly, during the period of time in which the older liturgical tradition was taken as authoritative—from the twelfth century, or from the fourth, depending on how you want to define it, down to the mid-twentieth century—and one for the rather shorter period since the 1960s or 1970s.

Liberal Catholic critics of the traditional movement tend not to be troubled by the idea that what they believe would have been rejected by the Fathers and Doctors and most of the popes and saints of the Church, but it is not surprising to find this idea being used against them by their opponents: that if the ecclesiology of the postconciliar era is different, then it must be erroneous.

The connection between this radical traditionalist claim and the progressive line of argument was borne in on me when I came to respond to a column in a UK Catholic newspaper, the *Catholic Times*, by a retired canonist, Msgr Basil Loftus. He quoted Archbishop (later, Cardinal) Angelo Benelli, addressing the President of the Una Voce Federation, Erich de Saventhem, in 1976. Archbishop Benelli wrote that "those who wish to retain the old Mass have a different ecclesiology." Loftus thought this a splendid stick with which to beat the traditionalist movement.

In searching for the source of this quotation (Loftus gave no citation), I found that it came from an article dating from 1982, preserved on the US website of the Society of St Pius X. The author, a certain Fr Wrighton, regarded this quotation as an equally splendid stick to beat the ecclesial establishment represented by Cardinal Benelli. Wrighton commented on Benelli's claim:

> The phrase *quod semper, quod ubique, quod ab omnibus* ("What has been believed always, everywhere, and by all")[100] as a criterion of orthodoxy had now been rejected in favor of a new Party Line which contradicted the Church's entire previous tradition. What was forbidden and condemned yesterday becomes lawful today, and mandatory tomorrow. What had always been seen as black, is now white, and vice versa—because the Party says so. This comes close to the Bolshevik criterion of morality: what is right or wrong is simply what helps or hinders the Party.[101]

It must be said that Fr Wrighton has a point, and indeed his language is echoed by a quotation I will later give from Cardinal Ratzinger. If there really is this discontinuity, Loftus and those sharing his position cannot go on to claim that traditionally-minded Catholics should submit to every jot and tittle of the new regime. If all the popes up to 1962 were fools and even heretics, there is absolutely no reason to pay any attention to the popes since 1962, any more than Loftus, like his fellow radical progressives, does in fact pay attention to Pope Paul VI's teaching on contraception (which

---

[100] A paraphrase of the famous principle of St Vincent of Lérins.

[101] "Roman Protestants," from the website of SSPX USA District: http://sspx.org/en/roman-protestants.

he dissents from)[102] or Pope Benedict's promulgation of the new English translation of the Novus Ordo missal (which he bitterly attacks).[103]

However, Fr Wrighton and Msgr Loftus had both got hold of the wrong end of the stick. The archives of the Una Voce Federation give a much fuller account of the conversation between Saventhem and Benelli, which was written up by the former and continued by letter; the extensive exchange of letters has now been published.[104] It is clear from this that Benelli's argument wasn't that the *theology embedded in the Old Mass* had been overturned by Vatican II. It was rather that the *desire for the Old Mass when the Holy Father does not want you to desire it* is wrong.

Here is an extract from Eric de Saventhem's own summary of the interview, in a letter which he sent to Benelli after it took place. The date of the letter (not the meeting) is October 26, 1976:

> Your Excellency has urged us to espouse as a matter of conscience the new forms of the Church's public cult, promulgated in the course of these last years by "the Apostolic See and the episcopal conferences, under the authority of the Holy Father conferred by Christ." You have reminded us of Our Lord's words; "What you shall bind on earth shall be bound in heaven," "Graze my sheep," "Confirm your brethren," and you insisted on the point that, for the government of the Church, Christ had given to Peter and to his successors a "charisma" which is to be considered as a gift both unique and indivisible. Although the character of irreformability only attaches to definitions, promulgated *ex cathedra* in matters of faith and morals, the assent due to the acts of the Sovereign Pontiff ought equally to express itself in humble obedience to those of his acts which merely concern the discipline or other nondoctrinal

---

[102] See "Loftus and the time-warp," *LMS Chairman*, December 21, 2014, www.lmschairman.org/2014/12/loftus-and-time-warp.html.

[103] See "1998 ICEL: a twitching dead horse," *LMS Chairman*, March 21, 2015, www.lmschairman.org/2015/03/1998-icel-twitching-dead-horse.html.

[104] Leo Darroch, *Una Voce: The History of the Foederatio Internationalis Una Voce* (Leominster: Gracewing, 2017), 127–41.

aspects of the government of the Church. For there also, you said, it is the same one and indivisible charisma which guarantees that all these acts cannot but be ordered towards the true and certain good of the Church. Consequently, you could only consider as reckless and irreconcilable with a proper ecclesiology all demands or initiatives which implied that the utility of such and such an act of government duly promulgated by the reigning Pontiff or under his authority could be a subject of discussion or even contestation.[105]

Cardinal Benelli does not dispute the accuracy of this summary in his response. What it amounts to—as Dr de Saventhem goes on to explain at some length, though not in these terms—is an extreme Ultramontanism, the view that imbues the reigning pope's *prudential decisions* with something close to infallibility, and his *wishes* with a force approaching that of Divine Law. As Benelli explains in his response to de Saventhem:

> You reiterate unceasingly the same arguments to withhold in effect compliance with that which is clearly wanted by the Church and by the Holy Father himself: the loyal and trusting adoption, by all the faithful of the Roman Rite, of the rite reformed under his authority and in application of the orientations laid down by the Council.[106]

"The Holy Father wishes it!" Then, it would seem, the matter is closed.

The "loyal and trusting" attitude towards the projects and preferences of the Holy Father was indeed one which characterized many conservatively-minded Catholics of the 1960s and 1970s. Such an attitude had long been held by many Catholics. For instance, the *Baltimore Catechism* Number 4—the teacher's manual, with the fullest treatment of each topic—gives a detailed summary of the doctrine of papal infallibility. Naturally it tells us that it only extends to *ex cathedra* statements by the pope on matters of faith and morals, and that on other matters, or in other statements, the

---

[105] Darroch, 128.
[106] Darroch, 132.

pope can err. But then it adds: "Nevertheless, whatever the Pope teaches on any subject you can be pretty sure he is right."[107]

Such a statement could be made only in an era of great theological stability, but even in the first half of the twentieth century this stability was not absolute. Pope Pius XII, for example, contradicted what had been said by some (but not others) of his predecessors about the admissibility of Confucian ceremonies in honour of ancestors: the "Chinese Rites" controversy.[108] Again, he would not have thanked Catholics for adopting a loyal and trusting docility towards the policy of Pope Paul V towards Rome's Jewish community, which included confining them to a ghetto and forcing them to listen to sermons. Certainly, earlier popes' condemnations of the Chinese rites and their hostile policies towards the Jewish people were not attempts to exercise the infallible teaching office of the papacy. But equally clearly, neither is the promulgation of a liturgical book.[109]

Benelli, it should be emphasised, was not saying that Saventhem or any other traditional Catholic rejected the *doctrinal content* of the reformed missal. His criticism was based simply on the fact that after its promulgation they still wanted to attend the older Mass.

It is not clear whether Benelli would have applied his argument to other matters, such as private devotions or theological schools of thought. If the pope is an Augustinian (like Pope Benedict XVI), may one be a Thomist? If the pope is a phenomenologist (like Pope John Paul II), may one be an Augustinian? In any case, if we take Benelli's principle to its logical conclusion, it suggests that all Catholics except the pope himself should sacrifice their intellectual and even their affective autonomy. They

---

[107] Rev. Thomas Kinkhead, *An Explanation of the Baltimore Catechism of Christian Doctrine for the Use of Sunday-School Teachers and Advanced Classes: Baltimore Catechism Number 4* (Rockford, IL: TAN Books, 1988; first published 1891 and 1921), 120.

[108] Pius XII, Decree *Plane Compertum*, December 8, 1939.

[109] See Thomas Pink, "Papal Authority and the Limits of Official Theology," *The Lamp* 13 (2022), 27–36, online at https://thelampmagazine.com/2022/12/02/papal-authority-and-the-limits-of-official-theology/.

should think like the pope, like the things the pope likes, and dislike the things the pope dislikes.

The pope can command those subject to his authority, and assuming the command regards something within his sphere of competence, his subjects are obliged to obey. Were he to command Catholics to fast on Christmas Eve, for example, or to define as a dogma the Blessed Virgin Mary's role as Mediatrix of All Graces, Catholics would be bound, in the first case to fast, and in the second, to believe. On the other hand, we would not be obliged to think that these acts were prudent for the Church as a whole in the circumstances of the day, and still less would we be obliged to believe that it is better all things considered for *us*, *personally*, to be bound in this way. The discipline and the teaching of the Church is one thing; the prudence of the way pope's authority is exercised is another.

The parallel with the liturgy would be that if we concede that Pope Paul VI has the power to reform the liturgy, it is a further step to concede that any reform he might promulgate would be for the good of the Church. And it is another step after that, to concede that this reform would be for our good *personally*, to the extent that we should *not even desire* to attend the traditional Mass.

In the liturgical case, all three steps can be questioned. First, there are clearly limits to the authority of the pope to change the liturgy, although I cannot enter into these here. Second, there is no guarantee that a prudential decision of a pope will be for the good of the Church, as a glance at the history of the Church would demonstrate. Third, even were this established, it does not follow that there must be absolutely no exceptions. As a matter of fact Pope Paul VI did allow exceptions. He allowed aged priests to continue to celebrate the old Mass, and, in 1971, prompted by Cardinal John Heenan, the archbishop of Westminster, allowed the bishops of England and Wales to permit occasional celebrations for the benefit of the laity. It would appear, therefore, that not even he accepted Benelli's argument.

We are called on to unite our wills with the will of God. What God does not demand, however, is for us to forfeit our personalities. As we know from the history of the Church, God wishes his saints to continue to have distinct interests, intellectual proclivities, and affections. What Benelli was proposing was something quite different: indeed, a personality cult around the pope of the day amounting to idolatry.

What I have shown so far is that the most famous criticisms about the theological deficiencies of Catholics attached to the traditional Mass, made by Church officials or in official documents, are not about the theological content of the old or the new missals. They are about the exercise of authority represented by the liturgical reform, and the attitude which this demands of Catholics. However, in 1988, in his Apostolic Letter *Ecclesia Dei Adflicta*, Pope John Paul II undercut this train of reasoning, writing that the desire for the traditional Mass was a "rightful aspiration." Loyalty to the Church does not demand that we not even *want* the traditional Mass.

It is after all not surprising that the traditional Mass is not subject to theological criticisms by the Holy See. The justification for the reform was not any theological inadequacy of the old missal, but pastoral considerations. Again, the theological authority of the ancient missal is such that official, direct criticism of it would be very difficult, without undercutting the authority of the Church itself: a point to which I shall return.

This has not stopped liturgical radicals from criticising it, but that is not our present concern. Such individuals, like Msgr Basil Loftus noted above, often also reject whole swathes of the teaching of the Church, and even the authority of the Holy See over the liturgy itself. While I'm happy to meet their arguments one by one—I addressed a great many of them in preparing Position Papers for the Una Voce Federation[110]—taken together they are not a real challenge to the orthodoxy of traditional Catholics.

Loyalty to the hierarchy

A third way of criticizing Catholics attached to the traditional Mass is the claim that, whatever the rights and wrongs of their views on the liturgy, they are characteristically over-critical of the pope and of the hierarchy. Many commentators think this claim is obviously true, but it rests on

---

[110] Subsequently published as *The Case for Liturgical Restoration* (Angelico, 2019).

a failure to compare traditionalists as a group with other groups in the Church. If we must talk in these terms of "groups" in the Church, as this criticism forces us to do, we should try to make fair comparisons. How do traditional Catholics compare to conservative and liberal ones?

Each group within the Church has recognisable leaders, institutions, and publications, so a comparison is certainly possible, even if there are some borderline areas between them. We are of course comparing people *within* the Church as a human institution, and without going too far into questions of schism and heresy we can leave out of account those elements which reject the authority of the pope and of the hierarchy. On one side we will pay no heed to sedevacantists, and on the other, to liberal Catholic splinter groups, whether these are Belgians who prefer to celebrate invalid liturgies in a secular meeting room, or groups claiming the Apostolic Succession even while ordaining female clergy, like the Liberal Catholic Church. Such groups, on either side, are numerically insignificant, in any case.

It is clear that, over the decades since the Second Vatican Council, the leading critics of the popes and of the hierarchy have been liberal Catholic individuals, organisations, and publications. These attacks reached an early crescendo over the issue of contraception, in the papacy of Pope Paul VI, but Pope John Paul II's reaffirmation of the impossibility of female ordination, and Pope Benedict XVI's promulgation of a revised English translation of the liturgy, were occasions for renewed, massive outpourings. Liberal publications regarded as mainstream, copies of which can be found on sale in churches, and in bishops' residences and seminaries, are very much part of this, as are liberal Catholic figures actually employed directly by the Church. The criticisms they make can be extraordinarily bitter, and even personal.

As an exercise, I once did a survey of the writings of Msgr Basil Loftus, already mentioned in this chapter, in the UK's Catholic press, and found that over a few years he had vented his spleen on four English bishops and five more further afield. Cardinal Ranjith of Colombo was described as a "Sri Lankan *cappa magna* fetishist"; Cardinal Müller as "not fit for purpose"; a remark of Bishop Davies of Shrewsbury "may even call for anger"; one of Bishop Alan Hopes of East Anglia was "deeply disturbing."

It is an interesting fact that this behaviour never seemed to merit any response from his victims, despite their being well aware of it. The English bishops were much less tolerant of criticisms made by conservative Catholics, such as those of the distinguished Catholic novelist Alice Thomas Ellis, whose column in the *Catholic Universe* was terminated at the insistence of the bishops in 1994.[111]

Msgr Loftus had a soft spot for Pope Francis, but this is not shared by all liberal Catholics. The former Irish President, Mary McAleese, described Pope Francis's cautious remarks on same-sex marriage as "unbearably vicious language,"[112] and called the Church an "empire of misogyny" because women cannot be ordained.[113] Following some remarks of Pope Francis about the impossibility of ordaining women, McAleese wrote the Holy Father an email, which she seems to have shared with the press. This portion was quoted in the *Irish Times:*

> It was reassuring and gratifying to observe the utter impenetrability of the reasons you offered, their ludicrous lack of logic or clarity, in short the fact that you offered just more unlikely misogynistic drivel. So nothing new then and nothing to fear. Thank you for giving us something to laugh at. If you ever come up with a serious and credible reason please do not hesitate to let us know. Meanwhile keep rambling on. It is such fun and the fun has almost gone out of faith!
> Best wishes and renewed thanks. Mary McAleese.[114]

---

[111] Richard Ingrams, introduction to Alice Thomas Ellis, *God Has Not Changed: The Assembled Thoughts of Alice Thomas Ellis* (London: Burns & Oates, 2004), ix.

[112] *Irish Post*, March 19, 2021, www.irishpost.com/news/mary-mcaleese-criticises-pope-francis-after-unbearably-vicious-and-cruel-ruling-that-church-cannot-bless-same-sex-unions-206874.

[113] *The Journal*, March 8, 2018, www.thejournal.ie/mary-mcaleese-catholic-church-3891496-Mar2018.

[114] *Irish Times*, December 12, 2022, www.irishtimes.com/ireland/2022/12/01/pope-francis-accused-by-mary-mcaleese-of-ludicrous-lack-of-logic-in-comments-on-women-priests.

McAleese has not been ostracised by her fellow liberals for her stance or her tone. On the contrary, Catherine Pepinster, a long-standing editor of the influential liberal weekly, *The Tablet*, commented in *The Guardian:*

> The language used by the former Irish president Mary McAleese, when she denounced the church last week as an "empire of misogyny," might have been extreme but it did articulate the frustrations of so many women that not only are they ignored, but also their talents are going to waste.[115]

Pepinster's article was headlined "Five years on, Pope Francis has failed to deliver on his promises," and this sentiment is widespread among liberal critics of the Holy Father.

On another occasion, Pepinster responded to Pope Francis's failure to propose the ordination of female deacons, following the Amazon Synod, and his remark that women should be "valued, not clericalised":

> Rather than warn about clericalising women, why doesn't the Pope seek to rid the Church of clericalism? This is grim on both counts— not finding new roles for women; almost an assumption clericalism is automatically part of priesthood.[116]

So much for the liberals. What about conservative Catholics, those who control so many publishing houses, universities, and respected charities and campaigning organisations in the Church? Some, certainly, have maintained a strict policy of public silence about their disagreements with the hierarchy, while complaining loudly enough about them in private. But by no means all.

Going back some time, the classic example is Fr Werenfried van Straaten and the organisation he founded, Aid to the Church in Need, which campaigns on behalf of Catholics under persecution. During the Cold War they were strongly opposed to the appeasement of Communism

---

[115] *The Guardian*, March 12, 2018, www.theguardian.com/commentisfree/2018/mar/12/pope-francis-catholic-church-child.

[116] February 12, 2020: twitter.com/CPsPepTalk/status/1227566840773316609.

which was the official Vatican policy under Pope Paul VI.[117] Later, the headline cases have been the UK campaigning organization Pro Ecclesia et Pontifice, under the leadership of Daphne MacLeod, which went into battle particularly over the orthodoxy of religious instruction in Catholic schools, and the UK-based pro-life organisation, the Society for the Protection of Unborn Children, which was frustrated by the limited support of bishops for the pro-life cause. Later still Deacon Nick Donnelly, who had created the blog "Protect the Pope" to defend the record of Pope Benedict XVI during the papal visit to the UK, was forced to close his blog down for his criticisms of bishops.

In some cases, people and organisations critical of the hierarchy have subsequently come closer to the traditional movement; in others they have not. Archbishop Carlo Viganò, for example, seems to have developed an interest in the traditional liturgy only after emerging as a major critic of Pope Francis over his handling of sex abuse allegations. Michael Voris and his foundation, Church Militant TV, had been a strong critic of bishops and cardinals long before becoming friendly to the traditional Mass, after initially being rather hostile to it. I do not know exactly what causal process is at work in such cases. It may be that finding oneself out of favour with the hierarchy stimulates some people to reassess their attitude towards others out of favour, even if for quite different reasons.

In other cases, however, critics of the hierarchy have kept their distance from traditionalism. A number of leading conservative theologians who criticised Pope Francis over the implications of his Apostolic Letter *Amoris Lætitia* simply have no particular interest in the liturgy. The late Professor Germain Grisez and Professor John Finnis are examples; their thirty-page open letter on the problems raised by *Amoris Lætitia* was published in 2016.[118] Cardinal Seán O'Malley, who famously implied that Pope Francis was not telling the truth about a case of clerical sexual abuse in 2018, is another.

---

[117] Joanna Bogle, *Fr Werenfried—A Life* (Leominster: Gracewing, 2001), 107.
[118] "The Misuse of *Amoris Laetitia* to Support Errors against the Catholic Faith," November 21, 2016, www.twotlj.org/OW-MisuseAL.pdf.

Others combine strong criticisms of the pope or hierarchy with attacks on the traditional Mass and its supporters. One example is Fr Thomas Weinandy OFM Cap, a former theological advisor to the US Bishops' Conference and member of the International Theological Commission. In July 2017 he wrote a thousand-word letter to Pope Francis about *Amoris Lætitia* and other matters, and later made this public. To give a flavour of this letter, he wrote: "You seem to censor and even mock those who interpret chapter 8 of *Amoris Lætitia* in accord with Church tradition as Pharisaic stone-throwers who embody a merciless rigorism. This kind of calumny is alien to the nature of the Petrine ministry." More recently Fr Weinandy has co-authored a series of five articles criticizing the traditional movement in rather harsh terms.[119]

Similarly, the well-known conservative figure, the convert priest Fr Dwight Longenecker, periodically attacks the traditional movement on his blog, but we get off lightly compared with what he says about the hierarchy. He wrote in 2015:

> Clergy can be devious and manipulative and secretive at times, and often they have a good reason to play their cards close to their chest, but a few members of the Catholic hierarchy in England and Wales (those Damien [*sic*] Thompson calls "the magic circle") are the most secretive, devious, duplicitous and schemingly oily inside operators I have ever come across.[120]

It is hard to imagine figures as respected and as central to the traditional movement as Weinandy and Longenecker are to Catholic conservatism, or

---

[119] In *Church Life Journal*, culminating on November 23, 2022. His co-authors were John Cavadini and Mary Healy. The entire series was published as a single long article: "A Synoptic Look at the Failures and Successes of Post-Vatican II Liturgical Reforms," December 1, 2022, https://churchlifejournal.nd.edu/articles/a-synoptic-look-at-the-failures-and-successes-of-post-vatican-ii-liturgical-reforms/.

[120] "Religious Sister Serves as 'Parish Priest,'" January 3, 2015, www.patheos.com/blogs/standingonmyhead/2015/01/religious-sister-serves-as-parish-priest.html.

McAleese and Pepinster are to Catholic liberalism, expressing themselves publicly in terms as disrespectful of the Holy Father or our bishops as they do. This is not to judge anyone, simply to state a fact.

It is certainly true that some people associated with the traditional Mass have criticised the hierarchy over the decades, and more recently Pope Francis. The major traditionalist organisations have not been among them, however. Not only have the traditional priestly institutes and communities remained extremely muted on these matters, but so has the lay movement which supports them, comprising the Una Voce groups around the world and the International Una Voce Federation which represents them internationally. As was demanded by the occasion, the Federation issued a statement in response to *Traditionis Custodes*,[121] the Apostolic Letter of Pope Francis which restricted the traditional Mass, and a little later an appeal was made to the bishops of France by the superiors of a number of traditional priestly institutes and communities,[122] but these documents were characterised by extremely mild language.

Interestingly, the Society of St Pius X (SSPX), which celebrates the traditional Mass and does not in practice accept the authority of the hierarchy, also had little to say about the issues raised by *Amoris Lætitia*, or even by *Traditionis Custodes*. I know of one senior priest of the SSPX who was forbidden by his superiors to sign a petition criticising Pope Francis over the former. The Superior General of the SSPX, Fr Davide Pagliarani, issued a public letter in response to *Traditionis Custodes* which refers to the "harshness" of the document, but rather remarkably makes no other criticism of it, nor of its author.[123] No doubt he had his reasons.

---

[121] "Official Statement of the *Fœderatio Internationalis Una Voce* regarding the Motu Proprio *Traditionis Custodes*," July 19, 2021, www.fiuv.org/2021/07/oficial-statement-of-fderatio.html.

[122] "Communique of the Superiors-General of the 'Ecclesia Dei' Communities," September 3, 2021, https://fssp.com/communique-of-the-superiors-general-of-the-ecclesia-dei-communities.

[123] Letter of July 22, 2021, https://fsspx.news/sites/sspx/files/letter_from_the_superior_general_en.pdf.

Individuals, independent journals, and publishing houses have both greater freedom and a wider remit, and naturally they represent a range of views and approaches. It would be unjustifiable to take the more trenchant critics of Pope Francis among these, such as the periodical *The Remnant*, as somehow representative of the movement, ignoring the more cautious ones, such as *The Latin Mass Magazine*. The traditional tendency in the Church is no more monolithic than the liberal or conservative tendencies.

To repeat, my purpose here is not to say whether any of these criticisms are right or wrong, or made in a reasonable and constructive way or not. I am concerned only to answer the charge so often made about the traditional movement, that it is a nest of particularly unrestrained critics of the hierarchy. My response is that those who make this claim need to get out more. They should read widely-respected liberal journals and websites. They should look at the histories of influential and well-resourced conservative Catholic organisations, and their relations with the bishops. And they should listen carefully to the kinds of conversations I have heard many times over the years: the things liberal clergy and intellectuals say about Pope John Paul II and Pope Benedict XVI; the things conservatives say about the bishops and about Pope Francis.

Those determined to hear only what they want to hear will ignore all this, but it is a fact. The criticisms made by traditional Catholics are different, of course, but not necessarily more bitter or unjust. An attitude of criticism bordering on despair over the hierarchical Church in its human aspect is, indeed, something that unites the more experienced leaders of all sections of Catholic opinion: a truly tragic situation, but one for which traditional Catholics are certainly not responsible.

Indeed, given how they have been treated by the hierarchical Church, it is remarkable how they have stuck with it. On this, readers need not take my word for it, but Joseph Ratzinger's, who pointed out in 2002: "Anyone who nowadays advocates the continuing existence of this liturgy or takes part in it is treated like a leper; all tolerance ends here. There has never been anything like this in history; in doing this we are despising and proscribing the Church's whole past. How can one trust her at present if things are that way?"[124]

Critics of traditionalists may have become confused by the fact that until *Summorum Pontificum* it was open season on trads and any old stick was good enough to beat them with. But once you take away the assumption that support for the traditional Mass is *itself* an act of personal disloyalty to the pope, then you can allow yourself to notice a much more complex situation.

The old Mass as bulwark of orthodoxy

There are people who like the Extraordinary Form but have heterodox theological views. There are, of course, many people who are orthodox in faith who don't even know about the traditional Mass, or know about it but don't particularly seek it out. It is nevertheless an observable phenomenon that traditional Catholics tend to be orthodox, and, conversely, that heterodox thinkers within the Church tend to dislike the traditional Mass.

A pilot study by Fr Donald Kloster conducted across five states of the USA in 2018 attempted to test this impression empirically. The survey gathered 1,322 paper responses from churches and 451 online from those attending the traditional Mass. To give just one result, only 2 percent of responders approved of contraception, whereas a survey of self-identified Catholics by Pew Research in 2016 claimed that 89 percent of Catholics did so.[125] Results in this ball-park surprise few commentators.

Confronted by this reality, critics of the traditional Mass often say that its congregations are self-selecting: that is, that Catholics with more orthodox views migrate to it. Of course, congregations at all flavours of the liturgy are self-selecting, at least in areas where there is a choice of Masses, but an explanation is still needed why Catholics who believe the

---

[124] Joseph Ratzinger, *God and the World* (San Francisco: Ignatius Press, 2002), 416.

[125] Fr Donald Kloster, "Traditional Lati n Mass National Survey," available at www.lifesitenews.com/wp-content/uploads/2021/03/Traditional_Latin _Mass_National_Survey_v.2.pdf

official teachings of the Church should cluster in celebrations of a Mass so consistently marginalised and denigrated by the Church's official organs and representatives. In any case, it is not at all the case that the traditional Mass is attractive only to those who can already tick all the right boxes in surveys of Catholic belief, since it does not attract people primarily through intellectual means.

This claim has also received some objective empirical support, in surveys of attendees at events organised for young Catholics in London in 2018 and 2019 by the Committee for the New Evangelisation of the Catholic Medical Association. Attendees were mostly, but not exclusively, trainee doctors and nurses. The events were billed as one-day conferences preceded by Mass; the Masses were the traditional Roman rite in the first case, and the traditional Dominican rite in the second. Although the numbers attending were not enormous, it was a rare chance to ask young Catholics who found themselves at the traditional liturgy more or less by chance what they thought about it. Of those (the majority) who liked it, the most common explanation by far was that it was "solemn," "beautiful," "reverent," or "prayerful."

Again, this would surprise no one familiar with the congregations at the traditional Mass, who will also have heard many stories of people changing not only their beliefs but their ways of life after discovering the ancient Mass. This, indeed, is part of what the liturgy is supposed to do: to support our ongoing formation. Catholics who discover a form of the liturgy they find engaging, and begin to attend it consistently, should be in a good position to deepen their understanding of the Faith and find the grace and social support to bring their lives into greater conformity with the Church's teachings. One aspect of the crisis in the Church today is that this does not seem to be happening, or happening enough, in a lot of parishes. Celebrations of the traditional Mass seem be doing well in this respect, however, so it is worth asking why.

The theology of the ancient missal

One reason why the traditional Mass might draw attendees towards greater orthodoxy is the obvious one: the theological content of the missal. People attending Mass, even regularly, do not study the texts in the way that liturgical scholars do, but nevertheless if they follow the collects, for example, in a hand missal, or attend to the Gospel passages, they will come away from the Old Mass with a somewhat different angle on the Faith than they will from the New, which may be helpful or unhelpful to their formation.

Elsewhere I have discussed a number of examples of texts and ceremonies in the older missal in relation to theology and how the faithful engage with them.[126] Here I will mention just two issues, both raised by Cardinal Ratzinger: the theology of sacrifice, and Pelagianism.

On the first, Cardinal Ratzinger, speaking in 2001, quotes a theologian, Stefan Orth, reflecting on the Mass as a sacrifice. Orth writes:

> In fact, many Catholics themselves today ratify the verdict and the conclusions of Martin Luther, who says that to speak of sacrifice is "the greatest and most appalling horror" and a "damnable impiety": this is why we want to refrain from all that smacks of sacrifice, including the whole canon, and retain only that which is pure and holy.[127]

Cardinal Ratzinger comments:

> A sizable party of Catholic liturgists seems to have practically arrived at the conclusion that Luther, rather than Trent, was substantially right in the sixteenth century debate. . . . It is only against this background of the effective denial of the authority of Trent, that the bitterness of the struggle against allowing the celebration of Mass according to the 1962 Missal, after the liturgical reform, can be understood. The possibility of so celebrating constitutes the strongest, and thus (for them) the most intolerable contradiction of the opinion of those who believe that the faith in the Eucharist formulated by Trent has lost its value.

---

[126] Joseph Shaw, *The Case for Liturgical Restoration.*

[127] *Looking Again at the Question of the Liturgy with Cardinal Ratzinger: Proceedings of the July 2001 Fontgombault Liturgical Conference,* ed. Alcuin Reid (Farnborough, UK: St. Michael's Abbey Press, 2003), 20.

For Ratzinger, then, the traditional Mass is an obstacle to the rejection of the orthodox Catholic view of the Mass, which has been abandoned by a large and influential section of opinion in the Church. These dissenters prefer the reformed liturgy because it does not remind them so forcefully of the traditional teaching.

The rejection of the sacrificial nature of the Mass is not something the dissenters have derived from the Second Vatican Council. Ratzinger begins his discussion with a quotation from *Sacrosanctum Concilium* which describes the Mass as "the divine Sacrifice of the Eucharist."[128] Indeed, that document uses the term "sacrifice" ten times, in three cases in the phrase "the sacrifice of the Mass": capitalised, in the Latin, as *Sacrificium Missæ*.

Since the ancient Roman Canon is included in the reformed missal, it is impossible to say that the reformed liturgy as a whole is silent about the Mass as a sacrifice, let alone that it denies it. Ratzinger's point remains valid, however, since celebrants don't have to use the Roman Canon, and many other passages using the language of sacrifice have been abolished, like the ancient Offertory prayers; edited out, like many Secret prayers; or are optional. Those attending Masses celebrated by priests who have adopted this fashionable error will, accordingly, find that the sacrificial nature of the Mass is very little mentioned. By contrast, those attending the traditional Mass are constantly reminded of it.

On Pelagianism, in an early work Ratzinger criticised the Vatican II document *Gaudium et Spes*, writing:

> The whole text gives scarcely a hint of the discord which runs through man and which is described so dramatically in Rom 7:13–25. It even falls into downright Pelagian terminology when it speaks of man "sese ab omni passionum captivitate liberans finem suum persequitur et apta subsidia . . . procurat."[129]

---

[128] *Sacrosancum Concilium* (1963), §2: "in divino Eucharistiae Sacrificio."

[129] Joseph Ratzinger, "The Dignity of the Human Person," in *Commentary on the Documents of Vatican II*, vol. 5, trans. W. J. O'Hara (New York: Herder and Herder, 1969), 138.

To translate a slightly longer section of the passage of *Gaudium et Spes* Ratzinger refers to:

> Man achieves such dignity when, emancipating himself from all captivity to passion, he pursues his goal in a spontaneous choice of what is good, and procures for himself through effective and skilful action, apt helps to that end.[130]

Without going into an extended discussion of the intended meaning of *Gaudium et Spes* (Ratzinger has much to say about the theological background of the drafters), it is enough to note that Catholics, subject as always to the influence of the world, are particularly in danger in modern times of forgetting the reality of Original Sin and the need for God's grace. It might be called a dogma of modernity that you can achieve anything, realise your dreams, and escape your limitations, just by relying on your inner resources: this is the message of millions of films and pop songs, a message which occasionally gives way, inevitably, to the darker side of Western culture: existential despair.

In this context, even theologians tasked with drafting official documents for an ecumenical council might fail to emphasise Original Sin and the need for grace as much as they could, and the same is true of theologians revising the prayers of the missal. This, at least, would explain the way that references to these things were systematically weeded out of the Collects of the missal in the course of the reform, as has been set out at scholarly length by Fr Anthony Cekada,[131] Lauren Pristas,[132] and in the ongoing work of Matthew Hazell. This phenomenon is undeniable, systematic, and on a grand scale.

The reform of the liturgy was a project to adapt the liturgy to meet the needs of the time. One difficulty such a project faces is that addressing the

---

[130] *Gaudium et Spes* (1965), §17.

[131] Anthony Cekada, *Work of Human Hands: A Theological Critique of the Mass of Paul VI* (West Chester, OH: Philothea Press, 2010).

[132] Lauren Pristas, *The Collects of the Roman Missals: A Comparative Study of the Sundays in Proper Seasons Before and After the Second Vatican Council* (London/New York: Bloomsbury T&T Clark, 2013).

favourite sins and theological errors of one's own generation and circle requires an unusual amount of moral courage. It is extremely tempting to understand the "needs of the time" in terms of what will not be embarrassing or off-putting to people of the day, rather than what they really need to hear.

Thus, congregations in a slave-owning society might be made uncomfortable by references to the equality of all under God. The last thing that society needs is a liturgy with all these references removed, but the temptation for liturgical reformers in such a society to remove them will be considerable. For this reason, a liturgy composed in an age with completely different social problems to one's own has its advantages: its creators may have included references, if not to all their own favourite sins, then at least to some of ours.

In this case, unlike in the case of the language of sacrifice, it might be possible to draw a line of influence between the text of Vatican II and the way the liturgical reform was carried out, and *still* think that the unreformed liturgy has value precisely insofar as it has not been subject to this influence. This is not because *Gaudium et Spes* is heretical: just because a liturgical text not influenced by the latest theological trend may be just what we need to counter the errors dearest to the modern heart.

The realities of sin and grace are constantly referred to in the traditional liturgy; they are not completely absent from the reformed one, but they come up much less often. Worshippers bombarded by the optimistic Pelagianism of modernity will not be instantly converted by hearing this contradicted in the liturgy, but with constant repetition there is some chance that the Church's message might get through.

> Stir up thy power, we beseech Thee, O Lord, and come: that from the threatening dangers of our sins we may deserve to be rescued by Thy protection, and to be saved by Thy deliverance. Who livest and reignest with God the Father in the unity of the Holy Ghost, God, world without end. Amen.[133]

[133] Collect of the First Sunday of Advent, translation from the *The Daily Missal and Liturgical Manual* (London: Baronius Press, 2004).

The ancient Mass and continuity

The second reason why the traditional Mass might favour doctrinal orthodoxy is of a rather different character. The statistic I quoted above, of the 2 percent rate of dissent from the teaching of the Church on contraception among those attending the traditional Mass, compared with 89 percent of self-identified Catholics, is not due to the texts of the ancient missal referring to this particular teaching, because they do not. There are other factors at work, one of which is that the traditional Mass represents continuity in the life of the Church.

It is an easily observable fact that progressive Catholics tend not only to dislike the traditional Mass personally, but oppose *anyone* having access to it. This seems puzzling, but there is an explanation. They find the texts about grace and penance and the intercession of the saints embarrassing not only for themselves but for the whole Church. They want them wiped from the Church's collective memory. But more deeply, they want to deny the *continuity* of the Church. They are opposed to the idea that anything worthwhile can be found in the Church's past. If they do look at the past, they prefer to look at isolated bits and pieces from the distant past, with which there is no lived continuity.

The reason is that in order to deny the Church's teaching you have to stop people from appealing to the teaching and also to the lived experience of Catholics over recent centuries up to Vatican II, in which our predecessors in the Faith struggled with many of the same problems as we do: "natural" theories of education, the theory of evolution, critical methods of interpreting the Bible, contraception, divorce, secularism, and so on. The liberals want to cut us off most of all from those parts of the magisterium which are most useful, and they want to destroy the prestige and authority of this teaching by ridiculing the Mass that went with it.

Anne Roche Muggeridge, in her book *The Desolate City*, explains the way that the "revolutionary" party in the Church gained dominance in a short space of time in the 1960s, in light of a parallel with revolutions in the secular sphere. Borrowing a phrase from a secular historian, Peter Shaw, she talks about "the rituals of the revolution":

These rituals are designed to diminish the power of existing authority by destroying its mystique during a process in which the symbols that inspire awe are mocked and degraded in "reversed ceremonies of legitimacy." The mocking reversal of sacred symbols serves as a psychological preparation for a transference of allegiance.[134]

She goes on to discuss the shocking liturgical abuses and parodies of the liturgy which took place in the 1960s, particularly in the context of get-togethers of dissenting priests, but in many parishes too. In order to destroy the allegiance of the faithful to the old doctrines, the liberals subjected the most holy and important symbols of the old order to ritualised mockery. Of course, this did not stop in the 1960s, but it had a special importance in that decade because almost the whole Catholic population had to be brought round from a strong habitual attachment to the old ways to an attitude at least of non-resistance to the revolution the liberals wished to push forward, of which the keynote issue was the rejection of the Church's teaching on contraception.

The end result was somewhat less than what the 1960s radicals had hoped for, which was the capitulation of the Holy See itself. Nevertheless, the process emphasises the connection between the liturgy and orthodoxy. For practical purposes there are no references to the Church's teaching on contraception in the traditional Mass. That wasn't the liberals' problem with it. They wanted to destroy the prestige of the ancient Mass because they wanted to destroy the prestige of the Church, since the Mass is the holiest thing the Church possesses. To express this in another way, they, like all revolutionaries, wanted to destroy the prestige of the *past*.

The ancient Mass is not simply a well put-together liturgy, cleverly combining this element with that one. It is something which has developed over many centuries, slowly enough to enable us to participate in a meaningful way in the spiritual atmosphere of the preceding generation of Catholics, and the one before that, and so on for many centuries. It is

---

[134] Anne Roche Muggeridge, *The Desolate City: Revolution in the Catholic Church*, rev. and expanded (New York: HarperCollins, 1990), 115. First published in 1986.

the product of the Church in a very deep way: not of a committee, even at some distant time in the past, but of the prayer and practice of innumerable popes, Doctors and Saints, and ordinary priests and lay people as well. We all know instinctively that, despite identifiable changes made in the decades up to 1962, it is essentially very, very old, and that this age is not the age of a pot-shard dug out from an ancient rubbish-tip where it has lain forgotten, but of a great public building or city square walked over and worked and lived in every day since its construction until today. And this lived-in age makes it venerable, worthy of respect.

The liberals of the 1960s needed to destroy this connection with the past, because they wanted to establish a new theology. The promulgation of the *Novus Ordo Missæ* at the end of the decade restored a degree of stability to the liturgical scene, but of course a lot of damage had already been done, and even at its best the new liturgical settlement was a striking break with the past.

The polemic against the traditional Mass, which is still heard today, is that it was "all wrong": it "excluded the people"; it made them "dumb spectators"; the theology, even, was misguided. If we allow that polemic to stand we are saying that the Church was wrong about her most intimate inner life, the shared liturgical life of the Christian community, for the vast majority of the Church's existence. It may be logically possible to say that she was wrong about that and right about all the doctrines, but it is *incongruous*. The two things just don't hang together.

It is not that anyone is incapable of distinguishing doctrine from liturgy, or is ignorant that the liturgy of the mid-twentieth century was not identical to that celebrated by the apostles. It is, rather, that the institution we should believe in doctrinally also brought us this ancient liturgy. If the liturgy is rubbished, then the Church is rubbished. The Church loses her credibility.

This is something expressed with great clarity by Cardinal Ratzinger:

A community is calling its very being into question when it suddenly declares that what until now was its holiest and highest possession is strictly forbidden, and when it makes the longing for it seem downright indecent. Can it be trusted any more about any-thing else? Won't it proscribe tomorrow what it prescribes today?[135]

As Ratzinger says, the ancient liturgy was not some indifferent thing, some petty regulation, but the Church's "holiest and highest possession": that is how generations of Catholics thought of it. Then again, this was not simply changed, but the older form was actually forbidden: the message seemed to be not at all that one petty regulation had been replaced by another, but that there was something profoundly wrong with the old one, so that even to desire it was "indecent."

Not only does this weaken confidence in the institution as a source of wisdom (to put it mildly), but, as Ratzinger indicates, it threatens the very existence of the community. This is because institutions have to have some markers of identity, and up to the time of the Second Vatican Council a major marker was the Catholic liturgy. If this is changed beyond recognition, the continued existence of the community as a sociological reality is called into question, because it has lost a key element of what gives it unity. This is a point developed in the last chapter.

For present purposes, the conclusion is a simple one. If we want to promote orthodoxy in doctrine in the Church, we have to reverse the process the liberals undertook in the 1960s: we have to reconnect Catholics with the ancient liturgy, restore the prestige of this liturgy, convince people again of its value. Only by doing this will we get them to accept the authority of the succession of Councils and the ancient Creeds and the Scriptures: the authority, in short, of the Church's continuous life over many centuries, or, even more briefly, of the past.

Constant harping by conservative Catholics about the difference between unchanging doctrines and potentially changeable liturgy has done nothing, over the decades, to reverse the collapse of orthodox belief in the Church. The connection between the liturgy and the Faith cannot be so easily shrugged off. If we want people to believe in what the Church teaches we have to allow them to believe in the *Church*, and that means

---

[135] Ratzinger, *Salt of the Earth*, 176.

rejecting the idea that the Church was dumbly devoted to liturgical nonsense for fifteen or more centuries

What I am describing is the restoration of the ancient liturgy to a *place of honour* in the Church. This would not solve all our problems, but it would help, for the reasons just explained, and moreover it is perfectly achievable. It was well on its way to being achieved, at least in large and influential regions of the Church, on the eve of Pope Francis's Apostolic Letter *Traditionis Custodes* in 2021.

This document seemed designed to put this process into reverse, and it is a testament to the negative importance of the traditional Mass to radical progressives that this seemed to them such an important objective. At the time of writing, however, there is little indication that this project of theirs will succeed.

9

The Traditional Latin Mass and Diversity

In an article in the *Illinois Times*, Massimo Faggioli, a theology professor at Villanova University in Philadelphia, is quoted as follows, of a specific traditional Mass location:

> It's not an accident that all of these Catholics at the old Mass are white, because one of the things that happened after Vatican II was an "inculturation" of the liturgy. . . . The Latin Mass is white and European by its definition, because it's a product of the Catholic Church of the 16th century. So, this is creating serious problems because it is never limited to the liturgy only, but it is always the first step to saying Vatican II was a disaster.[136]

Faggioli's theme was later reprised in *America Magazine*, where Kerry Weber opined:

> Too often, the descriptions of the Latin Mass as "more reverent" cite liturgical attributes that are inspired by European aesthetics and the sensibilities of overwhelmingly white congregations.[137]

I would far rather ignore these childish accusations, but I fear that if they are repeated frequently enough without rebuttal they will become established

---

A shorter version of this paper was published on *OnePeterFive*, October 11, 2021, under the title "Ethnic Diversity and the Latin Mass."

[136] Quoted in Scott Reeder, "Mass disagreement," *Ilinois Times*, September 30, 2021.

[137] Kerry Weber, "Stop saying the Latin Mass is 'more reverent,'" *America Magazine* online, November 17, 2022.

as part of the liberal narrative about the traditional Latin Mass. The reality is that in order to shoe-horn the movement for the ancient Mass into the role of the bad guys in some racially-charged political confrontation, these writers need to distort the past and ignore the present. Let's start with the past.

The traditional Mass and European culture

Faggioli claims that the Mass as experienced in celebrations of the pre-Vatican II liturgical books is the "product" of sixteenth-century Europe. Were it so, it would come from a milieu with completely different cultural and political concerns from those of current American politics, but let that pass, because the claim is false, as Faggioli must be aware. Readers can compare the first printed missal, of 1474, with sixteenth-century and later examples right up to 1962 to satisfy themselves that no major changes were made in the sixteenth century. Nor was it new in 1474: that was simply a printed version of what the Franciscans had been using since the thirteenth century, a version of the Roman missal for use outside Rome. The last significant changes to the Roman missal took place between the ninth and the twelfth centuries—things like the Preparatory Prayers and Last Gospel, and the development of Low Mass—but it was substantially complete in the eighth century, and its central components were in place long before that. The Canon of the Mass dates, scholars tell us, from the fourth century.

The fourth century is not even medieval: it is late antiquity. Before the Muslims conquered North Africa three centuries later, it would be anachronistic to contrast "European" with "non-European" culture, since the Mediterranean was not the dividing line between different cultures, but a conduit connecting a region of strongly interconnected cultures, which contrasted with the more remote hinterland in any direction: Germany in the north, Persia to the east, and the Sahara to the south. The ancient Roman Mass was a product of Jewish and Roman religious culture in this Mediterranean world, and it was closely aligned with the liturgical tradition of what the Romans called North Africa (as opposed to Egypt). The liturgy of other parts of the Roman Empire—Greece, Egypt, the

Levant, France and Spain—had their own lines of development, but each influenced and were influenced by the others.

When the reformers started pulling things out of the missal in the 1960s, they sometimes claimed that these things were "late" or "medieval." In some cases they were correct, but in other cases what they removed went back much earlier. The ancient cycle of Sunday Gospels, for example, entirely lost in 1969, provided the subject matter of sermons by Pope Gregory the Great in the year 490. The ancient orations, which the reformers of the 1960s didn't like because they talked about penance, sin, and grace, reflect the world of the Church's great African theologians, St Augustine of Hippo and St Cyprian of Carthage.

What of the reformed Mass? When, and by whom, was this created? It may come as a shock to Faggioli to discover this, but it was produced overwhelmingly by a small group of European liturgical experts, closely aligned in age, education, and attitudes. Notoriously, only a few of them were pastors; even fewer had experience of pastoral work outside Europe and North America. What they destroyed was something which had formed the Catholic culture, not just of Europe, but of Latin America, Africa, India, and China.

To a Catholic in Shanghai, in Goa, in Mexico City, or in Cape Town, the ancient Mass is *their* ancient Mass. It is the Mass which marked the life events of their parents, grandparents, and great grandparents. It is the Mass which evangelised their countries, often in the distant past, just as it evangelised England, Germany, and Ireland in the early Middle Ages. It is this Mass which inspired their native saints and martyrs. It is this Mass which formed the backdrop to the authentic Catholic customs and art of which they are justly proud, from the wonderful baroque architecture of Catholic Latin America to the exquisite devotional art of Catholic China.

Faggioli and his gang are determined to deprive them of this Mass, on the basis that he, and a handful of white American and European self-appointed liturgical experts, know better than they what is good for them. Sadly, since bishops all over the world are educated in Rome, a tiny clique of European liberals have outsized influence over what happens in other continents.

The International Una Voce Federation has members and contacts in the Philippines, in Malaysia, China, Taiwan, Japan, Korea, all over Latin America, and in a number of locations in Africa, and I know, because I have corresponded with them, that the reason the ancient Mass is more available in the USA than in these places is not because no one wants it there, but because getting permission for it there has been extremely difficult, even under *Summorum Pontificum*. The bishops have been given the idea, by the likes of Andrea Grillo[138] from his perch in Rome's Sant'Anselmo university, that the traditional Mass is not part of the officially approved programme. Sometimes from ambition, sometimes from loyalty to the Holy See, and frequently from a feeling that this is the path of least resistance, many bishops in Africa, Asia, and Latin America stifle the traditional Mass in an exercise of clerical power which in any other context Faggioli would be the first to condemn as clericalism. *Traditionis Custodes* has encouraged them to go even further, as we have seen with the complete suppression of the traditional Mass in Puerto Rico.

To be fair to the bishops of Africa, Latin America, and Asia, there are also practical constraints to the development of the traditional Mass in those places, similar to those in America and Europe but biting more sharply. The limited education in Latin of many of the clergy (contrary, be it noted, to the requirements of canon law); limitations on resources of time and places where the Mass can be said; lack of money for the support of dedicated clergy, from (for example) the traditional priestly institutes. Like Americans, Africans are willing to travel for up to two hours, if necessary, to get to church: but if you are doing that on foot, this gives you a range of about ten miles, rather than more than a hundred in a comfortable American car. Making provision for the traditional Mass in this context is an entirely different ball-game from making provision for it in the rich world.

---

[138] Prof. Grillo coined the phrase, applied to the 1970 missal, that it is "the unique expression of the Roman rite's *lex orandi*," which is found in Pope Francis's Apostolic Letter *Traditionis Custodes*, §1.

Despite all these difficulties, however, there are many points of light in the gloom: places where the faithful flock to attend the ancient Mass, and where they experience the same increases in personal devotion and vocations associated with the traditional Mass in Europe and America. The traditional priestly institutes have apostolates in several African countries and in parts of Latin America. The Apostolic Administration of Campos, an entire parallel traditional diocese in communion with the Holy See, is located in Brazil. The SSPX, thanks no doubt to the extensive missionary experience of Archbishop Lefebvre, have made Africa a priority in their work and have been present in multiple countries for up to fifty years.

Diversity in traditional Mass congregations

The wide appeal of the traditional Mass can be seen not only between countries but within them. In the multi-ethnic and multi-lingual cities of the rich world, Faggioli and Weber would presumably expect to find congregations at the ancient Mass lacking in cultural diversity. As many have pointed out, however, in response to these articles, this is far from being the case. It is common to hear people say that their local traditional Mass is far *more* diverse than comparable Novus Ordo celebrations. The point can be illustrated from all over the world, thanks to the contacts of the Una Voce Federation.[139]

A particular celebration of the traditional Mass in Italy, it is reported, "is frequented by people of all ages, several young couples with children, often Oriental (Sri Lankan) or even Africans (Congolese)."

A Canadian correspondent noted:

Families with young children are very well represented in the congregations of both the churches where the EF is celebrated on Sundays. At one, there are also many young adults and seniors; those attending also come from many national/ethnic backgrounds, e.g., Canadian, American, British, Chinese (China, Hong Kong), Filipino, Indonesian, Vietnamese, Indian, Polish, German, South

---

[139] The following three quotations were supplied by people filling out online forms in response to a request from the Una Voce Federation in 2019.

African, Australian, Korean, Trinidadian, Brazilian, Salvadorian, Mexican, Ivorian (Ivory Coast), etc.

An extended explanation is given by a correspondent from Luxembourg.

The population of Luxembourg is about 600,000 of which only half hold Luxembourgeois passports, but of these a great many came originally from Portugal, Italy and other places and many have never really integrated. As anyone who lives here will testify, Luxembourg is not a cultural melting pot like London but, rather, a ghettoised society in which each linguistic group sticks to its own.

A very significant contributor to this phenomenon is the vernacular Mass. The Luxembourgish Mass, the Italian Mass, the Portuguese Mass, the English Mass, the French Mass, the Polish Mass and so on are all focuses of attendance by the various expatriate communities. If you attend any of these you are unlikely to meet anyone whose native language is not that of the Mass you are attending.

It is at the TLM that you will find a real mixture of ethnic backgrounds. There, you can meet people of Luxembourgeois, Hungarian, British, French, Polish, Japanese, Belgian, Italian, Nigerian, Austrian, Dutch and Spanish nationality, united by the common language of the Church: Latin.

The advantage of Latin as a universal language is felt also in African cities, where recent migrants from the countryside can bring with them dozens of languages, and China, where Standard Chinese (Mandarin) is alien, and sometimes incomprehensible, to many millions of Chinese Catholic speakers of Cantonese and other languages. It would be totally beyond the resources of the local Church to use all these different languages liturgically, and even if that were somehow possible it would not solve the problem of multilingual congregations.

However, the diversity of Latin Mass congregations is not simply a matter of language, but of spirituality. As I wrote in an article for *The Pastoral and Homiletic Review:*

When migrants move from the countryside into the city, or from a less developed country into a more developed one, they are frequently (to speak in very broad terms) simultaneously making a transition from a more traditional society to a less traditional one. Those moving to Luxembourg, for example, from Portugal, let alone from Nigeria, may find the spirituality of the Church in their new home strikingly more individualistic and stripped down than what they are used to. It is not surprising that we should find some of them joining the ranks of those born into this culture who yearn for something more rooted, and who find it in the Extraordinary Form.[140]

This is, indeed, the fundamental issue, on which Faggioli and Kerry have got things completely upside down. The traditional Mass represents something quite alien to the elite culture of modern Europe and North America, and has done for at least two centuries, particularly in the most industrialised and urbanised parts of the English-speaking world. It is attractive to a wide range of people *precisely for that reason:* because, whether brought up to it or not, they find that elite culture forbidding, chilly, and sterile.

This explains a further way in which traditional Mass congregations are diverse, in the developed world. In places where there is a choice of *Novus Ordo* Masses, there is a tendency for Catholics to sort themselves into different congregations according to social class as well as by ethnicity and language. In contrast, there is very rarely a choice of traditional Masses to attend, and Catholics of very different backgrounds rub along in these congregations very well because they have a love of the traditional Mass in common, a love which can be found in a great variety of cultural backgrounds. The idea that people are drawn to a particular celebration because of a shared, specific, and exclusive aesthetic is applicable to the *Novus Ordo* in many Western cities, but much less so, if at all, of the traditional Mass.

---

[140] Joseph Shaw, "The Demographics of the Extraordinary Form: Young People, Families, Sex Ratios, and Diversity," *Homiletic and Pastoral Review*, January 14, 2021.

The traditional Mass and the European Enlightenment

What exactly is it about the traditional Mass which made it such a successful tool in the evangelisation of such contrasting cultures as Confucian China, Animist Africa, and the very varied cultures of Latin America? And where does the alternative model of worship, found in the *Novus Ordo Missæ*, come from?

The contrast between the two missals can be described in many ways, but a useful one in this context is between a rite focused on symbol and ritual, and one which, though it still retains these, shifts the emphasis towards verbal communication and spontaneity. A liturgy celebrated in a language most of the congregation does not understand, and partly silently, is clearly not relying very heavily on verbal communication to get its point across. It uses instead symbols and ritual, dramatic and repeated representations of the truths of faith and of the specific meaning of the rites through dramatic images: washing, genuflecting, incensing, kissing, and so on. The reform of the liturgy drastically cut down on these symbols, and compensated by giving the worshipper a great quantity of information through words, spoken aloud, in a vernacular language, some of it made up on the spot by the celebrant.

Now consider the religious culture of the countries outside Europe which the Church has evangelised in recent centuries, in Asia, Africa, and Latin America. These are, in their own ways, ritual cultures. Their native, non-Christian spirituality is expressed through symbols and ceremonies. The people who wanted to shift Catholic worship from a ritual to a verbal event certainly weren't inspired by native American or African shamans, Japanese Shintoism, or the sacred texts and rituals of Hinduism or Islam.

Instead, they were responding to something quite different: a critique of the traditional Catholic liturgy mounted by modern Europeans. The thinkers of the Enlightenment (the European philosophical movement of the seventeenth and eighteenth centuries) and their intellectual successors liked to pour scorn on elaborate ritual, silent prayer, and the use of sacred languages as obscurantist. They wanted things to be aloud, visible, simple, and easy to understand: a set of propositions that could be set out, analysed, and if necessary defended. They looked at the Catholic liturgy and saw something primitive and barbarous. When they encountered the religious traditions of non-European cultures, they thought these were even worse.

The reform of the Catholic liturgy was done as a concession to this critique. This is not controversial: in saying this I am not making a hurtful accusation, but simply stating a fact which was acknowledged by the reformers themselves. At the time, and since, many Catholics have defended this concession as absolutely required if the Church is to gain a hearing in the "modern world," by which they mean the world of European culture influenced decisively by Enlightenment ideas. I leave that argument in favour of the reform to others to make. What is undeniable is that this project produced a liturgy not at all desired by Europeans *less* influenced by the Enlightenment—both by those without a modern, rationalist education, and by those critical of the Enlightenment project, such as the many intellectuals, writers, musicians, and artists who signed petitions to save the traditional Mass.

It should be even more obvious that this new liturgy was light-years more distant from the authentic spiritual traditions of non-European cultures than the old liturgy had been. Yes, it is true that the reformed Mass is more flexible, and allows the insertion of non-Christian religious elements, as Faggioli noted in the quotation I gave at the beginning of this chapter. This flexibility has created an endless debate about syncretism (bad) *vs.* inculturation (good), which no one seems able to resolve. This does not change the reality that the reformed Mass is *in itself* something completely alien to the religious instincts of almost all non-Christian religions, which are able to find *specifically Christian* expression in the ancient Mass, in the sense that their yearning for the transcendent, their appreciation of mystery, and their appetite for ritual, can be satisfied very easily in the ancient Mass.

The setting apart of religious persons by their clothes and lifestyle; the use of sacred objects, words, and whole languages; the importance of sacrifice as a theological concept; the importance of ritual; the performance of key rites hidden from clear view: these are all things inherited by the Catholic liturgical tradition from the religion of the Old Testament, which it had in common with the paganism of the ancient Mediterranean world, and continues to have in common with Islam and Hinduism and the native spiritual traditions of Africa and Asia.

The attitude of reducing mystery, of explaining the rites in plain, vernacular words, of cutting and simplifying ritual, of simplifying vestments and aligning the lives of the clergy with those of the people they serve as much as possible, and of having everything take place under bright lights in full view of everyone: these things are specifically modern and European in origin. What is more, they are experienced as modern and European both by those of other cultures who want to be modern and European, and by those who react against this influence.

Elsewhere, I have written on the affinities of the ancient Mass with the religious culture of Africa, of China, and of the Islamic world.[141] I have done a podcast interview with an anthropologist on the relationship between the ancient Catholic liturgy and the spirituality of the native people of the Amazon region.[142] I have also written about its connection with the spirituality of the post-Enlightenment West: the New Age.[143]

We are now living in a time when Enlightenment thinkers and their ideas are being increasingly criticised for being euro-centric, for prioritising a specific model of rationality over all others, and even for being implicitly racist. There is, indeed, more than a little truth in this critique. These men were not the inspiration for the traditional Mass, however, but its enemies.

[141] Shaw, *The Case for Liturgical Restoration*, 255–73, 293–97.
[142] Iota Unum discussion with Dr Daniel Dolley, December 15, 2020, available on the Latin Mass Society's Spotify account.
[143] Shaw, *The Case for Liturgical Restoration*, 217–24.

10

Why Do They Call You "Rigid"?

What does it mean to call someone "rigid"? In common speech it might mean simply that someone was obstinate. In a Catholic context it might suggest the concept of the "rigorous," as in "strict," in the application of the moral law. However, it has come, at least in certain contexts, to mean something rather different, and very specific. Conservatives, it would seem, can be "rigid" in a way liberals cannot, and it is in this specialised sense that the word is used, particularly against traditional Catholics.

This notion of "rigidity" has very long roots. It is related to attempts to apply the tools of Freudian psychoanalysis to politics.

This talk is divided into three parts. In the first part, I will lay out the history of the terminology, in order to explain why the term has come to be used in the way in which it is used, and what it really means, both in general, outside the Church, and in the context of the Church, and in particular in Pope Francis's always perplexing idiolect. In the second part, I will bring out some difficulties of the theory lying behind these uses of the term. In the third part I will give some suggestions about how its victims can usefully respond to it.

What is the theory of the rigid personality?

Freudian politics

As everyone knows, Sigmund Freud liked to explain negative psycho-logical phenomena by reference to sexual repression. So powerful did this

This paper was delivered as part of the Iota Unum series in London, April 26, 2019.

explanation appear to his followers that it is only slightly caricatured by Thomas Mann when he presents in his novel *The Magic Mountain* a psychologist convinced that tuberculosis is a manifestation of sexual repression. It was natural that a later (and non-fictional) Freudian, Wilhelm Reich, should use the same hypothesis to explain political movements, in his 1933 book *The Mass Psychology of Fascism*. Here is an illustrative quotation:

> Suppression of the natural sexuality in the child, particularly of its genital sexuality, makes the child apprehensive, shy, obedient, afraid of authority, good and adjusted in the authoritarian sense; it paralyzes the rebellious forces because any rebellion is laden with anxiety; it produces, by inhibiting sexual curiosity and sexual thinking in the child, a general inhibition of thinking and of critical faculties. In brief, the goal of sexual suppression is that of producing an individual who is adjusted to the authoritarian order and who will submit to it in spite of all misery and degradation. Initially, the child has to submit to the structure of the authoritarian miniature state, the family, which process makes it capable of later subordination to the general authoritarian system. The formation of the authoritarian structure takes place through the anchoring of sexual inhibition and anxiety.

Reich applied his theory to Communism as well as Fascism, labelling it "Red Fascism," and was ejected from the Communist Party for his pains.

Reich's challenge to Nazism was answered by another psychologist, Erich Jaensch, just two years later, in 1935. Jaensch accepted something of the flavour of Reich's characterisation of Nazis, while giving it a positive spin, saying that they were clean-living, tough-minded, and anti-Semitic, and opposed to decadent artistic, ideological, and sexual trends. Jaensch offered his readers two personality groups, the good "J" and the bad "S," which were explained in terms of racial origin instead of Freudian theory.

After the war Theodor Adorno and his co-authors picked up the threads of this debate in their hugely influential work *The Authoritarian Personality*, published in 1950. Adorno et al.—just "Adorno" from now on—adopted Jaensch's two personality types, though they regarded the J type as bad, labelling it Authoritarian, Anti-Semitic, or high on the scale of Ethno-Prejudice;[144] the contrasting type was good. In their own terms, left-wing authoritarianism was a contradiction in terms. Like Reich, however, Adorno appealed to sexual repression as the origin of the Authoritarian.

Adorno's theory is truly a product of Hell's kitchen, combing ingredients from both Nazis and Communists. It has nevertheless been hugely influential. Here is the British psychologist Peter Kelvin writing about the authoritarian personality twenty years after Adorno:

> These tendencies reflect on a type of individual who needs to feel that his environment is highly predictable . . . he needs to know where he stands; and so he fastens on to norms: he does not "let himself go," for fear of where this might lead; he looks to authority as a guide. . . . [He also] relies very heavily on stereotypes in [his] perception of the social environment. Moreover, the stereotypes used by an authoritarian personality tend to be very clear-cut, and the characteristic inflexibility of this personality leads to relative inability to modify the stereotype once it has been formed.[145]

Just how widespread this approach became in the discipline of psychology is illustrated by Frank Furedi:[146]

> Psychology was harnessed to legitimate the claim that the concerns of conformist right-wing people were largely an expression of emotional "status anxiety." During the Cold War, leading

---

[144] See Norman Dixon, *On the Psychology of Military Incompetence* (London: The Folio Society, 2016), 245ff.

[145] Peter Kelvin, *The Bases of Social Behaviour: An Approach in Terms of Order and Value* (New York: Holt, Rinehart and Winston, 1970), quoted by Dixon, 254 (ellipses his).

[146] Frank Furedi, "Do You Have a Conservative Personality? Why Do They Say That You Are Sick?," in his Substack, November 25, 2022, https://frankfuredi.substack.com/p/do-you-have-a-conservative-disposition. The following two notes give internal references.

American liberal commentators such as Richard Hofstadter and Lionel Trilling claimed that conservatism did not need to be taken seriously since it had no important argument. Hofstadter's student, the historian Dorothy Ross recalled that the prevailing sentiment amongst fellow academics was that conservatives "had no mind."[147] Psychological studies of personality often directed their fire against those possessing conservative psychological traits. University of Pennsylvania psychiatrist Kenneth Appel stated that conservatism was itself a personality disorder. The liberal political commentator Arthur Schlesinger Jr insisted that American conservatives were guilty of "schizophrenia." Leading social scientists, such as Riesman and Hofstadter, defined "conservatism as a problem of abnormal psychology, a failure of intolerant, uninformed, and uneducated individuals to adjust to the complex modern world."[148]

These ideas were not limited to text-books; they are still reflected uncritically in journalism, and are embedded in popular culture. The lyrics of the 1979 Pink Floyd album, *The Wall*, contrasts the "bleeding hearts and artists," and the repressed, fearful, dull-witted, and aggressive types who hate Jews, blacks, and homosexuals. Similarly, in the Harry Potter series, J.K. Rowling sets up a conflict between the family-oriented, un-intelligent, and fascist-leaning character Draco Malfoy, and the creative, independent, rule-breaking Harry Potter. In both cases, the contrast is straight out of Adorno.

Pope Francis on the rigid personality

We similarly see Adorno's stereotypes and patterns of thought popping up in the Catholic Church. A characteristic expression of the Holy Father's thinking would be this remark, made in the context of an interview question, from Fr Antonio Spadaro, of why some people like the traditional

---

[147] Jamie Cohen-Cole, *The Open Mind: Cold War Politics and the Sciences of Human Nature* (Chicago: University of Chicago Press, 2014), 51.

[148] Ian Dowbiggin, *The Quest for Mental Health: The Tale of Science, Medicine, and Mass Society* (Cambridge: Cambridge University Press, 2011), 138–39.

Mass: "And I ask myself: Why so much rigidity? Dig, dig, this rigidity always hides something, insecurity or even something else. Rigidity is defensive. True love is not rigid."[149] It is characteristic of Pope Francis that the statement is full of undefined terms and pregnant with unspecified implications, but the forgoing discussion seems to give the key to its meaning. "Rigidity" is a reference to the authoritarian personality, and the pope relates this in textbook fashion to insecurity. The coy reference to "something else" presumably refers to sexual repression, and the disordered sexualities which Freud suggested may result from repression. Pope Francis, like many churchmen of his generation, is reciting a script handed to him by the likes of Adorno and Kelvin.

As has been apparent since the liturgical reform, and was again on view when Pope Benedict XVI promulgated *Summorum Pontificum*, some influential liberals in the Church regard the traditional Mass as a threat. They like to insist that only old ladies attend celebrations, but they seem fearful that they are wrong, and that the traditional movement will grow if allowed to take root, and cause all sorts of problems. Pope Francis's analysis is rather different. On his view, the traditional Mass is an outlet for a group of people with deep-seated anxiety issues deriving from sexual repression in childhood. This is a small minority of Catholics, and can no more grow by making converts than could a club for red-heads.

This helps to explain Pope Francis's *laissez fair* attitude to celebrations of the traditional Mass up to the time of his promulgation of *Traditionis Custodes* in 2021, when he changed direction. By contrast, his hostility towards traditionalist seminarians, and the bishops who wish to ordain them, has been a consistent thread throughout his papacy. This is because, on the view I have described, members of this unfortunate minority are clearly unsuited to pastoral ministry. Here, it is even clearer that the

[149] The interview was published with a collection of Pope Francis's sermons: *Nei tuoi occhi è la mia parola: Omelie e discorsi di Buenos Aires 1999-2013* (Milan: Rizzoli, 2016); in English, *In Your Eyes I See My Words: Homilies and Speeches from Buenos Aires*, 3 vols. (New York: Fordham University Press, 2021). The quotation was reported by *Catholic Culture*, November 11, 2016, www.catholicculture.org/news/headlines/index.cfm?storyid=29904.

problem he envisages with these candidates is a disordered sexuality, including paedophilia.

Assessment of the theory of the rigid personality

Nazism, conformism, and morality

Adorno's research methodology has been much criticised. Reading his book as a non-specialist I am astonished at the narrow range of data through which he appears to want to psychoanalyse the entire American population. However, within the limits of this chapter I would like to pick out two large-scale problems with his theory.

The first is the strangely influential role which it accords to the self-image of the Nazi leadership as ideal specimens of Germanic manhood. Most importantly, Jaensch's claim, which has passed without challenge into the thinking of Adorno and his popularisers, is that the Nazis were products of the traditional, hierarchical family, and represented traditional, middle-class morality, especially in the area of sexuality. Jaensch's motive was to make the Nazis reassuringly respectable; Adorno's project seems to be to denigrate this kind of respectability through its association with the Nazis.

The reality, however, as many people noticed at the time and since, was that the higher echelons of the Nazi party was filled with saddos and misfits, of all kinds of family backgrounds, often of dubious sexuality and even racial origin, who condemned what they called "bourgeois" moral principles, herded priests into death camps, and dabbled in the occult. They undermined the authority of the traditional family in favour of the state, by for example conscripting children into the Hitler Youth, and had little time for conventional sexual morality.

The second issue is to do with the Freudian explanation of the Nazi phenomenon. This is that sexual repression leads to anxiety, narrow-mindedness, and a strong aversion to taking risks. The difficulty is that the adoption of fascism in Germany was experienced not as an act of conformity to conventional rules, but as the violent overthrow of the political establishment, in favour of a programme of suicidally risky expansionism. The question of risk aversion needs to be treated at greater length.

Freudian military incompetence

The issue of risk aversion is central to one application of Adorno's ideas, that of Norman Dixon in his 1976 classic *On the Psychology of Military Incompetence*. Dixon suggests that a weak ego is indicated by conformism in relation to traditional middle-class morality, which is itself regarded as tantamount to authoritarianism. He accordingly ransacks the annals of military history in search of examples of incompetent generals who exercised sexual continence; he is the only person I have yet encountered who uses the word "womaniser" as a term of approbation.

On the Dixon-Adorno understanding, we would expect the Nazis to lack mental agility and be bound to robotic, submissive behaviour determined by an unbending authoritarian hierarchy. This might be a pleasing thought, but the implication that the Nazi war-machine was sclerotic and incompetent is hardly borne out by the facts. As is argued in detail in Marc Bloch's 1940 account of the defeat of France in the Second World War, *Strange Defeat*, it was not the Germans, but their opponents, who were incapable of adjusting their military principles to new circumstances, particularly in the opening stages of the war. Bloch, a medieval historian by trade, was a French Jew who fought in both World Wars. A short time after writing his book he was executed by the Germans for his part in the French Resistance. He wrote:

> Compared with the old Imperial Army, the troops of the Nazi regime have the appearance of being far more "democratic." The gulf between officers and men now seems to be less unbridgeable.... From highest to lowest there is a more clearly marked participation by all ranks in a general atmosphere of goodwill. That spiritual communion which is the outcome of the special brand of mysticism which is rife in modern Germany is extremely powerful, and we should not let the crudity of its origins blind us to that truth.[150]

---

[150] Marc Bloch, *Strange Defeat: A Statement of Evidence Written in 1940*, trans. Gerard Hopkins (New York: W.W. Norton & Co., 1999), 92. Originally published in 1968.

This national fellow-feeling was, after all, precisely what was attractive about Nazi racial ideology, a point also made by Dietrich von Hildebrand, in his autobiographical work *My Battle against Hitler.*[151]

A final point about Dixon is that, having found examples of the kind of generals he likes—ideally, as successful (as W.S. Gilbert expressed it) in the courts of Venus as on the field of Mars[152]—he is obliged to admit that in many cases they were far from being "let it all hang out" liberals, but were strict disciplinarians who expected their orders to be obeyed. He deals with this anomaly by making a distinction between people being *authoritarian* and their being *autocratic*, saying that being autocratic is actually a good thing, or at least a neutral one, though the difference between authoritarianism and autocracy is left vague. On gets the impression that the notion of an autocratic personality is simply an emergency lever Dixon can pull each time someone with otherwise authoritarian traits turns out to have imagination, open-mindedness, and military effectiveness.

Conformism, incompetence, rigidity, repression

Dixon does make a convincing case for the connection between conformism and incompetence. His argument is simple enough: that in a hierarchical institution like an army it is sometimes possible, at least in peacetime, to get promotion by toeing the line while lacking the self-confidence necessary to take risks, accept responsibility for mistakes, and tear up the rule-book when faced with an unforeseen situation. Three aspects of his account of what weak-ego conformists do when faced with difficulties seem particularly perceptive.

First, because a conformist craves affirmation from superiors and equals, he will strive to do what pleases them, even if this means sacrificing his subordinates. Second, a conformist may prefer to attempt either very simple or else impossible tasks. The former he is confident he will complete successfully; the latter he does not think he will be blamed for failing.

---

[151] Dietrich von Hildebrand, *My Battle Against Hitler: Defiance in the Shadow of the Third Reich*, trans. and ed. John Henry Crosby and John F. Crosby (New York: Image, 2014).

[152] W.S. Gilbert, *Patience*, Act I (the Colonel speaking).

Third, the conformist's desire to avoid getting the blame when things go wrong can lead him not only into sticking to the text-book, but also to refusing to give orders at all.

When we get down to the nitty-gritty of Dixon's historical examples, and generalisations of these kinds drawn from them, it is reasonably clear what Dixon is talking about. The key issue is extreme risk aversion, of which social conformism is simply one manifestation. Once we have this out on the table we can see that there is no necessary connection with the left-right spectrum of politics: communists in a communist system can be just as risk-averse as conservatives in a conservative environment.

As already indicated, the idea that Nazism is the political ideology of choice for risk-averse individuals needs only to be stated to be rejected. Once in power, of course, risks attach to rejecting it, but this will be the case for any politically dominant ideology which is aggressively enforced.

What Adorno and his followers attempted to do was to roll into a single phenomenon three elements: fascism (right-wing authoritarianism); traditional sexual morality; and "rigidity," by which they meant a lack of critical faculties and imagination combined with social conformism. What I have argued is that the active ingredient in the amorphous concept of rigidity is extreme risk aversion. With hindsight this is in fact strongly implied by the quotations I have already given of Kelvin and indeed Reich. Risk aversion, however, is neither conceptually connected nor obviously empirically correlated with the other two elements, fascism and sexual morality, nor are these two elements connected with each other. As already noted, the overthrow of liberal politics by Nazism in Germany is not an example of the politics of risk aversion. Nor were the Nazis favourable either to traditional social norms nor to the family structures which embodied and inculcated them. To state the obvious, what Hitler wanted was not independent-minded risk-takers, nor timid and risk-averse subjects, but fanatics indifferent alike to risk, morality, and death.

Supposing it is obvious enough that Nazism is not connected in any significant way with risk aversion or to sexual morality, Adorno's followers may insist that these two things—playing it safe and following conventional sexual norms—are at least connected with each other. This is, after all, the key element of the Freudian inspiration of the theory. I shall address that next.

The psychological evidence

Two lines of empirical enquiry shed some light on the relationship between these two ideas. The first is the investigation of healthy risk-taking, seen for example in entrepreneurism. One of the things which has emerged from this is that children with secure two-parent families have greater appetite for such risk in later life than others less fortunate.[153]

Traditional two-parent families are strongly correlated with positive life outcomes for children in many ways, so this finding is hardly surprising. But it is these families, if any, which must include that bogeyman of Freudianism, the supposedly cloying and unimaginative traditional family and the moral formation it gives children. The reality is that children brought up without this structure, with liberated parents moving between multiple partners, are more prone to have problems with their schoolwork and to display chronic anxiety.

The second line of suggestive research relates to pornography. If the fundamental Freudian claim were true—that sexual problems, not to say all problems, are due to sexual repression—then at least part of the solution to such problems will be providing people with a sexual outlet. This has led generations of Freud-influenced penal reformers to demand that rapists and other sex abusers in prison be provided with a supply of porn. The issue was held up by Joseph Fletcher, in his influential 1966 book *Situation Ethics*, as a prime example of how outdated and irrational sexual taboos cause real harm in public policy, contrary to his own enlightened and humane attitude.

What does the evidence say? One survey of the literature, whose author set out to test the effectiveness of rehabilitation plans for offenders which included the provision of pornography, admitted:

[153] Ross Levine and Yona Rubinstein, "Smart and Illicit: Who Becomes an Entrepreneur and Do They Earn More?," Working Paper 19276, National Bureau of Economic Research, August 2013, www.nber.org/papers/w19276.pdf.

My dilemma is that I find there is no research support for utilizing pornography in any type of treatment for violent and/or sexually violent offenders. The literature is rich, however, with information about the negative impact of pornography for the violent and sexually violent offender.[154]

As with the Freudian claim about sexual morality and pathological risk aversion, the claim that porn can facilitate a sexual outlet like a safety-valve for people of disturbed sexualities is not just off the mark, but the reverse of the truth.

Zombie Freudianism and the Catholic tradition

Freud's reputation has waxed and waned over the last century. Today, while he still has his partisans, attention has generally shifted to alternative models of the human psyche and alternative therapeutic approaches. As with many formerly influential theorists, however, he continues to shape popular thinking on his subject long after specialists have left him behind. We might call the continuing influence of Freud "Zombie Freudianism." Its key tenet is that sexual repression is the root of everything bad in the individual and in society.

Like all thoroughly bad ideas, this has found its way into a Catholic Church bereft of intellectual antibodies capable of identifying and expelling ideas hostile to the Faith. But as the Catholic psychiatrist Thomas Verner Moore observed in the 1950s, it should be obvious that this Freudian claim is incompatible with Catholic teaching about sexual morality and with the whole tradition of Catholic spirituality.[155]

In the Catholic tradition, all our desires, of which the most powerful are frequently the sexual ones, need to be controlled to conform with

---

[154] Scott Allen Johnson, "Use of Pornography with Sex Offenders in Treatment: A Controversial Conundrum," *Journal of Forensic Research*, September 30, 2015, www.hilarispublisher.com/open-access/use-of-pornography-with-sex-offenders-in-treatment-a-controversial-conundrum-2157-7145-1000309.pdf.

[155] Thomas Verner Moore, *Heroic Sanctity and Insanity: An Introduction to the Spiritual Life and Mental Hygiene* (New York: Grune & Stratton, 1959), 183–85.

the Natural Law. This law is not an arbitrary obligation, and the limits it places on our desires do not act as a kind of dam, as the Freudians imagine, behind which they will build up until they break forth with greater ferocity than ever. On the contrary, the Natural Law is the law of human nature, which not only protects others from our unmastered impulses, but preserves our own humanity by enabling us to rise above our animal passions, to subdue them, and to channel them into the objects which we value the most.

It is not surprising that opponents of the Church latch on to Zombie Freudianism to attack the Catholic tradition, saying, for example, that the clerical abuse crisis is the consequence of celibacy. What is more depressing is to find it expressed by people within the Church, as when Cardinal Reinhard Marx declared, on the subject of clerical celibacy, that "sexual freedom" is intrinsic to the "inner freedom of faith and orientation to the example of Jesus Christ."[156]

This kind of talk has been going on, in the Church, since the 1970s, though not until recently at such high levels. Just as Freudianism gave the sexual revolution intellectual respectability outside the Church, within the Church it has provided cover for clergy wishing to excuse their failure to maintain their vow of celibacy.

How to respond?

The continuing popularity of the Rigidity Theory, now long after its scientific basis has been called into doubt, raises the question of how one should respond to accusations of rigidity, whether directed at one personally, or at the movement for the restoration of the traditional Mass in general.

The first thing to note in this regard is the supreme irony of claiming that, today, those upholding the Latin liturgy, the supernatural realities of Church teaching, and a way of life in accordance with Natural Law, are

---

[156] Bree A. Dail, "Cardinal Marx: Issues of Celibacy & 'Sexual Orientation' Will Receive 'Synodal' Clarification," *OnePeterFive*, March 14, 2019, https://onepeterfive.com/cardinal-marx-issues-of-celibacy-sexual-orientation-will-receive-synodal-clarification.

social conformists. Having any such views is an act of radical rebellion against the entire cultural and political establishment: against what we have been taught in school, against the dominant attitudes of our peers in university and the workplace, against the favoured narratives offered us by the entertainment industry, and against the incentives of the tax and benefit system. Within the Church one may find the occasional hint that this massive consensus could be questioned, but few indeed are the bishops and intellectuals who will openly repudiate it.

So to those who claim that we are conformists, the first thing we can say is: to what are we supposedly conforming? Traditionalism today is not conformism, but rebellion. The words of D.H. Lawrence are apter than ever: "We know these new English Catholics. They are the last word in protest. They are Protestants protesting against Protestantism."[157]

A second point is about the very strategy of those who make use of the notion of the rigid personality. It is, as they must be at least dimly aware, a Freudian diagnosis, linking poor social functioning to bad childhood experiences. It medicalises those to whom it is applied, and today it is beginning to be recognised that this is not just an imprudent way of arguing, but an outrageous and abusive one. In 2017, the papal biographer Austen Ivereigh was forced to apologise for suggesting that converts to the Faith were suffering from a "neurosis" which engendered opposition to Pope Francis.[158] The accusation of "rigidity" is, however, a far more serious attempt to portray opponents as mentally ill. It is simple gaslighting.

A third approach to the accusation is to refer back to the characteristics of Adorno's two personality types. Most of the people talking about

---

[157] D.H. Lawrence, Letter to Lady Cynthia Asquith, quoted in Matthew Parris, *Scorn: The Wittiest and Wickedest Insults in Human History* (London: Profile Books, 2016), 33.

[158] Austen Ivereigh, "Pope Francis and the convert problem," *Crux*, August 9, 2017, https://cruxnow.com/commentary/2017/08/09/pope-francis-convert-problem and idem, "An apology for needless offense—and how to disagree better," https://cruxnow.com/commentary/2017/08/12/apology-needless-offense-disagree-better.

rigidity have probably never heard of Adorno, but, like Pink Floyd and J.K. Rowling, they think, for reasons they may not fully understand, that rigidity is opposed to artistic creativity, culture, and the intellectual life. It is therefore useful to point out the passionate support the traditional movement has always had from artists of all kinds, particularly poets, novelists, and musicians; the connection it has with Catholic culture, both high culture and popular culture; and the appeal it has for many intellectuals, including many of the brightest of the younger generation of Catholic scholars and writers today.

The list of signatories of the 1971 "Agatha Christie" petition in favour of the traditional Mass is one good source of material here,[159] as is the chapter on intellectuals' reactions to the liturgical reform in Joseph Pearce's *Literary Converts.*[160]

So powerfully obvious, indeed, are these facts, that opponents of traditionalism sometimes adopt the opposite approach, characterising traditional Catholics not as rigid and boorish but as stuck in an ivory tower. For present purposes it is enough to point out that they can't have it both ways.

Another aspect of Adorno's characterisation of the authoritarian personality can also be turned against its supporters. As I quoted Kelvin, the rigid individual is one who navigates through life with the aid of stereotypes: this may be what Pope Francis is talking about when he criticises people who like to "categorise" others.[161] What is the rigidity theory, however, but an attempt to classify the entire human race into two stereotypes? Followers of the theory believe themselves able to attribute a whole set of psychological features, together with a childhood

---

[159] See Shaw, *The Case for Liturgical Restoration*, 213–16; idem, "50 Years Ago: Non-Catholics Petitioned the Pope for the Latin Mass," *OnePeterFive*, November 8, 2021, https://onepeterfive.com/non-catholics-petition-pope-latin-mass.

[160] Joseph Pearce, *Literary Converts: Spiritual Inspiration in an Age of Unbelief* (San Francisco: Ignatius Press, 2006).

[161] John L. Allen Jr., "Pope blasts turning truth into an idol, wielding it to judge and classify," *Crux*, March 29, 2018, https://cruxnow.com/vatican/2018/03/29/pope-blasts-turning-truth-into-an-idol-wielding-it-to-judge-and-classify.

background, to anyone who likes the traditional Mass, without going to the trouble of actually talking to any of them. One might even say that those who apply to traditional Catholics the stereotypical characteristic of rigid personalities, namely of stereotypical thinking, are projecting onto an out-group a characteristic which they have themselves.

Further to this, my final suggestion about responding to accusations of rigidity is drawn from Norman Dixon's description of risk-averse conformists in leadership positions. For what we find, among many churchmen today, is a concern for the opinions of peers and superiors, at the expense of the welfare of subordinates. We see among them a preference for easy or impossible tasks over difficult and necessary ones. And we see a fear of accepting responsibility so intense that it can manifest itself in a refusal to lead at all.

These are the traits of what Dixon called the rigid or authoritarian personality. As will be clear from all I have said, I don't think those are very useful terms, but Dixon is correct to link these patterns of behaviour to risk aversion and conformism. This is not a description of traditional Catholics, but of the overwhelmingly liberal clerical and lay institutional leadership under which the Catholic community suffers today.

My proposal, then, is to turn the tables in this debate. It is not traditional Catholics who are fearful and unimaginative, seeking the comfort of established norms and structures. It is traditional Catholics who leave the comfort of the familiar and established, as a result of following their research and thinking into whatever scary territory it may lead. When they reach their ecclesial wilderness, where peers don't want to know you and superiors treat you with scorn, they can see clearly the deficiencies of those leaders and that structure—a creaking, outmoded structure too unimaginative to consider effective reform, with leaders clinging to the approval of each other while the rising waters engulf the souls entrusted to their care.

11

Clericalism and the Culture of Clerical Abuse

When I was at an English Benedictine boarding school, Ampleforth College, in the 1980s, I was, at around the age of fourteen, prepared for the reception of the sacrament of Confirmation by a monk later imprisoned for the sexual abuse of children. There were, indeed, several abuser monks in the community at that time, and they were also to be found in the communities of other monastic schools: at Fort Augustus in Scotland, at Ealing in London, and at Downside in the southwest of England, to name but three. Some of these passed through the Benedictine house of studies I later attended as a student in Oxford, and of which I was for some years a Fellow, St Benet's Hall.

Their enablers and protectors included more or less everyone in authority in those communities over an extended period of time. An official inquiry into child sexual abuse was later presented with a letter written by an Abbot of Downside, Aiden Bellinger, which included this passage:

> At the heart of the darkness in the community is the issue of child abuse which was "tolerated" by all my predecessors as abbot. I am particularly concerned that Richard,[162] who should have known better, attempted to protect Nicholas and Dunstan when he should have been protecting their victims.[163]

[162] Abbot Richard Yeo, Bellinger's immediate predecessor. Bellinger held office 2006–2014.

[163] Evidence presented to the Independent Inquiry into Child Sexual Abuse, December 11, 2017. The transcript is available online, on p. 73: www.iicsa. org.uk/key-documents/3537/view/11-december-2017-roman-catholic-church-public-hearing-transcript.pdf.

The problem is certainly not limited to the English Benedictine Congregation, of which the communities just mentioned were members, nor is it limited to the Catholic Church, or indeed to religious groups. Nevertheless, I feel the need to address the matter here both because it is an important aspect of the crisis in the Church, and because of the attempts which have been made to use the problem to attack traditional Catholic spirituality.

Abuse and the authoritarian personality

For quite a long time, a media narrative about clerical abuse appeared to be in operation, which had it that clerical abuse was a problem caused by "conservatives." This was suggested naturally enough by the idea, which I explored in the last chapter, that political and religious conservativism, including a belief in traditional sexual prohibitions, is the manifestation of a disordered sexuality: Theodore Adorno's theory of the "authoritarian personality." Put as starkly as that the idea seems preposterous, but a slightly more subtle formulation would be greeted by knowing nods in a lot of secular liberal circles, certainly until recently: that those who talk the loudest about sexual morality are sexually repressed, and these are the kind of people who present the greatest danger to others.

Since I have separately addressed the theoretical underpinnings of this idea, here I'll simply observe that this narrative has taken quite a battering from the facts. The different treatment of abusive prelates regarded as "conservative" and "liberal" by the media, particularly visible in the first decade after major stories began to break in 2002, was truly remarkable, but the weight of numbers of liberal abusers has finally begun to tell.

To illustrate, the influential liberal prelate, Archbishop Rembert Weakland of Milwaukee, sedulously protected the priest-abusers of his diocese, and settled a lawsuit brought against him by his own homosexual lover, or victim, with $450,000 of Church funds. The first fact was publicly established in a court case as early as 1984; the second emerged at the time of his retirement in 2002. These revelations did not prevent him from launching a self-justifying autobiography in 2009.[164] For some liberal commentators his coming out as homosexual—as he does in the book—appeared to make up for his shredding reports about abusive priests, telling complainants that their letters would be scrutinised by libel lawyers, accusing complainants of "squealing," breaking his vow of celibacy, and misappropriating diocesan money.

The media was somewhat less kind to Theodore McCarrick, sometime cardinal archbishop of Washington, and in his day the most powerful liberal prelate in America. He was stripped of his rank in 2019. Significantly, the Holy See did not open a canonical process against him until detailed and specific allegations of McCarrick's abuse of minors were presented in 2017: it is almost as if the abuse of seminarians was something that could be tolerated.[165] In truth, abusers have little interest in the age of consent.

A further landmark was the post-mortem destruction of the reputation of Jean Vanier, the founder of L'Arche, a chain of communities for the disabled. He died in 2019, and had been revered as a living saint by many liberal Catholics, but a report by L'Arche itself, published in 2020,[166] established that he had had a succession of abusive relationships with women.

Another shattering case was the conviction of Bishop Gustavo Zanchetta in Argentina in March 2022, for the sexual abuse of seminarians. Zanchetta had been appointed a bishop by Pope Francis, and strongly and repeatedly defended by him ever since allegations were formally presented to the Church authorities in 2016. There are, of course, many similar cases.

Another problem for the "conservative abuser" media angle was the way that stories of abuse spread from the Catholic Church, which was an initial focus of sexual abuse stories, into other denominations, and

---

[164] Archbishop Rembert Weakland, *Pilgrim in a Pilgrim Church: Memoirs of a Catholic Archbishop* (Grand Rapids, MI: Eerdmans Publishing Co., 2009).

[165] See Andrea Tornielli, "McCarrick Report: a sorrowful page the Church is learning from," *Vatican News*, November 10, 2020, www.vaticannews.va/en/vatican-city/news/2020-11/mccarrick-report-secretary-state-sexual-abuse-minors-church-pope.html.

[166] *Summary Report from L'Arche International*, February 22, 2020.

into all kinds of professional bodies, finally developing into the "me too" series of scandals that engulfed the film industry. On this narrative, it made sense that the Catholic Church, as a redoubt of sexual repression, should have also been a nest of sexual abusers, but this requires a contrast with other institutions. When it turns out that college athletics coaches, the Boy Scouts, the British Broadcasting Company, and Hollywood have also harboured sexual abuse on a large scale, the argument ceases to work.

This is not to say that abusers cannot be found among theological conservatives and traditionalists. Abusers can be found, unfortunately, in all kinds of places where they can carry out their abuse. The question is whether a theoretical or empirical connection can be made between a proclivity to abuse and some theological position or other.

The priesthood, Christ, and clericalism

One suggestion to this effect is that abuse is connected with a particular understanding of the priesthood. Thus, a letter in the UK's liberal Catholic weekly, *The Tablet*, criticising the founders of a conservative priestly association, the Confraternity of Catholic Clergy, lambasted "the theologically dubious description of the priest as being an image of Christ," which, the author claimed, is a "power-focused self-definition that has in part contributed to the abuse of power within the priesthood, including sexual abuse of children."[167] This connects a particular theological position, the traditional one, with clericalism, and with abuse.

There is a certain plausibility to this suggestion: anything which increases the prestige of priests can make it more difficult for victims to make accusations against them, or to get people to believe them. Then again, there is certainly an identifiable historical phenomenon of clericalism, which gives the clergy an exaggerated role vis-à-vis the laity. Nevertheless, the relationship between clericalism and the abuse crisis is more complicated, and the link between clericalism and the theology of the priest as an *alter Christus* is far from clear. In order to consider these difficulties, it is necessary to establish what is meant by clericalism.

---

[167] Letter from John Dunn in *The Tablet*, April 9, 2011.

What is clericalism?

Clericalism is seldom defined, but it presumably involves the clergy impinging on the proper sphere of the laity, which is the temporal sphere, as distinguished from the spiritual sphere. The Second Vatican Council expressed the lay role in the Church as follows: "The laity must take up the restoration of the temporal order [*ordo temporalis*] as their own special task. Led by the light of the Gospel and the mind of the Church and motivated by Christian charity, they must act directly and in a definite way in the temporal sphere."[168] This was not an innovation by the Council: it follows in essence from the principle of "Gelasian Dyarchy," the way Church and State were envisaged to cooperate by Pope Gelasius I, which was the basis for the standard Catholic understanding thereafter. His letter to the Eastern Emperor Anastasius I Dicorus, *Famuli Vestræ Pietatis* (also known as *Duo Sunt*), written in 494, says simply enough that the pope, and the hierarchy in general, are the spiritual leaders of Catholics; the Emperor, and lay rulers in general, are the temporal rulers.

It is not difficult to find modern examples of a tendency to extend clerical authority into temporal matters. For example, in 1867, John Henry Newman, at that time editor of the English Catholic periodical *The Rambler*, suggested that the bishops might like to consult the laity over negotiations with the Government on the question of Catholic schools. This ignited an enormous row; particularly alarming to some clergy was the support Newman gained from prominent Catholic laity. Msgr George Talbot wrote to Cardinal Manning in alarm: "What is the province of the laity? To hunt, to shoot, to entertain? These matters they understand, but to meddle with ecclesiastical matters they have no right at all ..."[169] Talbot regarded the question of Catholic schools as "a matter purely ecclesiastical."[170]

This, however, is a mistake. Catholic schools are part of the temporal sphere: they have temporal objectives which they pursue through

---

[168] Second Vatican Council, Decree on the Apostolate of the Laity *Apostolicam Actuositatem* (1965), §7.

[169] Quoted in Russell Shaw, *To Hunt, To Shoot, To Entertain: Clericalism and the Catholic Laity* (San Francisco: Ignatius Press, 1993), 10.

[170] Ibid.

temporal means. The distinction between spiritual and temporal should not be confused with the modern distinction between the religious and the secular, the American doctrine of the "separation of Church and State," or the French idea of *laïcité*. These ideas involve postulating a religion-free zone, which would have been incomprehensible in past ages. A Catholic school is not non-religious: it should by definition be run according to Catholic principles, in accordance with Catholic teaching, and mindful of the spiritual good of its staff and pupils, and its Catholic character should be expressed through collective Catholic worship. The aim of a school *as such* is nevertheless temporal, in the sense that schools aim to convey knowledge of science, literature, languages, and so on, and these are not spiritual matters. Knowledge of these subjects is gained by the "light of reason," or empirical study, rather than divine revelation. Knowledge of the natural world and humane studies are integrated into a complete Catholic culture, because a complete Catholic culture has both temporal and spiritual aspects, just as the Catholic community does. This integration can be compared to the relationship between an individual's body and soul, or the incarnation of God the Son, with a fully human nature, and it parallels the traditional cooperation of the Church with a Catholic state.

To be fair to Talbot, his dismay at the intervention of prominent Catholics on Newman's side in 1867 must have been coloured by his historical memory. In the last decades of the previous century, a group of Catholic aristocrats known as "the Catholic Committee" had formed to negotiate with the British Government over the dismantling of the anti-Catholic Penal Laws.[171] The Committee was led by laity, although three clerics joined it in 1788. In preparation for what was to be the 1791 Catholic Relief Act, the Government proposed an oath to be taken by Catholics, that some of the bishops felt obliged to condemn publicly, to the consternation of leading Committee members. In the end a compromise was reached, the Act was passed, and the Committee was dissolved, although some of its

---

[171] In the following paragraphs I draw on Mark Bence-Jones, *The Catholic Families* (London: Constable & Robinson, 1995), 66–73, and Fr Nicholas Schofield and Gerard Skinner, *The English Vicars Apostolic 1688–1850* (Oxford: Family Publications, 2009), 48, 50.

members then founded the provocatively-named Cisalpine Club: the Cisalpine position being in opposition to the pro-papal, "Ultramontane" one.

Although the final result was a good one, the Catholic Committee was seen at the time and afterwards as encapsulating the danger of influential lay Catholics trying to determine theological issues, such as what doctrines, formulated in what way, could be rejected by conscientious Catholics, notably concerning the power of the pope. The Committee was motivated in part by liberal principles. One leading member, Robert, Lord Petre, was a Freemason: although already condemned by the pope, this condemnation could not be promulgated in England, and so was regarded as not binding.[172] Another, Sir John Throckmorton, proposed that English bishops be chosen without reference to the Holy See. These tendencies were a faint echo of the reforms imposed by the Holy Roman Emperor Joseph II, the "Sacristan Emperor," which affected many areas of the life of the Church, including teaching in seminaries and the liturgy, and turned many contemplative religious out into the streets; earlier, the Jesuits had been suppressed by several supposedly Catholic monarchies. This unfortunate trend in the final decades before the French Revolution represents the opposite error to that of clericalism: it was an attempt by laity to invade the spiritual sphere.

By the 1860s, the position of the English Catholic bishops in relation to the laity was far stronger than it had been three quarters of a century earlier. A proper system of dioceses had been restored in 1850, and the role of private Catholic homes as bases from which the sacraments could be administered was much reduced. In this new situation it began to be possible for ultramontanists like Talbot to adopt an attitude of clericalism. What should be clear, however, is that this is not the Church's default setting, or a matter of the traditional theology of the priesthood. It simply reflects the ever-shifting balance of power between laity and clergy.

In a rather different way, following the British conquest of Quebec from France in 1763, much of the lay Catholic leadership of the French community there returned to France, creating a vacuum which could be filled only by the clergy. A similar shortage of educated lay Catholics pertained

---

[172] Bence-Jones, *Catholic Families*, 44.

in Ireland, and to a certain extent in the United States of America, in the nineteenth and early twentieth centuries. In all three countries conflicts arose between clergy and laity over the control of Catholic institutions with temporal aims, such as schools and hospitals. It was tempting, but of course false, for the clergy there to assume that the influence they had gained as a matter of historical circumstances was due to them as a matter of principle. This is a mistake we must not make ourselves.

This is not to minimise the importance of spiritual authority, which governs the more important of the two spheres, the soul in the body. Since our eternal fate is of greater significance than our temporal fate, temporal rulers are subordinate in an important sense to spiritual ones. It remains true, however, that the clergy are subordinate to temporal rulers with regard to temporal matters, even if temporal matters are of less ultimate importance. Indeed, the temptation to clericalism arises out of a worldly attitude that sees temporalities as the only things of real value. Clericalism inflates the importance of those things over which the hierarchical Church does *not* have authority.

In a similar way, it is common to see liberal Catholics demanding that lay people have more control over the hierarchical Church, or that women be ordained priests, as the only way in which they can be given a share of power within the Church. This is a clericalist attitude, inasmuch as it suggests that the only kind of power which exists in the Catholic community is clerical—as if the laity exercised no authority even in their own sphere.

Traditional theology, either of the role of the hierarchy or of priestly identity, does not, therefore, necessarily imply clericalism. On the contrary, it emphasises what is distinct about the priesthood, which is not power over temporal matters, but an identification with the spiritual sphere.

Clericalism and networks of abuse

Having defined what clericalism is, and identified historical clericalist tendencies in the modern Church, the question remains how exactly, if at all, it is related to clerical abuse. One hypothesis, already mentioned, is that by artificially elevating the prestige of the clergy, it makes it more difficult to call them to account for abusive behaviour. Consider Philip Lawler's account of the manner in which Cardinal John O'Connell ran the Archdiocese of Boston during his long tenure, which covered most of the first half of the twentieth century.

> Pastors were expected to run their parishes the way the cardinal ran the archdiocese: efficiently, decisively, avoiding all friction. Pastors who handled these responsibilities well were accorded a great deal of autonomy; they could make their own decisions about parish finances, programs, and personnel, provided that they did not violate the general policies of the archdiocese. If a conflict arose between a priest and a parishioner, the archdiocese invariably sided with the pastor. So the system arose in which complaints from the laity were funnelled first through the pastors, with priests protecting each other against any "interference" that came from outside the clerical ranks.[173]

The connection with the way clerical abuse complaints have been handled seems obvious, but there are a number of complications to be dealt with.

The first is that it is not only possible, but natural, to combine a high level of respect for an office or a class of persons—exaggerated or not—with highly restrictive entry requirements, coupled with a demand for higher standards of behaviour for those admitted to it, enforced by greater than normal scrutiny. Traditional monastic communities exemplify this, as do elite military units. What we find with the clergy in the era of clerical abuse is a slackening of entry requirements, standards, and scrutiny. I will examine this in more detail in the next section.

The second is that, while it is convenient to talk about the abuse of the laity by the clergy in Catholic institutions, the reality is not so neat and tidy. Younger members of the clergy, as well as seminarians,[174] have been

---

[173] Philip F. Lawler, *The Faithful Departed: The Collapse of Boston's Catholic Culture* (New York: Encounter Books, 2008; with new material, 2010), 35–36.

[174] Up to the time of the Council, most seminarians were regarded as being in the "clerical state"; afterwards, most were not.

among the victims of abuse. The Christian Brothers, whose educational institutions were notoriously abusive, is a religious order whose members are not ordained, and are therefore not clerics. Religious sisters have been both victims and perpetrators of abuse. And many lay employees and volunteers in Church institutions have also been drawn in to the privileged club of abusers, and then again, they have also been victims.

The third point follows from this. It is commonly assumed that the clerical abuse crisis is a matter of a series of individuals who fall to the temptations of the flesh, and are subsequently wrongfully protected. The explanations of why bishops and other superiors protect them include the abusers' clerical dignity, the scandal their fall from grace would cause to the faithful, or the harm their exposure would do to the reputation of the Church. An extra reason is sometimes suggested, that bishops and superiors are sometimes themselves morally compromised in some way, and are subject to explicit or implicit blackmail. However, these kinds of explanations cannot account for the willingness of bishops and superiors to degrade the dignity of the clergy, to scandalise the faithful, to destroy the reputation of the Church, and to create legal complications in which their own shortcomings come to be cruelly exposed, in the way they treat abusers: because this is what has frequently happened. Looking at the actions of bishops and others in authority, as described in court cases and public inquiries and investigations, what is remarkable is precisely their *lack* of aversion to risk. The risks they took in many cases seem quite insane.

A very common scenario is as follows. A priest-abuser generates complaints in a parish; after a certain point these complaints reach a pitch which can no longer be ignored. There are threats to go to the police or the press, or a danger that the stories will become notorious in the parish and beyond it. The bishop responds by moving the priest to a new parish, where the same thing happens all over again. Not only does this sequence of events get repeated an indefinite number of times with the same priest, but the bishop is simultaneously following the same procedure with other priests, and dealing with the consequences of this policy being implemented by his predecessor. In this context, it is impossible to claim that bishops in these cases simply do not realise that the abuse would be repeated. And yet, instead of keeping a lid on the scandal by quietly sending the priest into retirement, or somewhere where abuse is genuinely impossible, these bishops keep moving abusers around parishes and similar roles until a scandal ends up in court, with calamitous consequences.

Sometimes, bishops' behaviour goes even further than this. The journalist J.D. Flynn gives the example of Fr David Szatkowski SCJ of Allentown, one of the dioceses featured in the shocking 2018 Pennsylvania Grand Jury report into clerical abuse. Flynn notes that Szatkowski had been charged with the sexual assault of a minor in 2011. The incident took place in the street and there were witnesses, but the victim did not wish to press charges. Perhaps she assumed that, as a priest, Szatkowski would face serious sanctions from his superiors. However, he did not. Instead, Bishop Thomas Welsh appointed him to the diocese's "formation team," to work with young men aspiring to the priesthood. That is not all: "Three years after facing criminal charges for sexually assaulting a child, he was permitted by the bishop of Allentown to serve as the canon lawyer—the procurator and advocate, in technical terms—for Fr Michael Lawrence, a priest accused of sexually assaulting two adolescent boys."[175] This is not the behaviour of a bishop whose overriding concern is the preservation of his or the Church's reputation.

Nevertheless, the bishop was not insane. This pattern of behaviour does have an explanation, which emerges clearly with some of the more comprehensive reports, like that of the Pennsylvania Grand Jury, but can also be seen in smaller incidents.

A priest once complained to me about another member of his community, who was notorious as a bully. The latter had retired from one position, which had enabled him to dominate a large number of subordinates,

[175] J.D. Flynn, "'What do you want to know?' The Catholic reaction to bishops and sexual abuse," *Catholic News Agency*, August 16, 2018, www.catholic newsagency.com/news/39142/what-do-you-want-to-know-the-catholic -reaction-to-bishops-and-sexual-abuse.

and was given another, where, as things were working out at the time of this conversation, he was able to continue the abusive behaviour, albeit on a smaller scale. My interlocutor said that it was as if their superior had decided to make available to this man an opportunity to continue his abuse, offering up to him a new set of potential victims, "like a great plate of meat."[176]

This expression has stayed with me particularly because my interlocuter was himself an abuser. Although the two priests hated each other, they were in the same situation. Having come to the end of the possibilities of abuse in one institutional context, they were provided with another: an opportunity neither neglected. Bishops and superiors involved in such decisions are not sacrificing the interests of abuse victims because they are frightened of exposure. Something quite different is happening. They are sacrificing the interests of victims in order to provide abusers with fresh opportunities to abuse: "like a great plate of meat."

Bishops and superiors would not express it in quite these terms. They would say that they want to find a role for their priests, towards whom they feel an obligation, which would make them happy. Nevertheless, what we have here is not merely a failure to combat the problem with sufficient vigour. It is an abusive institution, an abusive network, whose objective is to find and exploit opportunities for abuse for its members.

A particularly chilling illustration of the systematic and self-confident nature of an abusive network is given by one of the cases investigated by the Pennsylvania Grand Jury. This involved George, who as a minor was photographed naked by a group of priests.

> George recalled that each of these priests had a group of favored boys who they would take on trips. The boys received gifts; specifi-cally, gold cross necklaces. George stated, "He [Zirwas] had told me that they, the priests, would give their boys, their altar boys or their favorite boys these crosses. So he gave me a big gold cross to wear." The Grand Jury observed that these crosses served another purpose

---

[176] Both of the priests concerned are now deceased.

beyond the grooming of the victims: They were a visible designation that these children were victims of sexual abuse. They were a signal to other predators that the children had been desensitized to sexual abuse and were optimal targets for further victimization.

It is not pleasant to write that major parts of the Catholic Church, as a human institution, have been instrumentalised for a criminal conspiracy. This is, nevertheless, the truth of the matter.

Abuse and sexual morality

It would seem that at a certain point the Cardinal O'Connell-style clericalist system of ignoring complaints was captured and utilised for systematic sexual abuse. Exactly how this happened no doubt varied from place to place, but a crucial step was a transformation in the official attitude towards sexual morality.

This is described in some detail, in the American context, by the Linacre Institute's important study *After Asceticism: Sex, Prayer, and Deviant Priests* (Author House, 2003). Judging by official statistics, priestly abuse increased enormously in the 1960s and 1970s. Not only was this the moment at which the sexual revolution undermined traditional sexual norms in the wider society, it was also the moment when the Church in general, and seminaries in particular, gave up on the traditional emphasis on spiritual self-discipline:

> It is a widely known fact that many of the traditional ascetical practices of laymen and clergy and the traditional Christian understanding of the nature of prayer were liberalized or abandoned altogether during the 1960s. This liberalization of behavioural norms regarding prayer, fasting, and other forms of self-denial, along with the scuttling of sexual decorum and the social assumptions of common living, must have had a profound impact on the cohort of seminary men who had been raised just before the onslaught of sexual permissiveness that swept the youth culture of the 1960s.[177]

---

[177] *After Asceticism*, 25.

The study illustrates the new attitude with numerous quotations from bishops, priests, and seminarians who, as the authors express it, "all betray the conviction that the spiritual effectiveness of the priest is disconnected from his moral integrity in general, and sexual inclinations in particular."[178] Many of the quotations are of *praise* for priests caught out in illicit sexual behaviour.

The study describes the theoetical background to the new attitude as the "therapeutic mentality": "Overcontrol of sexual passion is seen as much more of a problem than its undercontrol; sexual identity becomes the dominating feature of one's life, consistent with the notion that each man is his own measure of righteousness."[179] This is, in short, the kind of approach to mental health ultimately inspired by Freud, opposed to the "rigidity" discussed in the last chapter.

The same attitude is in evidence if we ask what the abusers themselves say about sexual morality. While some abusers present themselves in public as adhering strictly to Catholic teaching, the better to gain access to certain categories of potential victims, talk of traditional sexual prohibitions is not the most natural lead-in to grooming victims for sexual abuse. Abusers want their victims to go along with the abuse, and the first thing they do is to attempt to normalise abusive behaviour. They typically tell their victims that what they want to do to them is not wrong. If they are doing that behind closed doors, it is not surprising to see them commonly arguing something along the same lines in public as well.

This is easy to illustrate. Fr Thomas Philippe OP, the French Dominican who was the friend and mentor of Jean Vanier, was given a canonical trial for some of his crimes in 1956. One of his victims explained Philippe's attempts to give his abuse a theological justification. He quoted Philippe: "When one arrives at perfect love, everything is lawful, for there is no more sin."[180] A convenient doctrine.

---

[178] Ibid., 34.

[179] Ibid., 39.

[180] Quoted in *Summary Report from L'Arche International*, February 22, 2020, p. 8.

Fr Joseph Quigley of the Archdiocese of Birmingham, England, was convicted of sexual activity with a child, sexual assault, false imprisonment (he liked to lock children in a crypt), and cruelty; the crimes took place between the 1990s and 2008. He was also the author of the Archdiocese's controversial programme of sex education, *All That I Am*, published in 2004. Defending his programme against conservative critics, he made a very interesting remark: "If we talk about sexuality as a gift, clearly we want to introduce them to that at an appropriate level."[181] Quite so.

Bishop Kieran Conry, who had multiple affairs with emotionally vulnerable women in his diocese of Arundel and Brighton, England, and resigned in September 2014, said in his own defence "I have been very careful not to make sexual morality a priority [in sermons]."[182] Of course not.

For the sake of balance, I will give an example of an abusive priest who presented himself as a traditionalist. Just as liberal abusers commonly claim to be victims of conservative "rigidity" and homophobia, it is possible for some abusers to claim that complaints about them were really motivated by an animus against their traditionalism. Perhaps the best-known case, Fr Carlos Urrutigoity, was apparently able to get a bishop to disregard evidence against him because this evidence originated with the Society of St Pius X, which operates outside the structures of the Church, whereas he wanted to be reconciled with the Holy See. No doubt he claimed that they were biased against him.

Nevertheless, when explaining to his victims, and later to the wider public, why he had been sharing beds with boys at the school he was running in 2001, he played down the seriousness of the matter. Statements from members of his order—the Society of St John—pointed to the historical practice of members of families sharing beds. What Urrutigoity was claiming, just like his liberal fellow-abusers, was that those seeking to hold him to standard sexual *mores* were excessively uptight. Indeed, what else could he have said to reassure his victims? And once the facts had been established by witnesses, what other defence was open to him?

[181] Quoted in *The Tablet*, December 15, 2020.
[182] Quoted in *The Daily Mail*, September 28, 2014.

Not only is it natural for abusive clergy to play down the prohibitions of traditional sexual morality, it is natural for them to play down their clerical aloofness. The abuser priest who prepared me for Confirmation took his little group of *confirmandi* on a retreat away from the school, where we spent the night. In the evening, he enjoyed chasing some of the boys around the grounds. It struck me as a bit odd, at the time, but then that was the kind of priest he was. Of course it was. It's that kind of priest—informal, down with the kids, open to larking about with the boys—who is going to be able to find opportunities for abuse most easily, not the stuffy ones with a strong sense of their clerical dignity.

I could multiply instances indefinitely, but readers who search the internet for examples will not be disappointed.

The connection between abuse and a progressive theology of sexuality can also be illustrated at the institutional level. In 1947, Fr Gerald FitzGerald founded the Servants of the Paraclete in the USA to help priests suffering from a variety of psychological problems. He warned bishops who sent sex-abusers to him that these priests should not be returned to ministry: "charity to the Mystical Body should take precedence over charity to the individual," he wrote.[183] This policy was overturned in the 1960s, because it did not sit well with progressive views of sexuality which had invaded the Church from secular sources.

In the same decade the American bishops commissioned a study on the state of the presbyterate. The now-infamous report,[184] by a priest with psychological training, Eugene Kennedy, was delivered in 1972. It entirely ignored questions of spiritual practice among the clergy, but it encouraged the bishops to give their priests greater freedom: "There is little indication that American priests would exercise freedom in an impulsive or destructive way."[185] This of course was, if the statistics are any guide, precisely the

---

[183] Quoted by Lawler, *Faithful Departed*, 138.
[184] Eugene C. Kennedy with Victor J. Heckler, *The Catholic Priest in the United States: Psychological Investigations* (Washington, DC: United States Catholic Conference, 1972).
[185] Kennedy and Heckler, 139.

historical moment when clerical sexual abuse was increasing at a terrifying rate. Kennedy himself left the priesthood in 1977.

The question of moral teaching is central to the phenomenon of clerical abuse. In order for the abuser to justify the abuse to himself and others, and in order for superiors to justify to themselves ignoring the complaints, it is necessary for them to take the view that the terrible crimes being committed are not, in fact, very serious at all. Sometimes, indeed, we hear from abusers that the abuse is actually *good* for the victims. It is to an example of this that I turn in the penultimate section of this chapter.

Abuse and the liturgy

Not all abuse is sexual abuse. There are various forms of emotional and also spiritual abuse, and it is natural, in the context of the abuse crisis, that the abuse which was committed and covered up would encompass a range of manifestations. It is sometimes suggested that a driver of abuse is a homosexual network within Church institutions: Aiden Bellinger, when Abbot of Downside, referred to "the homosexual network which is too close to the heart of the community,"[186] and Pope Francis has spoken of a "gay lobby."[187] It is true that a large proportion of sexual abuse which has taken place in Catholic institutions has been against adolescent males and young men, although at the time of writing there are increasing indications of the systematic sexual abuse of religious sisters by priests in India and Africa. However, many kinds of abuse have flourished and been afforded the same protection. What unites the phenomenon is the abuse itself. In this section I want to take the principle of abuse into a new area altogether: the liturgy.

Liturgical abuse might be thought of as an abuse of the liturgy, but it is also truly an abuse of the faithful, who are deprived of access to the sacraments in a dignified setting, and are subjected to the whims of priests and their favoured lay assistants. This point has been repeatedly emphasised

---

[186] Independent Inquiry into Child Sexual Abuse, p. 72.
[187] Pope Francis, June 6, 2013, remarks in a meeting at the Vatican with a group, CLAR.

by the official organs of the Church. The Congregation for Divine Worship declared in 1980: "The faithful have a right to a true Liturgy, which means the Liturgy desired and laid down by the Church."[188] In 2005, the Congregation for Divine Worship produced an instruction, *Redemptionis Sacramentum*, condemning an enormous number of liturgical abuses in great detail. It notes, quoting Pope John Paul II's 2003 encyclical *Ecclesia de Eucharistia*:

> For abuses "contribute to the obscuring of the Catholic faith and doctrine concerning this wonderful sacrament." Thus, they also hinder the faithful from "reliving in a certain way the experience of the two disciples of Emmaus: 'and their eyes were opened, and they recognized him.'"[189]

I know that some readers of the last paragraph will be amused at the idea of taking liturgical abuse seriously, or perhaps offended by my drawing a parallel with sexual abuse. To make my point, I do not need to claim that liturgical abuse is on the same level of seriousness as sexual abuse, simply that it illustrates an attitude of disregard towards lay concerns which is also found in the other kind of case. Nevertheless, unless we want to adopt the contemptuous attitude towards victims held by abusers and their enablers, we should not treat liturgical abuse lightly. In its worst forms, it can be psychologically and spiritually manipulative, exhibiting many of the features of sexual abuse.[190]

In an earlier chapter I have quoted Ann Roche Muggeridge on the way liberal priests used liturgical abuse to destroy the faithful's attachment to the traditional teaching of the Church. A similar technique has been used in seminaries to break the spirit of orthodox seminarians. In *Goodbye, Good Men*, Michael Rose quotes one former seminarian: "It seems

---

[188] *Inaestimabile Donum*, Foreword; cf. *Code of Canon Law* (1983), can. 214.

[189] *Inaestimabile Donum*, Foreword.

[190] For parallel considerations, see "Liturgical Abuse, Sexual Abuse, and Clericalism" in Peter Kwasniewski, *Holy Bread of Eternal Life: Restoring Eucharistic Reverence in an Age of Impiety* (Manchester, NH: Sophia Institute Press, 2020), 203–13.

they wanted to break us of any 'romantic notions' we may have had of how Mass ought to be celebrated."[191] Rose goes on to quote Fr Andrew Walter of Bridgeport, speaking about St Mary's Seminary in Baltimore:

> Some seminarians were very reverent and pious towards the Eucharist . . . and one day at Mass, after Communion had been distributed, a faculty priest blew on the paten where there were fingernail-size pieces of the Eucharist on it. He did this to make a point to the guys who were pious, who believed in the teaching of the Church that Jesus is really present in the Host. He was asking the seminarians, "Why are you so rigid?" I'm not going to say this is *verging* on the demonic. That *is* demonic.[192]

This is an example of psychological abuse, using the liturgy as a means. The perpetrator, however, would no doubt justify it as something *good* for the victims, something helpful to free them from their hang-ups. Exactly the same kind of self-justification is made by priestly sex-abusers who have imbibed progressive theories of sexuality. In both cases, the end result can include the victim's loss of faith.

Pope Benedict XVI wrote to the world's bishops in 2007, explaining his liberation of the traditional Mass. He explained that one of the laity's motives for desiring the old Mass was the problem of liturgical abuse:

> In many places celebrations were not faithful to the prescriptions of the new Missal, but the latter actually was understood as authorizing or even requiring creativity, which frequently led to deformations of the liturgy which were hard to bear. I am speaking from experience, since I too lived through that period with all its hopes and its confusion. And I have seen how arbitrary deformations of the liturgy caused deep pain to individuals totally rooted in the faith of the Church.[193]

---

[191] Michael Rose, *Goodbye, Good Men: How Liberals Brought Corruption into the Catholic Church* (Washington, DC: Regnery, 2002), 118.

[192] Rose, 121–22.

[193] Benedict XVI, *Con Grande Fiducia* (letter accompanying *Summorum Pontificum*).

More than a quarter of a century earlier, Pope John Paul II had felt the need to offer a personal apology for the problem:

> As I bring these considerations to an end, I would like to ask forgiveness—in my own name and in the name of all of you, venerable and dear brothers in the episcopate—for everything which, for whatever reason, through whatever human weakness, impatience, or negligence, and also through the at times partial, one-sided, and erroneous application of the directives of the Second Vatican Council, may have caused scandal and disturbance concerning the interpretation of the doctrine and the veneration due to this great sacrament [*sc.* the Eucharist]. And I pray the Lord Jesus that in the future we may avoid in our manner of dealing with this sacred mystery anything which could weaken or disorient in any way the sense of reverence and love that exists in our faithful people.[194]

Despite Pope John Paul's heartfelt plea, and similar, earlier, calls by Pope Paul VI, the bishops of the world continued to ignore complaints about liturgical abuses, apparently impervious to the spiritual suffering it was causing to their own flocks.

Some bishops reacted to some particularly serious abuses, generally those which threaten the sacramental validity of the rite, but it is difficult to think of bishops who have gone further than this by attempting to stamp out liturgical abuse on principle. Even Pope John Paul II himself sat through liturgical abuses taking place in his own Masses, such as the blessing he received from a pagan priestess in Mexico City in 2002.[195]

The O'Connell system of ignoring lay complaints was particularly important in the context of the liturgical reform itself. The laity, of course, were not consulted about it, and many enthusiasts for the reform

---

[194] John Paul II, *Dominicae Cenae*, §12.

[195] August 1, 2002, at the Cathedral of Our Lady of Guadalupe, Mexico City. The occasion was the beatification of two martyrs of the Church in Mexico, Juan Battista and Jacinto de los Angeles.

admitted that the laity had no desire for it. Thus, Fr Clifford Howell wrote in 1966:

> In this country the people at large have not desired to have English in the liturgy because our liturgical movement has lagged far behind that of the Continent. Until very recently only a minority knew enough about the liturgy to realise that full, active, and intelligent participation in it cannot be attained by the use of Latin alone.[196]

The reformers assumed that they laity would come round to it, and that in the end it would be good for them, but in any case the concerns of the laity seemed to have had very little weight. Fr Bryan Houghton wrote that "the new reforms in general and of the liturgy in particular were based on the assumption that the Catholic laity were a set of ignorant fools."[197] Houghton goes on: "What passes belief is that I know of no book or article published within the last twenty years extolling the virtues and commiserating the sufferings of the Catholic laity. If they dared to remonstrate they were merely told that they were divisive, disloyal, and disobedient."[198]

Having said all this, there is, in fact, a particular category of complaint which, typically, bishops have not been ignoring, in the postconciliar period. They have tweaked the clericalist O'Connell system to produce an ideologically-slanted result. Those who want to associate clericalism with theological conservatism will be disappointed to see, however, that that the complaints bishops have tended not to ignore are not those from conservatives, but those from radical progressives. Lay complaints that priests are inventing their own eucharistic prayers, using invalid matter for the Mass, invalidly baptising babies, and other abuses so serious that, on many occasions, the Holy See had to become involved, have frequently

---

[196] Clifford Howell, in J.D. Crichton, ed., *The Liturgy and the Future* (Tenbury Wells, Worcestershire: Fowler Wright Books, 1966), 94, quoted in Michael Davies, *Pope Paul's New Mass* (Kansas City, MO: Angelus Press, 2009), 91.

[197] Houghton, *Judith's Marriage*, 7.

[198] Houghton, 8.

been ignored or downplayed by the responsible bishop, for years if not decades. By contrast, complaints that priests are celebrating the *Novus Ordo* Mass in a more conservative way, such as celebrating *ad orientem*, failing to use female altar servers, or using Latin—all things permitted by the liturgical rules—frequently led to swift and harsh responses. This is true above all when priests wish to start celebrations of the traditional Mass.

Examples of this tendency have been seen in the wake of Pope Francis's Apostolic Letter *Traditionis Custodes* (2021). This document restricts celebration of the traditional Mass, but it has occasioned restrictions by various bishops of liturgical practices within the rules of the *Novus Ordo*, such as those just mentioned, and even the use of Roman-style vestments.[199] There is no indication that practical steps are being taken against common liturgical abuses.

An example from an earlier moment of the postconciliar period is given by a report from a press conference addressed by Archbishop Weakland, in his capacity as the head of the Bishops' Committee on the Liturgy in the United States, in 1979. A journalist present, John Mulloy, noted Weakland's understanding for those who changed the words of the liturgy, against the rules, because of their desire to use "inclusive language," and asked him about those who, again against the rules, attended the traditional Mass.

> It became apparent that only those who objected to what they called "sexist language" in the liturgy were the object of the Archbishop's sympathy. It was only these people he had in mind when he spoke of the need for action "to alleviate any hurt, or feeling of alienation of a large segment of the assembly," not those who wished to retain the liturgy in the Latin Tridentine form. So far as Archbishop Weakland was concerned, these latter had no call upon him whatsoever—they had shown by their disobedience to liturgical norms that they were outside the Church community for which the Archbishop felt a responsibility.[200]

[199] Notably by the Bishops' Conference of Puerto Rico, in a Decree of July 21, 2021.

[200] Quoted in Davies, *Pope Paul's New Mass*, 236.

Strikingly, this tendency, to give weight to complaints coming from liturgical progressives but not to those of liturgical conservatives, is found not only among bishops who personally favour progressive liturgies, but also among many of the more conservative ones. They appear to feel themselves prisoners of a consensus in favour of a progressive liturgy, enforced by a combination of their own senior priests, their fellow bishops, and the noisiest elements of Catholic public opinion. As early as 1964, Cardinal Heenan expressed the problem in a letter to the novelist Evelyn Waugh:

> The hierarchy is in a difficult position. We have not yet lost the respect of ordinary Catholics but the constant nagging of the intellectuals and their tireless (tiresome?) letters to the Press and articles in the Catholic papers may eventually disturb the ordinary faithful. Most of us would be content to delay changes but the mood of the Council compels us to act. Otherwise the attack from our own people would become ever more bitter: *inimici hominis domestici scies* [*recte: ejus*].[201]

The Welsh novelist Alice Thomas Ellis expressed it less sympathetically some decades later:

> Catholic bishops at the moment remind me of those shy wild animals you occasionally catch a glimpse of—wide-eyed in the headlights before they scurry back to the hedgerow and the security of their own kind. They detest scrutiny, evade questioning and refuse to explain the twists and perversions of doctrine they seek to impose.[202]

There are, indeed, examples of bishops who have tried to swim against the stream, and have suffered for it: in terms of their relations with their

---

[201] "A man's enemies shall be of his own household" (Matt 10:36). Letter dated August 20, 1964, in Alcuin Reid, *A Bitter Trial: Evelyn Waugh and John Carmel Cardinal Heenan on the Liturgical Changes* (San Francisco: Ignatius Press, 2011), 62.
[202] Ellis, *God Has Not Changed*, 9.

fellow bishops, attacks by the liberal Catholic press, and even loss of office. Notwithstanding this, the substitution of the good opinion of an elite, for the good of those they govern, as a bishop's ultimate objective, cannot be justified: it is contrary to the nature of the office. Giving way on this is an example of the phenomenon of the weak-ego conformism I discussed in the last chapter. It is also an indication of the way bishops and others in authority are integrated into an abusive network. They don't have to agree with the abuse themselves, but somehow the system not only makes it impossible for them to do anything about it, but obliges them to act to prevent anyone else undermining the system.

Catholics must unfortunately thank journalists and the secular legal system for exposing, at least, important aspects of the grotesque system of abuse under which we have suffered so long.

Conclusion

As I noted at the outset of this chapter, the claim has been made repeatedly by liberal commentators inside and outside the Church that conservative or traditional Catholics have some special connection with clerical abuse, particularly through the phenomenon of clericalism. I have argued that clericalism is not the product of traditional Catholic theology; that the association between conservative or traditional Catholics and abuse is unjust; and that abusers commonly try to justify their actions in terms of a liberal understanding of sexual morality. Finally, I have argued that the asymmetry of the treatment of conservative and liberal complaints about the liturgy reveals not only a power imbalance in the Church but an opportunity for large-scale spiritual abuse—something identified by both Pope John Paul II and Pope Benedict XVI.

My argument has not been that liberal clergy are abusers, or that conservative and traditional clergy are not. It is more helpful, I believe, to think about clerical abuse from the point of view of the abuser himself. He asks, consciously or not: Where are there opportunities for access to children or vulnerable adults? What are the rhetorical strategies which can be employed to groom them, and to defend aspects of abusive behaviour which come out in public?

Particularly under the protective cloak of clericalism, opportunities for abuse by priests exist in all sorts of contexts, from religious orders with the reputation for conservatism, such as the Legionaries of Christ, to those with a liberal reputation, such as the Jesuits, and everything in between. It is nevertheless a fact that a progressive understanding of the priesthood, and of sexual morality, present particularly tempting opportunities, which have been exploited by a great many abusers. If liberal Catholic commentators would care to acknowledge this, we could perhaps have a more productive debate about how to address the problem.

I passed through my school years without being molested; not all of my contemporaries were so fortunate. The issue of clerical abuse calls for redress, indeed it calls for anger, the emotion that serves justice. It is imperative that this anger be directed to its proper object, and we not allow it to be manipulated and instrumentalised for the ends of ecclesial politics: this would be a further betrayal of the victims. "And where the offence is, let the great axe fall."[203]

---

[203] William Shakespeare, *Hamlet*, Act IV, scene 5.

12

Sex Education and the Ethics of Consent

The following was presented as a talk on sex education in schools. I include it in this collection since its discussion of the sexualisation of children follows naturally from my treatment of the claim that traditional Catholics are sexually repressed, and of the clerical abuse crisis, in the last two chapters. It completes the argument of those two chapters, that contrary to the popularised Freudianism so widespread in our culture, the rejection of sexual norms does not lead to some new Eden, but to the sexual exploitation of the vulnerable. This idea will be taken up again when considering Louise Perry's book, *The Case Against the Sexual Revolution*, in chapter 16.

Once upon a time, there was doctrine in the English law that while the legal character of *some* actions would be completely changed by the victim's consent, this was not so with others. Thus, if Adam took away the property of Beatrice, this was theft if Beatrice did not consent, but not theft if Beatrice did consent. On the other hand, if Adam caused Beatrice actual bodily harm, or killed her, it made no difference if Beatrice consented. Adam could wave any kind of signed or sworn declaration by Beatrice, that she wanted him to do what he had done, in front of judge and jury, and they would find him guilty all the same.

Many people will tell us that today we live in a more fortunate age. If Bea is tired of life, or wants to experience being harmed, we are well on our way to her consent being alone enough to make that legally, and indeed

This paper was delivered to a conference organised by the Society for the Protection of Unborn Children, December 7, 2019.

morally, permissible. The fast-moving world of bio-ethics has already gone beyond this rather simple idea. Now patients can be killed without their consent as well as with it, and doctors are increasingly obliged to harm their patients, if the patient should demand it: first in the case of abortion, but soon in that of gender dysphoria, with bodily-integrity disorder, when people want healthy limbs amputated, a little further down the road.

Once you get rid of the traditional prohibition on killing in cases where the victim consents, why, after all, stop there? Why not move on to cases where the victim does not consent to be killed, but where duly authorised people think that it would be a good thing to kill him regardless? This is the direction in which the legal and medical establishment is inclined to go, under the influence of Utilitarianism: the theory that we are obliged to bring about the best possible outcome. For them, the ultimate goal is bringing about good outcomes, not personal autonomy. The good outcomes are themselves measured in Utilitarian terms, which means in terms of satisfying as many preferences as possible.

The educational establishment, on the other hand, seems content to rest at the intermediate stage of conceptual development: that consent is the key, and consent must be mutual, be outcomes good, bad, or indifferent. This attitude is very much on display from social workers in the now numerous reports of public inquiries into child sex abuse rings. The pattern is that they acknowledge that child victims of abuse were making terrible choices, but this fact didn't warrant intervention. On the contrary, they saw it as their job to prevent parents from intervening. Consent is everything, outcomes can go hang.

In this presentation I want to explore the way consent is being used here: where it comes from, what it implies, how it interacts with other aspects of morality, both traditional and progressive, and how it works in practice.

Consent and moral scepticism

The first question is where the idea comes from. As I have already indicated, the appeal to consent is a substitute for the prohibitions of traditional morality and law: not to kill, for example, or to restrict sex to marriage.

Such prohibitions have long been attacked for restricting our freedom. Before the end of the eighteenth century William Blake imagined the Garden of Love spoiled by the building of a chapel, which had "Thou shalt not" written over its locked door:

> And Priests in black gowns, were walking their rounds,
> And binding with briars, my joys & desires.[204]

The problem with the old prohibitions that Blake is concerned about is not that they prevent clever and benevolent doctors and lawyers bringing about the best possible outcomes—the Utilitarian instinct—but rather that they impede self-realisation. We might call this the Romantic instinct.

Romantic self-realisation may, of course, involve harm to others, like the painter Gauguin abandoning his wife and five children to pursue his art: it seems probable that Mrs Gaugin's self-realisation as a wife and mother was impeded by this action. One way of responding to this difficulty is to insist on mutual consent. If I want to do something, then that is presumptively okay, but if it affects others then I should gain their consent.

In this way it is hoped that a world without the traditional moral prohibitions will not immediately descend into a dystopian nightmare, where the strong exploit the weak. Perhaps consent can become the one and only moral principle: perhaps we can squeeze the whole of morality out of this one idea, in the way that Jeremy Bentham, the founder of Utilitarianism, tried to squeeze it out of benevolence, and Immanuel Kant out of rationality.

The concern with consent can in this way be set into the context of the collapse of traditional moral and cultural values. The putatively objective claims about history or English literature taught to our parents and grandparents, such as that the First World War was a just and necessary response to German aggression, or that Shakespeare thought Shylock was a bad person, cannot be taught to our children because, to generalise, academics and schoolteachers have not only lost their confidence in those claims,

---

[204] William Blake, "The Garden of Love," www.poetryfoundation.org/poems /45950/the-garden-of-love.

but more significantly they have lost their confidence in any putatively objective claims they might put in their place. Never mind reassessing the causes of the First World War, or rehabilitating Shylock: today there is no true or false interpretation at all, just our own reaction to it.

So they show children a photograph of the trenches of World War I, or a poem or story, and ask them to emote about it. In the same way, children are presented with the prospect of sexual relations, and asked what they *feel* about it. In each case it is a substitute for an informed judgement based on substantive principles. People who have lost confidence in substantive moral principles are clearly not going to have any confidence in the judgements they generate, and background information becomes equally irrelevant. All we have is the reaction of the onlooker, the reader, or the agent. A positive reaction makes whatever is being reacted to good; a negative one makes it bad. Naturally, what one person thinks is good another person may think is bad, but this is no real contradiction, since we are not dealing with objective judgements, but with free choice.

The modern conception of consent grew up in the context of legal contracts, and in this original context one can lay down some tough criteria. The parties must know what they are doing; they must be of sound mind; they must not be under the influence of drugs or alcohol; they must be of a certain age; in some cases we can insist that they have independent legal or financial advice, and in cases of doubt we might even want to see a letter from a psychiatrist affirming a party's mental capacity. All these things are possible in the context of agreeing to complex financial transactions, or marriage, or major surgery, because generally speaking it is possible to delay the agreement until all the requirements can be satisfied. Most people won't have to give or seek consent in this elaborate fashion many times in their lives.

If, on the other hand, consent is going to be the key issue in every day-to-day interaction, it is going to have to be a rather watered-down version, or else those interactions are going to become impossible: or perhaps both. If some kind of consent is going to be necessary for Adam to tell the longsuffering Bea an off-colour joke in the lunch break, for example, it is pretty difficult to imagine how that could be arranged. If consent is going to be the key to whether Adam can touch Bea on the wrist late one evening in a bar after a few drinks, then Adam has a problem.

Social conventions

Before moving on, you may be wondering what the alternative to consent as the key to these sorts of interactions might be. The answer is social convention. There is a wide consensus that some kinds of behaviour are reasonable or unreasonable, polite or rude, or gallant or abusive. If we think of such a consensus as establishing rules of behaviour, this takes a lot of pressure off the concept of consent.

Thus, it doesn't matter if a stranger doesn't consent to my interrupting his daydreams to ask for directions, because asking directions from a stranger is a perfectly reasonable thing to do. Nor is it necessary for us to know that a young lady waiting for a bus does not consent to a crude sexual advance from a stranger, in order to say that such an advance is wrong, because we know that such an approach is inappropriately invasive and rude, given its social context and content.

If we can't rely on these social conventions, my asking for directions, and some yob propositioning a girl at a bus stop, come out as structurally parallel situations. The yob and I have the same difficulty. It would be impossible for me to gain the stranger's consent to interrupt his daydreams without interrupting his daydreams. In exactly the same way it would be impossible for the yob to determine whether the girl consents to hearing his crude advances without making her hear them. I labour the point because it is so obvious that one is okay and the other is not, that we can lose sight of what makes it obvious. It is obvious because of social conventions.

Social conventions, like the laws of warfare, apply fundamental moral principles to the complexities of real life. They evolve to meet new situations, and there is extensive mutual influence between such conventions and the law of the land. Even when not expressed in law, they set our expectations and form what we regard as reasonable and unreasonable when a person's behaviour puts at risk his job or reputation. They aren't infallible, of course, and it isn't always a simple matter to apply them to particular cases, but they are more widely understood and endorsed than the ethical theories academic philosophers pride themselves upon, and they are democratic, in the sense that conventions are always open to criticism, re-negotiation, and self-righteous defiance.

Although they need make no claim to absolutism or universality, social conventions have been the victims of moral scepticism just as much as the Ten Commandments: indeed more so, as they tend not to be defended so fiercely by social conservatives. This is understandable, but it has been a tactical mistake. Something intermediate between fundamental moral principles and daily life is absolutely necessary.

For example, telling young people not to break the Sixth Commandment is a wholly inadequate way of preparing them for the dating scene. Telling them to get home by 10pm, what it means, and does not mean, for a man to pay for a girl's drinks, and what sort of clothing signals sexual availability, are contingent and indeed arbitrary rules, but they are the kinds of things we need to know if we are to understand *how* to obey the Sixth Commandment in our own society. They are interpretations of the Sixth Commandment, for a highly specific social context, with the force of custom, and they are a major component of culture.

Consent and liberation

To return to the new world of the ethics of consent, the idea was that fundamental moral principles as well as social conventions should be set aside both because of scepticism about their validity and in the interests of personal freedom. For reasons I have already indicated, gaining consent can be difficult in everyday interactions, and this whole approach has often been ridiculed for bringing in, not Romantic libertinism, but its very opposite, a new Puritanism: perhaps from now on, critics say, flirtations will have to take place in the presence of a chaperone. Difficulties are particularly acute where alcohol has been consumed, and indeed at a certain point of inebriation it is obvious that a person cannot meaningfully consent to anything.

There are, however, some people who are permanently in a cognitive state in which consent is problematic: namely, the mentally handicapped, and children.

The educational establishment and social services, however, do not want to hear that their charges are incapable of giving consent. The object of the exercise was to loosen the bonds of traditional moral prohibitions, not to tighten them. They want the individuals under their charge to be able to do whatever they like. Given the limitations on their agency, however, this tends to mean that they want their charges to do whatever they themselves want them to do. Whether that is self-stimulation, or attending climate demonstrations, teachers and social workers can claim that their charges have consented, while ensuring that they are exposed to only one side of any argument. Even for people with normal adult mental faculties, an artificial information environment of this nature would be enough to undermine the moral significance of such consent.

This weakening of the notion of consent is not consistently applied. The stereotypical undergraduate rugby lad is told that he can do anything if everyone consents, but that a few glasses of wine effectively mean that he can't do anything. School teachers, school nurses, and social workers, on the other hand, are told that they can infer a child's consent to sexual relations and to abortion on the basis of a decision which falls a lot more than a few glasses of wine short of an adult's informed consent, because of the immaturity intrinsic to the state of childhood, and because of the deliberate and selective withholding of information. This is to say nothing of social pressures, to which I am going to turn in a moment.

There is also a particular paradox which arises over the teaching of the ethics of consent. As I have explained, the theory of consent has the ambition of taking over large areas of morality, if not the whole of it, and schools set themselves the task of teaching it to children. This requires a critique of any *other* basis upon which behaviour, especially sexual behaviour, can be criticised or justified. Thus we get the now-notorious Stonewall lesson plans designed to humiliate children who are insufficiently zealous with their accusations of homophobia. These lessons, we can be sure, are acutely uncomfortable experiences for many of the children. Have they consented to these experiences? This is a question which is not asked. It seems legitimate to wonder, however, how the sacred importance of consent can be taught effectively in a class which *itself* violates the principle of consent.

In this way, we can begin to see a strange alliance between the ethics of consent, and behaviour which is actually abusive. It is this I wish to discuss next.

Consent and the abuser

The replacement of substantive moral principles and social conventions with consent has not brought in quite the liberated idyll that some hoped. The "serious case review" into the Oxford sex abuse ring noted, among other things, that the desire among teachers and social workers to avoid value judgements about sexual behaviour created "an environment where it is easier for vulnerable young people/children to be exploited. It also makes it harder for professionals to have the confidence and bravery to be more proactive on prevention and intervention."[205]

This was about the sexual exploitation of children by adults. Of equal concern is the abuse of children by each other. In 2017 the BBC revealed that over the previous three years, police in England and Wales received reports of 2,625 sexual offences, including 225 alleged rapes, taking place on school premises.[206] This is twenty-three offenses for every week of school. One can only imagine the number of sexual assaults which were not reported, which in many schools are simply endemic. One piece of research reported:

"I was in a French lesson in year 8 [aged 12]," one girl told researchers, "and a boy sitting next to me kept groping my bum and tried moving his hand to my front." "They think they can touch us

---

[205] Quoted by Norman Wells, *Unprotected: How the Normalisation of Underage Sex Is Exposing Children and Young People to the Risk of Sexual Exploitation* (Middlesex, Family Education Trust, 2017), 44.

[206] "'It's Just Everywhere': A Study on Sexism in Schools—and How We Tackle It," published by National Education Union and UK Feminista, 2017, https://ukfeminista.org.uk/wp-content/uploads/2017/12/Report-Its-just-everywhere.pdf.

whenever they like," said another. "They slap our butts and touch our breasts." "They lift our skirts up and whistle." "They touch girls in corridors, at lunch and at break times," said a teacher. "And they all seem to think it's just normal."[207]

This particular report was jointly published by a group called UKFeminista, which looks at the phenomenon through the lens of sexism. They focus exclusively, therefore, on the abuse of girls by boys. This is, however, only one facet of the situation. For example, pressure to engage in premature sexual activity is exerted on both girls and boys by members of their own sex and peer group. The broader picture is that telling children that there are no moral rules, that everything is permitted, that the adults in charge will never judge you, and that there are no effective mechanisms of discipline, has not made children into little angels who never hurt each other or never get drawn into abusive relationships.

Are children not also taught that consent is necessary for actions to be okay? Yes, they are, but this important qualification to the moral nihilism of the educational establishment doesn't seem to be holding back the tide of sexual exploitation.

The fact is, as I have already indicated, the official view that consent is necessary for every interaction is completely unworkable, and therefore simply cannot become an established part of children's social lives, however many lessons on consent they are taught. Furthermore, when sexually abusive children are confronted about their behaviour, they tend to claim that they thought their victim consented. This turns a sexual assault into an unfortunate misunderstanding. Here is another quotation from the same report: "'Why didn't you stop when she was crying?' a teacher asked a fourteen-year-old perpetrator. 'It's normal for girls to cry during sex,' he replied."

There is, however, more to say about the effect of the ethics of consent upon the culture of schools, which I want to approach in a slightly different way.

[207] Blanche Girouard, "School Sex Ordeals," *Standpoint*, January 29, 2018, https://standpointmag.co.uk/counterpoints-february-2018-blanche -girouard-school-sex-harassment.

Children under pressure

Over the years I have given a few talks about philosophy in schools, and on one occasion not long ago I arrived at a private school in London to find the headmaster somewhat agitated about my talk. It seems that a previous speaker, a Catholic priest, had caused discomfort among the pupils, and he didn't want that to happen again. I was able to reassure him that the topic I had prepared didn't stray into personal morality, so the issue did not really arise, but in the course of our conversation one remark of his struck me: he said that the pupils felt under tremendous pressure. The problem with the earlier talk had been that it increased the feeling of pressure.

What I think he meant was this. Schools are conformist environments. We can all remember peer pressure to dress in certain ways, for example; in some schools there is pressure not to work too hard. This peer pressure may well be counter to various kinds of pressure being applied by teachers and parents. The school conformist likes to think of himself as a rebel.

Nowadays there is pressure to act sexually in certain ways, and it can be intense; there is counter-pressure from what we might call the natural sexual reserve of children. What the headmaster was worried about is that I would say something which would make the pupils feel guilty about what they had done or were contemplating doing: that I would increase one side of the pressure, making their dilemma more painful.

Now, the entire tenor of modern education—I don't say, of sex education, but of education in general—is that sexual reserve is irrational, because after all any and all sexual behaviour is okay if it is consensual. In other words, it tells children that if they *feel* bad about sexual activity, their feelings have no objective justification. They are just feelings. In theory, that should make them worthy of respect, but as a matter of fact sexual reserve is not respected.

One obvious way in which it is not respected is pupils' exposure to sexually explicit material in the classroom. But even aside from that, the constantly reiterated claim that sexual reserve is *just a feeling* itself fails to respect it, because such reserve actually presents itself to us as a moral intuition: an intuition that some acts are objectively wrong. To respect that moral intuition would imply accepting the possibility, at least for the sake of argument, that the intuition is correct. This, however, would be incompatible with the claim fundamental to the ethics of consent, that there are *no* valid moral prohibitions, and one can do anything if everyone involved consents.

Schools are told, with increasing shrillness, to ensure that pupils are taught to respect every lifestyle choice. "Respect" here does not mean not bullying, or denigrating, or openly criticising, other people for their decisions: it means affirming them, recognising them as good, good because expressive of each agent's choices, and therefore part of each agent's self-expression and identity. The approved lesson plans make it clear that to think that another person's sexual behaviour is potentially susceptible to criticism, on the basis of objective moral principles, is incompatible with respecting such choices.

The implication is that criticising others' decisions is wrong because the principles underlying such criticism are wrong. If the moral principles are invalid, then not only can we not use them to criticise other people's decisions, we can't use them to criticise our own decisions either. If *I* am even allowed to *believe* that there are objective moral principles which guide and limit my own decision-making, then I would have to be allowed to *believe* that those same principles would apply to other people's actions. That cannot be allowed. It must be conveyed to pupils, instead, that their feelings are just their feelings.

In order to establish this brave new world in which we all respect each other's lifestyle choices, the moral instincts which are common to the major world religions and form the basis of human civilisation and culture must be torn up by the roots.

So, where does that leave school children who find themselves under pressure to engage in sexual acts? Recall the headmaster I mentioned who was fretting that a visiting speaker at his school might suggest that some decisions are bad for some reason. Let us imagine he manages to banish such heretical ideas from his school. Children will hear from their teachers that all sorts of lifestyles should be affirmed and celebrated, with a stress on those which children may feel a bit uncomfortable about, with the message that their discomfort is wrong. It is difficult to avoid the implication of these lessons that sexual activity is the basis of pretty well all forms of self-realisation worthy of the name. This message will be reinforced by the Freudian narrative, long absorbed by popular culture, that sexual abstinence is a mark of immaturity, repression, and even mental illness. It will be further leveraged by their peers in terms of what is grown-up, cool, and fun, and what is the opposite of these things.

One might think, at this point, that this is not an environment in which children are encouraged to trust their own feelings, and to resist pressure to act against them. But this is only half the story, because it is only half of the children's feelings. Sexual pressure itself creates feelings: of shame, loneliness, fear, and a desire to fit in and be normal. Those feelings are no less real than feelings of reserve. The difference is the moral basis for the feelings in each case: sexual reserve derives, as we believe, from the instinctive knowledge of the moral law which is common to humanity. The feelings of shame and humiliation arising from being bullied and ostracised for not taking part in the sexual free-for-all of the school community, on the other hand, are an understandable reaction to a highly contingent and artificial environment, a modern British school.

We are not allowed to talk about this difference, however. We are told that there is no moral basis to our feelings, and no way of judging some to be more authentic witnesses of our true nature than others, unless it is a matter of shedding inhibitions. There is no reason to place the feelings of shame caused by a sexually depraved peer group into a wider context, for example, in which it might not seem quite so valid as a guide to action. Feelings are just feelings.

This is indeed, to repeat my quotation of the report about the Oxford child abuse ring, "an environment where it is easier for vulnerable young people/children to be exploited." The net result of the competing forms of pressure is that children come to understand that feelings of reserve are barriers to full and normal participation in the school community. Shedding them is a sign of maturity, of coming of age, and the sooner one does that, the better. This is a gift to those adults and peers who wish to engage in the sexual exploitation of vulnerable children.

In the context of abortion, we have of course all heard this before. Women in crisis pregnancies typically have mixed feelings, feelings which point them in different directions. While claiming to respect women's feelings and validate their decisions, the abortion industry, including its tentacles inside schools, seeks to undermine feelings of moral compunction about abortion, leaving such feelings as financial worries in possession of the field. Anyone who attempts to alleviate the latter kind of feeling, by offering practical advice or financial assistance, is accused of making things more difficult for women. The contest of feelings is not given much of a level playing field.

Conclusion

I would like to summarise what I have said today under two headings.

First, if schools want to stop children abusing each other, or allowing themselves to be abused by adults, they need to stop talking about consent, and talk instead about inappropriate behaviour: behaviour which is inappropriate *even if* the victim has been pressured and brow-beaten into going along with it.

As repeated court cases and public inquiries have indicated, an exclusive concern with consent places all responsibility on the child victim of abuse. If the victim caves in to what may be intense pressure to acquiesce, if alternatives to going along with abuse seem lacking or unattractive, then it is the victims who are then blamed for any bad outcomes: dropping out of school, pregnancy, and so on. To state the obvious, children are no more ready for this kind of responsibility than they are ready to handle their own financial affairs. To place this kind of responsibility on children is, in fact, *itself abusive.*

Second, if we want to prepare our children for life, not just in school, but in the wider world, memorising the Ten Commandments, while commendable, is insufficient. Going beyond what I have said myself in this chapter, the best way of coming to understand the place of sexuality in a complete life is to experience as a child a family life founded on sexual exclusivity and openness to life, a stable and loving environment where Catholic culture and spirituality are able to flourish. This is not a lesson easily learnt from a textbook of moral theology: the Catholic family must be experienced, and it must seep into our bones. If we want to know what we can do about the current crisis, for parents there is always this: to live our vocation more faithfully.

Part 3

Family

13

Understanding the Feminisation of Christianity

Rates of religious practice and belief on the eve of the cultural and sexual revolution of the 1960s were at an historic high point in the English-speaking world, to which they had been climbing for a century and a half. In Britain, we think of the Second Spring, the Catholic Church's revival which led to and benefitted from the restoration of the hierarchy in 1850, but this has to be placed in the context of the progress being made by all varieties of religion. Only patchy statistics exist for the nineteenth century, unfortunately, but it is clear that the vast efforts of church-building, house-visiting, tract-distributing, street-preaching and so on by all denominations between 1800 and 1960 were not entirely in vain. In 1900, for example, the proportion of marriages in Scotland celebrated in church reached a point, at over 95 percent of the total, which probably could not be exceeded, and which declined only very slightly in the period between 1950 and 1960.[208] It seems reasonable to see this 150 years of progress as following a historic low-point of morale and evangelical effectiveness in the late eighteenth century, when, among other factors, population shifts had moved vast numbers of people out of reach of a place of worship. The century and a half in the sun was followed in turn by the abundantly documented catastrophic decline in religious practice and affiliation with which we are all familiar, and which has continued to this day.

A talk delivered to the Roman Forum at Gardone Riviera, July 2018, under the title "The Feminisation of Religion and the 1930s."
[208] Callum Brown, *The Death of Christian Britain: Understanding Secularisation 1800–2000*, 2nd ed. (Abingdon: Routledge, 2009), 167.

The Liturgy, the Family, and the Crisis of Modernity

This chapter seeks to examine one aspect of the religious revival, which had particular significance for the subsequent collapse: the increasing identification of religion with the feminine realm, which I will call "feminisation" for short. Events in the 1930s exemplify this trend and gave it a special spin for the last decades of the process.

I am going to focus on Britain, which I know best, and for the most part leave it to others to say how well my analysis fits with other countries. Furthermore, a lot of what I am going to say is first and foremost applicable to the non-Catholic denominations which have for five centuries dominated public perceptions of religion in Britain, as they do in the United States.

This chapter is frankly speculative. I am not a sociologist of religion, and while statistics exist to prove at least important aspects of the pattern which needs to be explained, they do not provide the explanation. There are always many factors at work, and there are also local and regional variations. Somewhat presumptuously I take up a task which has been left incomplete by the real sociologists: to propose some suggestive correlations and conceptual connections. I hope at any rate to express clearly a thesis which can in time be proved wrong. In any case, ultimately, the sociology of religion is too important to be left to sociologists.

I shall proceed by explaining what I mean by feminisation, and establishing that this was indeed taking place. I will then consider three explanations for feminisation, two of which do not explain why it grew more marked, and not less, during and after the inter-war period. I will consider the place of the Catholic Church in this process. And finally, I will note the significance of feminisation in the context of the new conception of femininity popularised in the 1960s.

Religion and gender

The sociologist Callum Brown summarises what I am calling feminisation in this way:

> From the sixteenth to the eighteenth centuries, a wife's femininity was perceived as a threat to piety and household, and a husband

established his moral status by controlling her. From 1800 to 1950, by contrast, it was a husband's susceptibility to masculine temptations that was perceived as a threat to piety and household, and the wife established a family's respectability by curbing him. Exemplars of piety changed sex, from being overwhelmingly male to being overwhelmingly female, and the route to family harmony no longer lay in the taming of the Elizabethan shrew but in the bridling of the Victorian rake, drunkard, gambler and abuser.[209]

To summarise, in Brown's words: "As femininity and piety became conjoined in discourse after 1800, the spectre arose of masculinity as the antithesis of religiosity."[210]

These are very large generalisations, but Brown has an impressive set of data to support them. He notes, for example, that as the nineteenth century gets going the sex-ratio of obituaries in religious publications shifts from domination by men to domination by women. The content of these mirrored the fictionalised stories found in religious tracts, handed out on street corners and in railway stations, of pious females and men in need of conversion. These, again, are paralleled by systematic treatments of temptation and sin in religious publications. Brown picks out one example.

During 1887 and 1888 the religious newspaper the *British Weekly* published some forty articles on "Tempted London," a series concerned with the moral condition of men and women in the capital. Men and women were dealt with separately—men during the first thirty articles, women in the last ten. The nature of moral weakness in the two sexes was conceptualised very differently. The articles on women were organised on the principle that occupational exploitation corrupted women. . . . The iniquity of the trades in which the women worked were studied in detail, focusing on low wages, home working, long hours and the exploitation of employers and merchants. . . . The women themselves were not deemed "immoral" . . . but as victims. . . .

---

[209] Brown, 88.
[210] Ibid.

The men's articles were organised around three headings: drink, betting and gambling, and impurity.[211]

I shall call the identification of the sinful with the masculine "religious misandry" for convenience. One remarkable aspect of this attitude is the extent to which evangelical Protestantism continues the same misandristic tone to this very day. This is a milieu in which I have to take my evidence second-hand, but the conservative evangelical blogger Dalrock has made something of a study of it, in its American incarnation. Following Father's Day in 2018, Dalrock found seventeen online sermons from what he regards as conservative evangelical Protestant preachers. With two exceptions, these sermons were characterised by the following themes (I quote from Dalrock):

- mocking of fathers, following the lead of feminists who for decades have portrayed married fathers as (at best) useless oafs;
- blaming fathers for the single-mother revolution and the host of social maladies feminism has wrought;
- blaming fathers for children (and fathers) falling away from the anti-father church;
- telling men to man up and/or accusing them of being bad fathers;
- joking about how Father's Day is less important than Mother's Day.[212]

I don't want to get involved in Dalrock's complex arguments about the origins and nature of evangelical misandry, but clearly if it was going on in the 1880s, 1960s feminism is not the whole explanation.

To return to Callum Brown, the typical narrative of the edifying fictional stories of religious tracts and magazines, and equally of obituaries, had it that men had to struggle with their masculine urges in order to repent and convert. The great spiritual project of a woman's life, on the other hand, was to struggle with her men, whether husbands or sons,

---

[211] Ibid.
[212] "Father's Day sermons are the symptom, not the disease," *Dalrock*, June 12, 2018, https://dalrock.wordpress.com/2018/06/12/fathers-day-sermons -are-the-symptom-not-the-disease.

to get them to repent and convert. To be irreligious was typically to be male, rough, and undomesticated. To be religious was to be feminised and tamed. The danger for men was sin; the danger for women were sinners, male ones, who might abuse, exploit, and betray them.

While insisting that religious misandry is a continuous theme of Evangelical Protestantism through the otherwise momentous changes between the early nineteenth century and the present day, it is important to stress that it does not go back to the origins of the movement. From the sixteenth to the eighteenth century, as Brown notes, the dominant religious narrative was that it was women, and not men, who put sound religion at risk, and it was characteristically female, and not male, vices which dominated religious polemics. It is not difficult to fill in the details. We hear a great deal, in that period, about the sins of the tongue, of gossip and scolding; sins of frivolity, of vanity and extravagance; sins of irrationality, of superstition and witchcraft; and sexual sins, notably of prostitution: all identified especially as sins of women. This was the era of the scold's bridle and the ducking stool, implements to repress the vices of feminine garrulousness, to say nothing of the witch-panics. It is perfectly true that drinking and gambling were not favoured pastimes among Puritans, but that was not because masculinity was being used as a marker for sinfulness. Indeed, I think it would be fair to say that the reverse was the case, and we may describe the attitude of this period as religious misogyny.

One aspect of this of passing interest to a Catholic audience is the way British women from the time of the Reformation up to and through the eighteenth century maintained customs following childbirth which appear to have been attempts to continue or substitute for the Catholic ceremony of Churching, the blessing after childbirth, which had had great cultural and social significance in the pre-Reformation period. This was a prime example of what was regarded as female superstition by Protestant preachers of the period.

An aspect of the older, misogynistic attitude is occasionally still visible in the nineteenth century, and even later, in polemic directed against the Church of Rome. The practice of Confession, the use of Indulgences, the role of the emotions in devotions and religious art, and the cult of Mary are bundled together in the characterisation of Catholicism as excessively *soft, indulgent,* and *effeminate.* By contrast, Protestantism is represented as being disciplined, plain-speaking, and virile. This picture, which is noted for example in John Henry Newman's *Apologia,* continued to be evoked long after Protestantism had itself flipped from a masculine to a feminine ideal.

We may illustrate the later attitude, again, from Newman. In one of his *Sermons Preached on Various Occasions,* which were published as a book in 1858, Newman recognised, lamented, and strove to oppose the stereotype of religion as feminine, in the context of religious anti-intellectualism. He represents the Devil as whispering to young men "that somehow or other, religious people are commonly either very dull or very tiresome: nay, that religion itself after all is more suitable to women and children, who live at home, than to men."[213] I will return to this very perceptive remark as the argument of this paper unfolds.

This can be balanced by evidence from a very different milieu: mid-twentieth-century working-class Newcastle, where oral history archives captured a Catholic remarking: "It's a bit cissy to be a Christian in this area."[214]

My next task is to examine a number of explanations for the phenomenon of feminisation. I will consider the Fun Police, conversionism, and the public engagement of religion.

The "Fun Police"

Leon Podles, who has written extensively on this topic, has proposed[215] that men have over a very long period of time been put off religion by what he calls the "Fun Police," whose policing of fun has generally been particularly hard on masculine pursuits. Podles has certainly identified a real phenomenon. As well as restrictions on sex, we also find in late-nineteenth

---

[213] John Henry Newman, *Sermons Preached on Various Occasions* (London: Longman's, Green & Co, 1913; reprint of the 3rd ed. of 1874), 8.

[214] Archer, *Two Catholic Churches,* 105.

[215] Particularly in his talk on the New Emangelization website. The transcript can be seen here: www.newemangelization.com/discussion-with-dr-leon -podles-author-of-the-church-impotent-the-feminization-of-christianity -transcript.

century British Protestantism a distaste for dancing and even sports. Sports, despite the efforts to co-opt them as innocent Christian pastimes by public schools, the scouting movement, and in general by "muscular Christianity," were condemned by many nineteenth century evangelicals as pagan, dangerous to the health, and apt to disrupt the Sabbath.[216]

Sundays, indeed, were an opportunity for the screws to be tightened in lots of ways, and while it seems amazing to repeat it today, it really is true that in parts, at least, of Britain, local government employees would padlock children's swings in the parks to prevent them being used on the Lord's Day. Not content with putting the facilities for childish effervescence out of commission, children were dressed for the day in clothes which made playing outside impractical as well as naughty.

Evidence from oral histories confirms what is perhaps obvious: little girls loved their Sundays clothes and little boys hated them. The campaign against sports also impinged more on men than on women during our period. Above all, the long nineteenth-century campaigns against drink and gambling come into the same category. Gambling and drinking are not exclusively male vices, but as already noted, they were perceived as characteristically masculine during this period.

It is worth taking a moment to remind ourselves of how powerful these movements at one time were. Americans, perhaps, are less likely to forget the power of the temperance movement in their country than we in Britain, but although the stuff was never actually banned in the UK, the British movement was nevertheless massive and influential. Britain's fine Victorian suburbs, such as have survived the philistinism of the planners, are still dotted with spacious buildings, now converted to other uses, intended to provide wholesome entertainment, such as snooker, without the assistance of alcoholic lubrication, emblazoned with the words "Temperance Hall" and the like. There were also temperance hotels, temperance beverages, and people signing the pledge and wearing temperance badges. The entire Baptist movement took the pledge, so to speak, and stopped using wine in their communion services.

---

[216] Brown, *Death of Christian Britain*, 97.

The Liturgy, the Family, and the Crisis of Modernity

The difficulty for Podles's theory is that the temperance and anti-gambling movements came to an end, for practical purposes, in the 1930s. Following the Great War, and in light of the experiment of Prohibition from 1920 to 1933 in the United States, the British temperance movement ceased to be an influential social force, something that could influence public opinion or local or national politics in a significant way, and it ceased to be a major part of the preaching and self-understanding of Protestant communities.

On the subject of gambling, the great defeat of the anti-gambling movement was in the Royal Commission on Lotteries and Betting that sat between 1932 and 1933, and which, after some agonised debate, rejected further legislative restrictions. This was the end of the anti-gambling movement's ambitions, and, again, led to its disappearance as a social and political force. By the time of the next Royal Commission on the subject, in 1949, the movement was a spent force, and the Commission's conclusions were straightforwardly permissive, even if its legislative recommendations did not appear on the statute book until 1960, when off-course betting was finally licenced.

The end of these twin campaigns presumably comes as a relief to the male Christians whose characteristic pleasures had been frowned on for the previous century. However, the easing off of the Fun Police was not accompanied by any discernible increased religious enthusiasm on the part of men. On the contrary, boys' magazines, which had long combined adventure stories and Boy Scout-type material with religious stories and references, dropped their religious content in the 1930s, or, in the case of the *Boy's Own Paper*, ceased publication altogether, something that girl's magazines did not do for another twenty years. The sex ratios of boys and girls receiving Anglican Confirmation is another indication of what Callum Brown calls a "final squirt" of feminisation in the 1940s and 1950s.

Not only can Podles's Fun Police thesis not explain what happened in and after the 1930s, it cannot explain the shift from male to female religiosity at the beginning of the nineteenth century. It is obvious that the Fun Police were active before religion became identified as feminine, even if they were not so exclusively concerned with male fun. The religious

kill-joy instinct on its own doesn't seem to have to have any negative cor-
relation with male religious engagement.

It is a fact, indeed, which can be observed in other contexts, that official
restrictions on characteristic male fun in an institution do not necessarily
put men off that institution. They can, indeed, even give an institution
a certain *cachet* as tough, as well as giving the fun, when you do get it,
whether within the rules or outside them, an extra *frisson.* The armed
forces and Islam provide contrasting examples of this phenomenon, to
reinforce the case of seventeenth-century Puritanism.

To clarify, it is hardly surprising to find the identification of (what are
thought of as) male characteristics and activities as sinful, and the identification of (what are thought of as) female characteristics and activities as
virtuous, associated with a society where men are less engaged in religion
than women. The problem with Podles's thesis is that the Fun Police are
only one aspect of the situation just described. Fun Police as such can be
misandrist, they can be misogynist, and they can, as far as the sexes go, be
even-handed. Even if the Fun Police are focusing their attention on one
particular group, it doesn't follow that that group is going to be turned
off religion: it may be that this group is regarded as a religious elite. Male
Orthodox Jews rejoice in being subject to more religious obligations than
women or, for that matter, than gentiles: being held to a higher standard
can be a sign of a higher valuation. While a superficially attractive idea,
focusing on the Fun Police is the wrong way of analysing the situation.

Conversionism

The second thesis I wish to consider is the phenomenon of "conversionism."
This is the view that a serious moral and religious life should invariably
start from an identifiable moment of conversion, a special moment when
God vouchsafes the grace of repentance. This moment will ideally be accompanied by strong feelings and public witness.

I should emphasise that the idea that a new, purified life can begin
with a more or less spectacular moment of conversion is widespread and
perhaps universal among different religious traditions. What I am referring
to here is the attitude that an identifiable moment of conversion, marking

a watershed moment in one's personal story, is an *obligatory* feature of life: that you can't be a serious Christian without it.

The way it worked among evangelical Protestants in the nineteenth century, and to a large extent before and after, was that during religious meetings, or perhaps in a more intimate, but still public, after-meeting, there would be an opportunity for sinners to make a profession of their desire to change their lives for the better. It was well described in 1810 by the poet George Crabbe, in the words of a sinner, Abel Keene, attending such a meeting, referring to the preacher:

> His cried aloud, till in the flock began
> The sigh, the tear, as caught from man to man;
> They wept and they rejoiced, and there was I
> Hard as a flint, and as the desert dry.[217]

Callum Brown reports the words of a woman who was attempting to use this approach to evangelise the soldiers at Aldershot, in reminiscences published in 1888. It was, unsurprisingly, an uphill struggle: "Many a man would rather encounter the enemy's fire in open line, 'than be laughed at in the barrack room.' He would 'die for his colours,' but he cannot live for Christ."[218]

Conversionism presented a double problem for men. First, the kind of emotional display required went very much against the grain for men, and especially soldiers, and increasingly so as the "stiff-upper-lip" conception of masculinity took hold as the nineteenth century wore on. Even without that, a *relative* masculine reluctance to display inner states through public displays of emotion, whether in words, tears, or other gestures, is a very widespread cultural phenomenon.

Secondly, while the women of the time might have been expected to find it easier to engage in these kinds of emotional displays, as the nineteenth century progressed this was not required of them, because they were

---

[217] George Crabbe, "Abel Keene," from his *The Poor of the Borough*; www.poeticous.com/george-crabbe/the-poor-of-the-borough-letter-xxi-abel-keene.

[218] Brown, *Death of Christian Britain*, 93.

not regarded as needing conversion. To put it crudely, men were expected to behave like women to an extent that women themselves were not.

The problem was recognised by religious leaders, and a great effort was made to adopt a masculine *tone* in addressing men in religious tracts and preaching, of which "muscular Christianity" was the most thoroughgoing example. This might be characterised as a disciplinarian tone, which might be combined with an admission by the speaker or writer that he, too, had struggled with masculine temptations. The Christian life might be likened to a battle; the example of King David was a favourite one.

However, the fact remained that what male sinners were being invited to *do* and to *be* was simultaneously identified as feminine. Again and again, these same tracts and sermons would invoke the addressee's *mother*, her example, and her expectations. It was unnecessary to ascertain whether the mother in question was a model of piety: she was one *by definition*, simply by virtue of being a female and a mother. If a man were to model himself on his *mother*, then obviously he is going to bid farewell to his outstanding masculine attributes.

The rhetorical approach is satirised in Gilbert and Sullivan's opera *Patience:*

> GROSVENOR. But you would not do it—I am sure you would not. (*Throwing himself at Bunthorne's knees, and clinging to him.*) Oh, reflect, reflect! You had a mother once.
> BUNTHORNE. Never!
> GROSVENOR. Then you had an aunt! (*Bunthorne affected.*) Ah! I see you had! By the memory of that aunt, I implore you to pause ere you resort to this last fearful expedient.[219]

Can conversionism explain the feminisation of religion in our time-period? As with the Fun Police thesis, it is superficially attractive as an explanation, but actually it doesn't fit the facts. It is not a universal feature of religiosity in the nineteenth century, being largely limited to evangelical and

---

[219] W.S. Gilbert, *Patience or Bunthorne's Bride*, Act II. First performed in 1881.

dissenting communities. It also doesn't fit historically. It is found before the identification of religiosity with femininity, in the seventeenth and eighteenth centuries, and indeed during that time we find women felt the need to repent as well as men: to this extent, conversionism seems as much a victim of feminisation as a cause.

In the later part of our period, we find the heat going out of conversionism. The process is not as dramatic as the failure of the temperance movement: Billy Graham was still making successful appeals for public witness conversions in the UK in the 1950s. But as a standard part of a major component of British Protestantism, it was on its way out, and as it faded we do not see a greater interest in religion by men, but, as already noted, even less than before.

Public engagement

My third and last explanation of male disengagement with religion in our period turns on the question of the degree to which religion was engaged in public issues, by which I mean in questions of public morality, political reform, and so on.

Much as one might deprecate the choice of campaigning issues, we must recognise that the twin campaigns for temperance and against gambling were in their day serious attempts by Christians as a body to shape the public sphere. They were practical and political issues, involving attempts to influence politicians and legislation. The public and political sphere was, throughout our time period, predominantly conceptualised as the masculine sphere, by contrast to the female private and domestic sphere.

It followed from this conceptualisation of the two spheres that even if men were the primary sinners in relation to drink and gambling, if these sins were going to be restricted by law and discouraged by public initiatives—as indeed they were in the 1906 Street Betting Act and the restrictions on pub opening hours during the First World War—it would be by the intervention of men. What the collapse of the temperance and anti-gambling campaigns, as major components of religious activity, meant, was a withdrawal of Christianity from the public sphere, and its increasing restriction to the domestic sphere.

Unlike the putative explanations considered earlier, of the Fun Police and of conversionism, public engagement fits the facts historically. Since the English Revolution of 1688, religion had been increasingly driven from the public square in Britain, and the growing identification of religion with domesticity after 1800 fits in with that. With the campaigns against drink and gambling, nineteenth-century religious leaders found issues on which they could attempt to re-engage with the public sphere, with some degree of success: not so much success in getting their favoured outcomes enacted in public policy, but success in the sense that they were at least talking and campaigning about public issues. The failure of these campaigns represented a very significant setback, a new stage of religious withdrawal from public life, and it was followed by an even greater privatisation and feminisation of religion. Religion ceased, even more than before, to be of significance or interest to men, who identified their interests with commerce and politics.

At this point I need to say more about domesticity and femininity.

Domesticity and the female sphere

It may seen obvious that the domestic sphere would be associated with the female. In Shakespeare's *A Comedy of Errors*, the wife of Antipholus of Ephesus asks, about men, "Why should their liberty than ours be more?," receiving her sister's reply: "Because their business still lies out o' door."[220] Part of the comic action of Shakespeare's play, as of the work of the classical playwright Plautus[221] that was its inspiration, is the inappropriate exclusion or inclusion of men by women into their homes, which seem to function as a symbolic extension of their persons. Nevertheless, until the Industrial Revolution the home was a centre of production, and not just consumption, and often production by men, whether as artisans, scholars, shop-keepers, professionals, or farm labourers with a private vegetable plot. We might even say that the home itself was domesticated—it became what we think of as domestic today—with the removal from it of the means

[220] William Shakespeare, *The Comedy of Errors*, Act II, scene 1.
[221] Plautus, *The Menaechmi*.

of production, starting with those means characteristically employed by men. Just as men and their work disappeared from the home with industrialisation, so women and their work disappeared from the labour market. This process made far more stark than had been the case, say, in the late medieval or early modern periods, the contrast between the female home and the male public and commercial world. It is not surprising that at a certain point in this process, in 1830, British women were deprived of the vote, even in the unusual circumstances (of being a head of household) in which they had previously exercised it. Public affairs, the attitude was, were not for women.

In the meantime religion was retreating from public life. This, again, is very much a matter of degree: it is not as though religion has ever disappeared from politics completely. The degree, however, is considerable. Milestones in this process would include the failure of Puritanism as a political movement in the seventeenth century, and the policy of toleration in the eighteenth century, which benefitted non-conformist Protestants at the beginning of the century and Catholics at the end of it. The failure of the political campaigns against booze and gambling in the 1930s marked further steps down this long road.

At the very same time as the domestic sphere became more and more closely identified with a particular conception of femininity, so the religious sphere became more and more closely identified with the domestic. If the domestic sphere is feminine, then so must religion in general be. This, in fact, is Callum Brown's major thesis: that the religious, the domestic, and the feminine, became fused in the course of the nineteenth century, an iron triangle of logical implication. To be feminine, as a woman, was to be domestic and pious; to be domestic was to be pious and feminine; to be pious was to be feminine and domestic. Note that what we are dealing with here is not simply the artificial limitation of feminine influence to the domestic sphere, but a specific conception of femininity: of what it means for a woman to be feminine. This has little in common with the *mulier fortis* of Proverbs 31, or the educated and independent women found in Shakespeare: to repeat, when we speak of the feminisation of religion in the context of nineteenth and early twentieth century domesticity, we are talking about an historically specific conception of femininity, one which has been aptly summarised as "the angel in the house."

To be "a man of affairs," on the other hand, was too easily seen, as Newman indicated, as a matter of putting religious matters to one side. To take religion seriously, as a man, was to take a step away from one's public, masculine role in life.

Misandry and patriarchy

One thing to notice in this set-up is that there is no incompatibility between a misandrist religiosity, associating masculinity with sinfulness, and patriarchy, understood as the masculine leadership of home and society in political and commercial matters. On the contrary, the two principles feed off each other. The public sphere is understood as essentially an irreligious sphere, a compromise with wickedness, and this is the masculine sphere: the sinful world. The master comes home in the evening to a refuge, a feminised, pious, and good home, where women, children, and perhaps servants, keep the dark at bay, by their very innocence of that wicked world and its ways. If he wanted to spend the evening discussing public or business affairs, he would go to an all-male club or public house.

This image of the home is a thing of religious magazines, soft focus photographs, and pious claptrap. The time period of which I have been speaking was inhabited by real people possessed of common sense, people of both sexes who were acquainted with the complexities of human nature from close acquaintance with it. It included people who could make fun, in particular, of this idealised conception of femininity. I have already quoted Gilbert and Sullivan. Fifty years later, Somerset Maughan wrote: "We know of course that women are habitually constipated, but to represent them in fiction as being altogether devoid of a back passage seems to me really an excess of chivalry."[222]

Nevertheless, while Victorian and Edwardian homes may not have attained the ideal, the *power* of the ideal, in contrast with other possible

---

[222] W. Somerset Maughan, *Cakes and Ale, or, The Skeleton in the Cupboard* (Harmondsworth: Penguin Books, 1948; originally published in 1930), 103.

ideals, made some options attractive and others unattractive. The idea that for a man to become serious about religion is some kind of a denial of his masculinity need not be *true*, it need not even be *believed*, to have its effect: it need only be in the air, influencing one's idea of *what the chaps might say if they found out*, as it did for the soldiers in Aldershot.

However, what concerns me most is not the effects of this on men, which is perhaps sufficiently obvious, but its effects on women, as time wore on. But before I deal with that, I want to bring the Catholic Church more clearly into the picture.

The Catholic Church and feminised religiosity

I have been saying throughout the above account that I am referring to British Protestantism. The question arises to what extent the Catholic Church went along with the trends and ideas I have described.

The Catholic community in nineteenth and early twentieth century Britain was not in a position to influence national cultural trends. The most we can hope to see is a principled stand against some things, and a quiet practical exception to others, alongside a certain amount of jumping on the dominant religious bandwagon, if the bandwagon doesn't in itself appear to be bad.

Temperance was a cause famously close to the heart of, for example, Cardinal Manning (d. 1892), so much so that a public house a stone's throw from his Westminster residence called itself "The Cardinal," with his picture as its sign, purely to annoy him. Manning was, of course, a convert, and it was undeniable that alcohol was a major social problem at that time. On the other hand, Manning's decisive intervention in the Docker's Strike of 1889, on the side of the dockers, set the tone of the English Church's concern with social and political issues for many years. This was not least thanks to the work of Hilaire Belloc, whose mother was one of Manning's converts, and was very influenced by him.

The deep concern with politics, albeit on the part of a community with very limited political influence, was a recognisable feature of the English Catholic Church in the late nineteenth and early twentieth centuries. The sociologist Anthony Archer notes it as a factor in attracting industrial workers to the Church in this era. He expresses this in terms of the Church's relationship with the political establishment: unlike Anglicanism, it was not *of* the establishment; unlike much non-conformism, it was not seen as a club for respectable clerical workers either. To the dismay of some aristocratic Catholic families, who were busily (and with some success) attempting to regain their hereditary role in public life with the easing of anti-Catholic prejudice and legal restrictions, Manning and his successors took on a somewhat antagonistic attitude towards the ruling class and its institutions.

Although the temperance movement and the anti-gambling drives of the nineteenth and early twentieth century never enjoyed the favour of the political class, they were certainly a great deal safer, politically, than the critique of monopolists, unjust employers, and enclosures, not to mention industrial action, which were the leading subjects of Catholic political activism of this era.

This linking of Catholicism with deep and also very practical concerns about social justice and public affairs was furthered, as I have already noted, by Hilaire Belloc, and others of his generation of Catholic apologists who promoted Distributism, "back to the land" projects, and related thinking. What is interesting to see is that Belloc, in particular, and the inseparable G.K. Chesterton, very clearly distanced themselves from the temperance movement, and their work popularised what we might call the Catholicism of Good Living. Belloc's amusing speech to the House of Commons in 1906 on the subject of beer deserves to be quoted. The official record of the House of Commons at this time used the third person:

> He would not say that no one had been brought to ruin by drinking pure English beer, or good red wine, or long-matured spirit; but the effect on character, the creation of a craving, and the general deterioration from the moderate to the heavy drinker were mainly produced, after the tied-house system, by the badness of the liquor consumed.[223]

---

[223] House of Commons, 1906: "Pure Beer Bill," second reading.

In terms of public perceptions of Catholicism, the concern with social justice more than made up for a lack of enthusiasm for temperance or the anti-gambling drive as a form of public engagement.

If one wants to think in terms of misandrist Fun Police, the Chesterbelloc phenomenon gave the Church a clear edge in being attractive to men. The same is true of another phenomenon related to the public-private, masculine-feminine distinction, which was noted by Newman in the brief quotation I made above: of the association of religion with anti-intellectualism. Rationality can very easily be identified with science and public affairs, in contradistinction to the domestic, feminine, and religious. Newman was determined to oppose this identification, and the Catholic intellectual tradition made such opposition much easier for Catholics than for other Christians of the period.

Finally, on the question of conversionism, it should be obvious that this was not a characteristic of Catholic spirituality in this period. Writing just before the Great War, Msgr Hugh Benson addressed the accusation that in the Catholic Church there was an "alienation of the men," an accusation deriving, I suppose, from the by then somewhat archaic stereotype of Catholicism as emotional and irrational compared to Protestantism. On the contrary, Benson points out:

> There is no "alienation of the men" [in the Catholic Church]; on the contrary, in this country, as also in Italy and France, I am continually astonished by the extraordinary predominance of the male sex over the female in attendance at Mass and in the practice of private prayers in our churches. At a recent casual occasion, upon my remarking to the parish-priest of a suburban church of this phenomenon, he told me that on the previous evening he had happened to count the congregation from the west gallery and that the proportion of men to women had been about as two to one. This, of course, was something of an exceptional illustration of my point.[224]

---

[224] Robert Hugh Benson, *Confessions of a Convert* (Notre Dame, IN: Christian Classics, n.d.; first published 1913), 100.

Again:

> Amongst Catholics emotionalism and even strong sentiment is considerably discouraged, and . . . the heart of religion is thought rather to reside in the adherence and obedience of the will. The result is, of course, that persons of a comparatively undevout nature will, as Catholics, continue to practice their religion, and sometimes, in ungenerous characters, only the barest minimum of their obligations; whereas as Anglicans they would give it up altogether.[225]

It is a pity that George Crabbe's imaginary sinner, in the quotation earlier, never had the opportunity to meet Msgr Benson or other Catholic priests of this temperament. Crabbe's poem is, in fact, a critique of conversionism. The sinner, who felt no *emotional* response to the preacher's words, became convinced that he had been reprobated by God and hanged himself.

As I have argued, interesting though the phenomena of the Fun Police and conversionism are, the trend of feminisation is being driven in our period by the progressive loss of public engagement. Further to his own thesis that the Catholic Church has been feminised since the High Middle Ages, Podles quotes the French Trappist Debryne, writing in 1842, against a rigorist approach to wives who tolerated the practice of *coitus interruptus*.

> One should give serious attention to this; that one should not alienate women through an imprudent rigor; the matter is one of immense importance. The coming generation is in the hands of woman, the future belongs to her. . . . If the woman gets away from us, with her everything will disappear and vanish into the abyss of atheism—faith, morality, and our whole civilization.[226]

---

[225] Benson, 101.

[226] Leon Podles, *The Church Impotent: The Feminization of Christianity* (Dallas: Spence, 1999), 25. Podles is quoting from Claude Langlois, "Féminisation du catholicisme," in *Histoire de la France religieuse*, vol. 3, *Du rois Très Chrétien à la laïcité républicaine*, ed. Jacques Le Goff (Paris: Éditions du Seuil, 1991), 303.

Podles sees this as evidence that Catholic doctrine was being bent out of shape by feminisation. What it suggests to me, however, is that in the context of the exclusion of the Church from politics during France's Second Republic, Debryne is placing his hopes for the future of the Church in the only place left: the domestic sphere. What was perhaps not evident in 1842 was that Catholic political activism in France still had a long and vigorous life ahead of it.

We see a similar phenomenon in Germany, Spain, and Italy, where the leading political movements of the day were anticlerical, and furthered by all-male Masonic associations. At some times and places more than others, naturally, one can see an identification even in Catholic societies of the religious with the feminine and domestic, and the political with the masculine and public. However, I cannot explore that process further here.

On the question of the degree to which British Catholicism bucked the trend of feminisation, in addition to the factors I have just discussed I would also suggest that the use of spiritual and cultural sources from a wider span of time protected Catholic clergy, apologists, and ordinary laity alike from the distortions of the spiritual life to which Protestantism seemed to be a prey. Nevertheless, Catholicism could not fail to be influenced by wider social attitudes, for example by the rise of Romanticism in the early nineteenth century, which paralleled the invocation of feminine goodness in a religious context. It isn't difficult to find instances of feminised angels, for example, in Catholic devotional art as the twentieth century progresses, and even sentimentalism; and of the invocation of the mother as the *fons et origo* of the religion of the domestic church.

Domesticity as a substitute for activism, and feminism

After the 1930s, Callum Brown detects a shift of focus in popular religious literature from questions of morality and conversion, to domesticity. One may look at it like this: religion, with its moral and spiritual concerns, is first *identified* with the feminine, domestic sphere, since its moral and spiritual concerns tend to idealise the feminine and reprobate the masculine. Masculine traits and activities are public and bad; feminine ones are domestic and good. In the second stage, public campaigns against the masculine vices of booze and gambling fail, and these causes cease to be closely associated with religion. In the third stage, with the disappearance of these moral imperatives from the religious domain, what is left are simply the values of domesticity: lovingkindness and good manners, looking inward rather than outward to the public sphere. I don't say that this was all that was left of British Christianity, or Protestantism, by 1960, but it was an important aspect of the public perception of religion. Public, political campaigning was now being done above all by the Labour movement.

It should be noted that the substitution of domesticity for moral concerns with any sharp public edge to them was, for a time, perfectly successful, in terms of holding up levels of religious practice and affiliation. Women's magazines were full of domestic concerns: to achieve femininity was to be domestic, to have the latest refrigerator and the best clothes, and to maintain heart-warming family traditions such as church-going, at least on Christmas Day, when it would be their task to drag their menfolk along, just as it was their task to get them to wash.

1950s men had a reason to humour their wives or mothers by going to church, because of the identification of religiosity with hearth and home, respectability and domestic happiness.

The problem is that, to the extent that this really was the case, not only was it a hollowed-out religion, it was one radically dependent upon a very specific conception of femininity. If women began to be presented with a conception of femininity which replaced domesticity with other kinds of worldly success, together with an attack on the value of the domestic ideal itself, then the whole thing would collapse like a soufflé. And that, of course, is exactly what happened.

Conclusion

It is not possible in this paper to weave in the other factors involved in the collapse of religious observance in the course of the 1960s and 1970s, and thereafter. My concern has not, indeed, been to provide an explanation for that complex phenomenon, but rather to analyse one aspect of social and cultural change which is relevant to it. To say that people stopped going to church because women had started taking an interest in the world of work outside the home would be simplistic to the point of absurdity. But it remains true that the complex relationship between the home, the public sphere, and conceptions of masculinity and femininity, are part of the complex picture, influencing and being influenced by a host of other factors.

In chapter 4 I quoted Pope Paul VI's justification for the vernacularisation of the Catholic liturgy: it was, he said, among other things an attempt to reach "the world of labour and of affairs."[227] Paul VI wanted to break out of the private sphere to which religion had been confined as a result of secularism and anti-clericalism. He was prepared to destroy the reassuring, domestic associations of the liturgy in order to do this: "the comfort of feeling faithful to our spiritual past, which we kept alive to pass it on to the generations ahead."[228] It was as if Pope Paul did not wish to wait for the proponents of feminism to destroy the pious domestic ideal, which would not happen for a long time in many Catholic countries. He wanted to get in there first, and do it for them.

But vernacularisation did not make the liturgy more acceptable to the masculine world of labour and affairs, which women were beginning to join in 1969. Pope Paul succeeded only in destroying the ritual, transcendence, and mystery which, as I have argued elsewhere, appeal particularly to men, replacing it with a strong emphasis on verbal communication, which is more acceptable to women.[229] At the same time, his determination to abandon the Church's political claims led to the systematic and worldwide collapse of the Church's engagement in public affairs.

No image, I think, summarises this process more eloquently than this vignette of Cardinal Jorge Bergoglio from 2010. The participants in a major demonstration in Buenos Aires against same-sex marriage planned to hold an all-night prayer vigil outside the legislature. Bergoglio spoke to the organiser as follows: "It seems like a wonderful thing to me that you should pray. But the fact that you want to spend all night in the plaza. . . .

---

[227] Paul VI, General Audience, November 26, 1969.
[228] Ibid.
[229] See Shaw, *The Case for Liturgical Restoration*, 225–30.

It will be cold, go home, pray at home, as a family!"[230] The domestic here swallows up the political.

With the wisdom of hindsight, we can try to manage things better for the next half-century. As Newman expressed it: "Youths need a masculine religion, if it is to carry captive their restless imaginations, and their wild intellects, as well as to touch their susceptible hearts."[231]

---

[230] Víctor Manuel Fernández, *Il progetto di Francesco. Dove vuole portare la Chiesa* (Veronia: EMI, 2014); the passage is quoted by Sandro Magister, "Bergoglio, the General Who Wants to Win without Fighting," March 10, 2014, http://chiesa.espresso.repubblica.it/articolo/1350737bdc4.html.

[231] Newman, *Sermons Preached on Various Occasions*, 14.

14

The Male Priesthood and Patriarchy

The priesthood of the Catholic Church is a sacramentally-bestowed character enabling a person to represent Jesus Christ in offering the sacrifice of the Cross. What Our Lord offered once and for all in a bloody manner, on the Cross—namely, Himself—the Catholic priest offers again in an unbloody manner in the Mass. The priest, and the bishop who enjoys in a certain sense simply the fullness of the sacrament of Holy Orders, also have the role of governing the Christian community in spiritual matters, and the corresponding sacramental graces to assist them in doing that.

The identification of the priest with Christ in the priest's liturgical, sacramental, and governing roles is so close that it has made sense, over many centuries, for only male candidates for the priesthood to be considered for ordination. It seemed obvious to our predecessors in the Faith that it made sense for men alone to be sacrificing priests, and to exercise that authority over the community which is called "spiritual paternity," spiritual fatherhood. The cultural attitudes which made that seem obvious have, however, seriously eroded over the last century.

In this chapter I shall attempt to explain two things. Why we have an all-male priesthood is the first question, but a secondary question will, I think, emerge at the same time: why the usual arguments about this issue are so superficial, and indeed unconvincing. To give you a sneak preview of the second question, it is because the real theological reasons for the

A talk delivered in the parish of Holy Trinity, Hethe, Oxfordshire, January 19, 2019, under the title "Why a Male Priesthood?"

all-male priesthood are too unfashionable, or even scary, to be useful in public debate.

A superficial argument about the all-male priesthood

The usual, non-scary argument about the priesthood goes like this. Since Jesus chose only men to be apostles, despite having a good many female followers, and since these apostles were the first priests and bishops, the Church feels bound to follow this example. Indeed, the constant teaching of the Church is that it is *impossible* to ordain women to the priesthood: it just wouldn't take. When bishops go off the rails and start ordaining men priests, or even bishops, in hotel bedrooms and the like, without authorisation, the Holy See, however reluctantly, regards those men as validly ordained, if the proper prayers have been said. When bishops go off the rails and ordain women on boats in the Danube, or wherever, the Holy See does not regard it as a valid ordination: it simply excommunicates everyone involved.

In reply to this argument, proponents of the ordination of women point out that Jesus also chose apostles exclusively from the Jewish race, and yet the Church does not regard herself as bound to exclude non-Jews from Holy Orders. Similarly, Our Lord's choice of males was clearly connected with the attitude to gender roles in first-century Palestine and the ancient world in general. For example, as I understand it, twelve men were required for the foundation of a new synagogue, something with very obvious symbolic resonance for the role of the apostles, and rabbis were always men. However appropriate or even necessary for the mission of the nascent Church the choice of men, and indeed Jews, as apostles might have been, the Church does not regard every aspect of the ancient Jewish attitude to gender roles as binding for us.

What aspects of those gender roles are supposed to be binding, and why?

The nature of theological argument

I should say at this point something about the nature of theological argument. Every academic discipline, and in a small way every subdiscipline, has its own way of arguing—its own ideas about what constitutes a good argument—and this is conditioned by the kinds of arguments which are possible in that discipline. As far as theology goes, when push comes to shove it is difficult to say that, for example, God *could not* have saved the human race without the atonement, or that the Immaculate Conception was absolutely, logically, necessary for the Incarnation. What one has to say instead is that certain connections, inferences, or parallels are overwhelmingly appropriate, or, as the Scholastics said, *conveniens.* It just would not have been right for God to forgive humanity without their being able to plead in satisfaction the Sacrifice of Calvary: it wouldn't have sat right with God's justice or man's dignity. Similarly, it just would not have been right, it wouldn't have been appropriate, for Christ to have been born of a sinful woman, a women under the dominion of Satan. It would have been bizarre, undignified, it would have been *inconveniens.* A logician might think these are weak arguments, but they are not: they are overwhelmingly powerful considerations, from a theological point of view. They are the most powerful kinds of arguments, generally speaking, which are available within the discipline of theology.

So we aren't looking for a knock-down argument that God could not, in His omnipotence, have arranged things in such a way that women could be priests. What we are looking for is an understanding of the symbolic meaning of male and female which makes an all-male priesthood overwhelmingly appropriate.

Attempts to defend the all-male priesthood

What happened, as the debate about the ordination of women within Anglicanism heated up, in the late 1980s and early 1990s, is that Pope John Paul II, as well as teaching that the Catholic Church *could not* ordain women (*Ordinatio Sacerdotalis*, 1994), composed a document, *Mulieris Dignitatem* (1988), which tried to put some flesh on the idea of women having a special and distinct role in the economy of salvation. The key idea of this document is the "naturally spousal predisposition of the feminine personality" (§20), which Pope John Paul understands in terms of a special gift, vocation, or talent of self-giving.

Since the Church has a spousal or bridal relationship with Christ, St Ambrose (as quoted by Pope John Paul) could describe the Blessed Virgin Mary as the icon of the Church—the ultimate symbol of the Church. This is also why the vocation of consecrated virginity is possible only for women: because they are uniquely able to consecrate themselves as spouses to Christ.

The odd thing about this argument is that the theological explanation or justification for the all-male priesthood must be sought not in the special role of women but, obviously, in the special role of men. The vocation and symbolic role of males in the economy of salvation, however, is something which Pope John Paul is less willing to address. Elsewhere, he repeatedly insists that the priest is "configured" to Christ as "the head and shepherd, the servant and spouse of the Church,"[232] yet the link to maleness is left obscure. Feminists, understandably, ask: What is it about *men* that makes them uniquely suited to being "configured to Christ" in this way? Instead of explaining what it means to say that men are uniquely able to represent Christ at the altar or to exercise spiritual paternity over a parish or diocese, Pope John Paul seems to be offering women a sort of consolation prize of their own special vocation. His project does not seem to offer us a complete or balanced account of what the roles of the sexes in the economy of salvation are or should be.

The one-sided nature of the response to the movement for female ordination is continued beyond the magisterial level by popular and academic writers alike. The theologian Manfred Hauke, whose book *Women in the Priesthood?* is generally considered the best orthodox treatment of the subject, does say that men are uniquely able to represent Christ at the altar, because they represent the authority of Christ over the Church, whereas women represent the obedient Church. But he puts it in a curious way:

> As members of the Church, the office bearers are, in the first instance, receptively and cooperatively active like all other believers.

[232] Apostolic Exhortation *Pastores Dabo Vobis* (1992), no. 3; cf. nos. 15, 22, 29.

> In their specific representation of Christ, they are also distinct from and in contrast to the Church, but only as "intermediaries" and "instruments." They represent the Lord, from whom they themselves are different. Mary, by contrast, does not only represent the Church but is herself the "Church in its origin."
>
> In an analogical way, therefore, women, too, are representative and embodiments of the Church. As opposed to men and the male priesthood, they symbolize a reality with which they are themselves identical.[233]

In other words, men *represent* Christ *under whose authority* they live as individuals, but women represent the Church, obedient to Christ, *of whom they are members as individuals*. Men represent something they are not, whereas women represent something which they actually are.

One thing Hauke appears to have forgotten is that priests and bishops do, in fact, *exercise* the authority of Christ in governing the faithful in spiritual matters, most obviously in the sacrament of Penance when they forgive, or retain, sins. The authority of Christ is not just a mask they put on to say Mass: they are incorporated into it in a more fundamental way.

The other thing Hauke is reluctant to say is what Pope John Paul II says in *Mulieris Dignitatem* but does not follow up on: "Grace never casts nature aside or cancels it out, but rather perfects and ennobles it" (§5). If, in the order of grace, men are uniquely suited to representing and indeed exercising the authority of Christ, and women as obeying that authority are representative of the self-giving community governed by Christ, then there must be something parallel going on in the order of nature. The superstructure of grace must have a foundation of nature.

To summarise, what is needed to complete the argument made by theological conservatives like Pope John Paul II and Manfred Hauke is an explanation of the male side of the male-female specialisation of roles in the economy of salvation. Not only must they allow themselves

---

[233] Manfred Hauke, *Women in the Priesthood? A Systematic Analysis in the Light of the Order of Creation and Redemption* (San Francisco: Ignatius Press, 1986), 324.

to claim that men are better suited, symbolically, to represent Christ at the altar and in the spiritual government of the Church in terms of the *exercise of authority*, but also, if it is to make sense, this must be based on a connection between the exercise of authority and maleness in the order of *nature*, a connection in ordinary life which *makes* it appropriate to make that connection in the order of grace—in the Church and in the sacraments.

The all-male priesthood in the New Testament

These supplementary steps are not just my hypothetical filling-out of the case for an all-male priesthood: it is indeed what we find in Scripture, above all in St Paul. The closest thing we have to an explanation of the all-male priesthood in the Bible is St Paul's account of the parallel between the relationship between Christ and the Church and the relationship between husband and wife, in Ephesians 5:22–33. What Paul has to say about marriage, and what he has to say about the relationship between Christ and the Church, are inseparably entwined. I quote the Douai-Rheims version, lightly adapted.

> Let women be subject to their husbands, as to the Lord: Because the husband is the head of the wife, as Christ is the head of the church. He is the saviour of his body. Therefore as the church is subject to Christ, so also let the wives be to their husbands in all things.
>
> Husbands, love your wives, as Christ also loved the church, and delivered himself up for it: That he might sanctify it, cleansing it by the laver of water in the word of life: That he might present it to himself a glorious church, not having spot or wrinkle, or any such thing; but that it should be holy, and without blemish. So also ought men to love their wives as their own bodies. He that loveth his wife, loveth himself. For no man ever hated his own flesh; but nourisheth and cherisheth it, as also Christ doth the church: Because we are members of his body, of his flesh, and of his bones. For this cause shall a man leave his father and mother, and shall cleave to his wife, and they shall be two in one flesh. This is a great sacrament; but I speak in Christ and in the church. Nevertheless

let every one of you in particular love his wife as himself: and let the wife respect her husband.

St Paul presents a parallel: the relationship between Christ and the Church parallels the relationship between husband and wife. The first relationship is characterised in terms of three points:

1. The supernatural reality of Christ saving the Church's members by sacrificing himself for them;
2. the Church's being Christ's own body;
3. Christ being the head of the Church, and having authority over the Church

All these points have parallels in the marital relationship: the husband sacrifices himself for his wife, who represents also his family, the community he is to love, nourish, save, and govern; this family is his very body, his wife being one flesh with him.

Out of this parallel we can draw some conclusions about the priesthood, which can be understood as a third, parallel, institution. Clearly the Christian community needs a visible head, as well as the invisible head, Christ: a visible head who will represent Christ to the community, the Church, in a number of important ways, both sacramentally and in terms of spiritual government. The bishop and priest who, at their respective levels, perform this function, are to see their community as their body and their spouse; their own role involves not only authority but self-sacrifice, a preparedness to die, if necessary, for the community, as a husband and father must be prepared to die for his wife and family. The whole *raison d'être* of the priest and bishop is the nourishment and salvation of this community.

St Paul's parallel between Christ and the *paterfamilias* does not come out of nowhere: its roots go back to the earliest parts of the Old Testament, where in contrast to the paganism of the Near East, the Divine is not understood as a sexually fertile *couple*—a male god with a female consort—but as a masculine deity in relationship with the worshipping community, and with the whole cosmos. God's *fatherhood* of Israel, whether Israel is considered a son, a daughter, or a wife, is the key controlling metaphor of the Hebrew Scriptures.

Occasionally God is compared to a mother, but this is clearly a secondary metaphor. It is evidently important to the scriptural authors to maintain in the forefront of our minds, when talking about God, the things associated with the *paterfamilias*: not only love, but protection, discipline, and authority. By the same token our relationship as individuals, and the community's relationship, with God, is not, primarily, that of a child to a mother, but of a son or wife to a father or a husband. (To be exact, individuals are thought of primarily as sons, the community can be understood as a spouse.) One nice implication specifically of a son-father relationship is that, as St Paul reminds us, sons are the *heirs* of their father (Romans 8:17). When St Paul says this, the implication is that *all* Christians, not just the male ones, should see themselves as having this privileged relationship with God, of *sons*, and therefore of heirs.

Objections to taking St Paul too seriously

All this, objectors will say, is the creative metaphorical use of the family as understood in the ancient world to explain the nature of God: it is not, necessarily, an endorsement of the patriarchal family model. Similarly we find St Paul adopting ancient Greek athletic competitions or the equipment of a Roman soldier as metaphors for theological issues, without implying that either athletics or Roman weaponry has any permanent, normative role in Christian life.

There is, however, a twofold difficulty with this objection: first, that there does not seem any alternative way of understanding the relationship between God and the cosmos, or Christ and the Church, than through this metaphor; and secondly, that the patriarchal family is very much endorsed in Scripture as normative for the Christian household. I have already quoted the longest and most explicit passage on this subject, but there are many others, above all in the Epistles.

Both parts of this counter-objection are in evidence when St Paul remarks (Eph 3:14): "I bow my knees to the Father of our Lord Jesus Christ, of whom all paternity in heaven and earth is named." What St Paul is saying is that it is not that he or others apply to God a metaphor of fatherhood derived from the common experience of human family life as it happens to be lived in his day. No: on the contrary, the paternity discoverable in creation is a reflection, a dependent, derivative consequence, of God's fatherhood.

It is this passage which inspires the Scholastic theory that the key theological concepts applicable to God are not, in fact, metaphors drawn from merely human experience, but truths about God which find some imperfect reflection in the created order, a reflection which can enable us to grasp in some measure, analogically, the perfect exemplar represented by God. To use, as the Scholastics used, a Platonic term, human father-hood *participates* in divine fatherhood, as the imperfect and dependent participates in the perfect and self-subsistent.

Or, to put it in other terms: the patriarchal human family reflects the right ordering of things at the cosmic level. As the ancient saying had it: As above, so below.

Attempts to play down patriarchy

Now we all know that St Paul can be a bit old-fashioned in his social attitudes, and we've learned to make allowances, but what I've been suggesting is that it is not possible to separate the social practice of patriarchy from the theology of the all-male priesthood. In this, I am agreeing with the more radical feminist thinkers.

Exactly what Pope John Paul II thought he was doing I would not want to say—perhaps he was just trying to be diplomatic—but it is clear enough that many of his theological followers are concerned to separate the issues of patriarchy and the priesthood, and insist on the second while going so far as to criticise and reject the first. I have mentioned the distinguished theologian Manfred Hauke; the more popular version can be viewed on websites such as *Catholic Answers*.

The problem with this approach is very easy to state: as the feminists do not fail to notice, the all-male priesthood just *is* a patriarchal institution. It is a highly specialised one, to be sure, but it imbues the whole hierarchical Church with a very clear patriarchal character. Catholics live in a Church where spiritual authority is exercised by older men over everyone else. This makes sense, of a kind, in a society where temporal authority is exercised, as a rule, by men: the authority of priest, bishop, and pope is then balanced by the authority of the father, the magistrate, and the emperor. But the decline of the patriarchal hierarchy in temporal affairs has left the Church's sacramental priesthood looking anomalous.

The response of many who wish to defend the all-male priesthood has made it more anomalous still. In the 1974 *General Instruction of the Roman Missal* women were forbidden to enter the sanctuary of churches: if they were going to read a reading or the bidding prayers, they had to do so from somewhere else, at least in theory. Female altar servers were forbidden right up to 1992. The sanctuary of the church, as Hauke explains, represents heaven: the nave, the Church on earth. This symbolism was reinforced by the exclusion of females from the former. Today, this distinction has long gone. Instead of priests being the ultimate example of a general principle, that men better represent Christ, God, or heaven, and women the community of the Church, earth, or creation, we find today that there is no general principle of the kind, just an isolated claim about priests.

The admission of women to the sanctuary of the church as servers, readers, and Extraordinary Ministers, and also the banishment of headcoverings for women, are all concessions to those who object to patriarchal symbolism. Those making these concessions—from about the mid-1970s—thought that they were conceding ground difficult to defend, the better to defend what absolutely must be defended, the all-male priesthood. But what they were conceding was, essentially, the defensibility of patriarchy: and the all-male priesthood, to repeat, is simply another example of patriarchy.

It is true that there is a difference between these different cases. The theologians in Rome could never concede the all-male priesthood because, they will tell us, according to principles which they do not have the authority to overturn, the ordination of women would be invalid. They can concede on the other issues: for women to serve at Mass, for example, an immemorial tradition had to be overturned, but that can be done by the appropriate legal authority. But this way of thinking loses sight of the key issue, which is: *why* does the priesthood have to be all-male? Unless we are going to say that it is merely because of an arbitrary decision by

Our Lord, it must be fitted into a wider view about the roles of men and women in the Church and in society. If you reject that wider view, the all-male priesthood may continue to be sacramentally necessary, but it becomes theologically incomprehensible.[234]

How bad is patriarchy?

I should, at this point, say more about what patriarchy actually is. Just how bad is it? I will saying more about this in the next chapter, so here I will limit myself to some brief points.

First, the question of patriarchy should be separated from side-issues such as female participation in the workplace, female education, and the fluctuating and complicated history of the status of women's property, before, during, and after marriage.

What is essential to patriarchy is the idea that, in marrying, husband and wife create a hierarchically-ordered community. We tend to think of marriage in terms of just two people, but the patriarchal model is more about a *household*, which may include children, servants, farm-hands and other employees, other family members, and guests. When, in a patriarchal society, we say that in the hierarchy of the household the husband has the first place, it is important to stress that the wife has the *second*. She is the second in command, and assumes complete command in the absence of the husband.

The housewife's symbol is the bunch of keys: she is in charge of the valuables, the household supplies, and therefore of the domestic budget. She is in charge of the household in the absence of the husband. This absence may be regular, prolonged, or even permanent. The patriarchal model does not exclude women in principle from the exercise of authority, any more than it excludes them from the ownership of property, paid work, or education.

---

[234] For an extended *apologia* on behalf the tradition of all-male sanctuary ministry in the Church, see Peter Kwasniewski, *Ministers of Christ: Recovering the Roles of Clergy and Laity in an Age of Confusion* (Manchester, NH: Crisis Publications, 2021).

We are obliged to free ourselves from the stereotypes that derive from the social and economic circumstances of the early twentieth century: of the idle high-status wife, or the unpaid cook and cleaner of the working classes. The *mulier fortis* of Proverbs 31 undoubtedly lived in a patriarchal society, but she is in charge of the household, buys land, and engages in commerce. She is not an aberration, but a model for imitation.

It is only once we have the sense that a household is rightly ordered as a hierarchy, with the *paterfamilias* at its apex, and that this reflects the relationship between God and the Church, and between God and creation as a whole, that the appropriateness of the all-male priesthood is revealed. For what Christ did in instituting the all-male priesthood was to create a parallel patriarchal structure to that of the family and the temporal order in general. The functions of the priest must, in fact, in a more rigid way than in temporal affairs, be carried out by a man. But the parallel remains: in terms of St Paul's description in Ephesians, the priest, like Christ on the one hand and like the *paterfamilias* on the other, is the head of the community, and is bound to it as to his own body, exercising authority and willing to shed his blood for it.

In both cases, of course, as already noted, this authority is itself derived from a higher source: God. This serves to emphasise that there is no implication that the authority of *paterfamilias* or priest should be regarded as absolute or arbitrary. It is limited in scope and can be exercised only for the good of the community to be governed. The cosmic hierarchy gives everyone a place: and human beings do not have a very exalted one.

Conclusion

Nothing that I have said changes the fact that the idea of patriarchy, or male headship of the household, has very numerous and vociferous opponents today. It remains the case, however, that, as many of these opponents of patriarchy have noticed, the all-male priesthood of the Catholic Church is a patriarchal institution, and its roots and explanation can be understood only in terms of its parallels with a patriarchal conception of the household and of the cosmos. It is difficult to see how attempts to defend the all-male priesthood while dismissing patriarchy in general are going to succeed.

15

Headship and Hierarchy

I want to start with a couple of disclaimers. First, I would like to say something of substance, and not just dance around the subject, but at the same time I have no intention of criticising the life-choices of anyone hearing or reading this chapter. What I have to say is about principles and generalities, and differences of culture, circumstance, and personality are such that these principles can by applied in a wide variety of ways. As for those who reject these principles, that is their business, not mine. I want to elucidate the principles for the purposes of understanding them, and of understanding those individuals, in the present and in the past, who have chosen to live by them.

Second, I am aware that there are people who claim to follow traditional principles on the family but combine these with anti-natalist, misogynistic, or racist ideas. The same difficulty arises for progressive principles on the family, which are in some cases espoused by people who have unpleasant other ideas, particularly in the area of racism and eugenics. To explore these detestable theories on either side of our debate would be to give them too much credit, and would take too long. I will simply set out what I believe to be an authentic understanding of the traditional family, and we can let the loonies howl at the moon if they want to.

Feminism

Any discussion about the ordering of the family has to contend with feminism. This paper is about an un-feminist understanding of an institution

Delivered as part of the Iota Unum series of talks, April 24, 2020.

already highly suspect in the eyes of feminists: the family. So I want to start by saying something about feminism.

It would be too simple to say that feminism is the view that men and women are equal. Equality of dignity and value is not in itself incompatible with socially recognised gender roles, but feminism opposes these because it holds that they reflect and reinforce the oppression of women by men. On this view, almost all human institutions up to the present have been tools of such oppression. Feminism's avowal of the equality of the sexes is qualified, therefore, by the view that throughout history men have oppressed women, implying that they are almost universally, and perhaps innately, morally depraved and dangerous.

A consistent feminist cannot view the traditional family as anything but an evil which needs to be destroyed. We may talk about what individual members of the two sexes actually want, or their loving collaboration to achieve their life goals, but differences of aspiration between men and women are themselves regarded as further evidence of oppression: in the case of women, of internalised misogyny. Not just our psychological makeup, but our biological nature, is something which needs to be ignored or else counterbalanced in order to achieve the perfect 50/50 society: fifty per cent of chief executives, cabinet ministers, Anglican bishops, and so on, being women.

Feminism starts by saying that it wants women to be able to do what they want, but ends by saying that certain options should not be on the table, notably indissoluble marriage, non-participation in the labour market, and holding traditional cultural and religious views on the family. Thus Simone de Beauvoir: "No woman should be authorized to stay at home and raise her children. Women should not have that choice, precisely because if there is such a choice, too many women will make that one."[235] Ignoring what people are like, and what they want, in order to remould them to become citizens of a radically new society, is a recipe for totalitarianism.

In its own historical context, feminism was a reaction to the Victorian "pedestalising" of women: treating women as virtuous but extremely fragile.

---

[235] "Sex, Society, and the Female Dilemma," 18.

Betty Friedman's influential book *The Feminine Mystique* is an attack on that mystique. She wanted women to be down to earth and allowed to take their place alongside men. The "angelic female" idea had developed in the early nineteenth century, and feminism has this much justification: this view of women was accompanied by a narrowing of opportunities for women, and even if it had not been, it is patronising and absurd. Women are not more morally upright than men by nature, nor are they more feeble-minded. The first thing we must do in responding to feminism, therefore, is to take a longer historical perspective.

Feminism is itself under attack today, from an ideology which takes feminism at its word in wishing to deny the differences between men and women. The challenge to the traditional family remains the same, however: it is the idea that sex-specific roles are inherently bad. I have already hinted at my initial response to this challenge: men and women want what they want, and it is not for cultural commissars to tell us that we should not want it. If we want to live according to the principles of the traditional family, we are entitled to do so.

Childbirth

We are pushed towards the traditional model not only by inherited and perhaps outmoded ideas, or by unfashionable evolutionary instincts and drives, but by the realities of family life, and in particular by childbirth. Childbirth, along with gestation and lactation, is problematic for a model of the family based on equal and interchangeable roles, since it is not something which men can do, and it is in the most obvious and literal way fundamental to the existence of the family. It is of vast importance, it is hugely demanding, and in most societies—if not in our own—it brings with it important social status.

If everything except childbirth is up for grabs between the parents, and they share out earning money, mowing the lawn, and doing the washing up, there is no prospect of finding for fathers anything which can remotely balance the importance of childbirth, even if they take on a bigger share of these other tasks. Those tasks do not have the necessary importance or status, and they are not things uniquely assigned to men.

The solution found in traditional societies, which matches the psychological and physical characteristics of men and the needs of the family, is to balance maternity with paternity, a concept which assigns to the father the primary role in protection, provision, and authority.

The central idea of the traditional family, therefore, is not only that the roles of mother, father, and children are not interchangeable, but also that they are ordered hierarchically, with authority and responsibility matched by respect and obedience. Almost every society known to history and anthropology places the husband and father in a position of authority over the household.

St Paul

This hierarchical family is on display throughout Scripture, but it is St Paul who has the most to say explicitly about it, drawing on the Old Testament imagery of God as a father and a husband, *viz-à-viz* creation in general and the Chosen People in particular. God provides for and protects them; St Paul adds that in Christ, he suffers and dies for the Church. In return, creation, the Chosen People, and the Church, must love, honour, and obey.

A natural response to this would be to say the following: these metaphors are effective expressions of theological truths about the nature of God in the context of the way the family functioned and was understood in the ancient world. St Paul also uses slavery, Roman military equipment, and athletic contests as metaphors of the Christian life, without bequeathing to us an obligation to maintain those things.

St Paul anticipates this argument, however, and turns it on its head. It is not that he and the other inspired writers have created a handy metaphor out of the contingent form in which the institution of the family existed in their day. It is, rather, that the way the family is ordered, when it is properly ordered, is a reflection of the relationship between God and creation, which is intensified in the relationship between God and Israel, and Christ and the Church. We do not call God "Father" in a secondary sense, based on our experience of human fatherhood. It is God's fatherhood which is primary, and human fatherhood secondary. As St Paul expresses it in the Letter to the Ephesians, "I bow my knees to the Father of our Lord Jesus Christ, of whom all paternity in heaven and earth is named" (Eph 3:15).

Nor should this surprise us. Unlike the metaphors about running races and the like, what St Paul has to say about male headship in 1 Corinthians 11 is not that Christ is like a loving human husband and father, but rather that the human family should conform to the example of Christ in his relationship with the Church. Just as Christ loves and suffered for the Church, is the head of the Church, and should receive obedience from the Church, *so too* should husbands love their wives, sacrificing themselves for them as necessary, and wives should obey their husbands as their head.

Plato and St Paul

In addition to Christianity, the Western tradition has also been fundamentally, though unevenly, influenced by the views of Plato, who developed a theory of authority as growing out of superior expertise. He believed this approach could be applied to the authority in the state as well as within the family, and equally to the authority of Greek slave owners over their barbarian slaves, and even to the authority of the gods over men.

It is a constant theme in Plato, found throughout his writings, that the person who knows more should be in charge: of a chariot in a chariot race, of a household, a *polis*, or of an agent who might benefit from guidance, like an invalid, a child, a slave, or someone merely lacking knowledge or rationality. The knowledge at issue might be technical expertise in some cases, but when it is a matter of the guidance of human beings, the knowledge prominently includes moral knowledge: virtue. It is a familiar thought in Plato that moral deficiency is a form of ignorance. We can say, then, that for Plato, A should be ruled by B if and only if A is rationally and morally inferior to B.

Plato takes it for granted that women are intellectually inferior to men, and they don't feature as partners in philosophical discussions, except in the fictionalised form of Diotima in the *Symposium*. In that dialogue one character praises the love of boys over that of women on the grounds that boys are more intelligent (181c). In the *Republic*, famously, Plato proposes to abolish specialised gender roles within the ruling elite, but this does not imply equality. Following his analogy between the ruling class and guard-dogs, Socrates's interlocuter declares that "they should take up all duties, though we should treat the females as the weaker, and the males as the stronger" (451e). At any rate, for present purposes it is enough to say that on the Platonic view, *if* a wife is to be subordinate to men, the only justification would be that she is cognitively inferior to him.

Not only is this explanation not appealed to by St Paul, but there are several reasons why the Platonic view does not fit comfortably with a Catholic understanding of the male headship of the household.

First, although in relation to God, ancient Israel and the Church may seem both mentally and morally wanting at certain moments, to put it mildly, this is not the core meaning of their cosmic marriage to God. Yes, these brides make mistakes, but their marriage and obedience to God is not a remedy for their deficiencies, as authority is for Plato, but on the contrary a reward for fidelity. The marital state between God and his people, which reaches its fullest form in heaven, is a privileged state of union with God, not a necessary evil. As St Paul writes, "I have espoused you to one husband, that I may present you as a chaste virgin to Christ" (2 Cor 11:2). St Paul notes in the next verse, and as the prophets of the Old Testament often said about the Chosen People, the sinfulness of this bride implies not an intensification of husbandly authority, but a decay of the conjugal union.[236]

Similarly, the marriage of Adam and Eve was not necessitated by the Fall, but preceded it. St Augustine, who considered political authority in terms of the restraint of vice, cannot give a unified account of authority, since evidently paternal authority from Adam onwards does not parallel the explanation he gives of political authority. St Thomas Aquinas, on the other hand, can generalise about authority in the household and authority in the state because he thinks that the state has more to do than simply restrain vice: it looks after the common good, which is conceived

---

[236] St Paul continues: "But I fear lest, as the serpent seduced Eve by his subtilty, so your minds should be corrupted, and fall from the simplicity that is in Christ."

positively as well as negatively. Two particularly interesting aspects of Aquinas's conception of the common good of a human community are its internal ordering, like (as Aquinas says) the ordering of an army, and the promotion of civic friendship.[237]

On the first, while the utility of the hierarchical ordering of an army is evident, on the medieval view the hierarchical arrangement of a society seems to be good for its own sake. It is fitting that a society should have its king, nobles, merchants, artisans, and peasants. In this hierarchical arrangement it reflects the society of heaven.

On the second, the harmony and fellow-feeling among the members of a society is a key component of its well-being. Those exercising authority over the community do well to protect the community from whatever might undermine this, and to promote it as much as possible.

Is it necessary for authority to be exercised by a single person? Aquinas and other medieval political theorists thought that a single person was more likely to give a single, coherent, and consistent direction to his community, and that a hierarchy with a single apex was best suited to the avoidance of intractable disagreements.[238]

Plato had very definite ideas about the ideal state, which was to be governed by an ideally virtuous and rational class of philosopher-kings. Aristotle, more attuned to the variations found in real life, thought that it would be appropriate for a community to be governed by a king if it contained an outstandingly rational or virtuous individual. If there is a class of rational or virtuous people, then the ideal constitution would be aristocracy, or a democracy if the class encompassed the *demos*. Evidently, on this way of looking at things, only if men are consistently more rational and virtuous than women does it make sense for men to have authority over their wives.

This is not how Aquinas and his contemporaries saw things. A ruler need not be superior to the members of the community he rules, however ideal that might be. Rather, the community needs to be ruled by one, so

---

[237] Paul Weithman, "Augustine and Aquinas on Original Sin and the Function of Political Authority," *Journal of the History of Philosophy* 30.3 (1992): 353–76.

[238] *De Regimine Principum*, Bk. 1, ch. 2.

that one can attend to the common good while others are left to tend to their particular goods. The ruler should identify his interests with those of the community: he should think of an injury done to any part of the community as if it were an injury done to his own body.

St Paul's image of the wife as the body, and the husband as the head, of the family, is in this way applied to the discussion of the body politic.

Again, if we think of the Holy Family, the head of the family is St Joseph, the only member of his three-person community who was subject to Original Sin. At the other end of the family hierarchy was the young Jesus, whose human nature was hypostatically united with the Godhead. And yet St Joseph governed this family: it was he who was warned by the angel to flee the wrath of Herod the Great (Matt 2:13), and then to return to Israel on Herod's death (Matt 2:19), and a third time to avoid the Judean dominions of Herod's son, Herod Archelaus (Matt 2:22). The Angel took his information to the responsible person: the head of the family.

Head and Body

If St Joseph was the head of the Holy Family, the Blessed Virgin Mary was its body or heart. In this she was, as St Ambrose suggested, a type of the Church. By parallel with the mother of a natural family, Our Lady is the mother of Christians, as Eve was the mother of all the living.

We should pause to consider that the Church, as Christ's mystical Body, is in this way represented not, or not only, by Christ the Head, but by Mary, as the type of the body itself. There is, naturally, a certain dignity attached to the notion of authority, but there is another kind of dignity in representing the family unit itself.

This is reflected in the idea we find in traditional societies in the ancient and in the modern world of the wife and mother, the matriarch, being the embodiment of the family's honour, and accordingly being the object of the most elaborate reserve and protection, both symbolic and literal. The hiding away of the matriarch inside the tent and behind veils in the Islamic world, or out of sight during ancient Greek dinner parties, and with variations in other traditional cultures, is not an indication of her low status, but of her great importance. Contrary to a superficial modern reading of these cultures, it is low-status women who are allowed, or compelled, to go about unveiled, to dance at dinner parties, and to take the vegetables to market, the last of these activities being made a jibe against the mother of the Greek general Themistocles, who was not of noble birth.[239] High-status men, on the other hand, do not practice reserve in the same way. Although they may well be veiled, as with the Arabic headscarf, the *ghutra*, it is their role to go out of the home to transact business and to defend the family in war.

This is obviously connected practically and symbolically with the importance of childbirth, as discussed earlier.

The Latin Catholic liturgy of the traditional marriage service and Nuptial Mass also expresses the dignity of the bride as the representative of the family. In the marriage service the bridegroom symbolically gives his property to the bride, handing over, in a custom of England and Wales also found, with small variations, in a number of other countries, gold and silver, with the words: "With this ring I thee wed, this gold and silver I thee give, with my body I thee worship, and with all my worldly goods I thee endow." The bride has nothing equivalent to say to the bridegroom: it is for her to receive, not to give, because she is receiving these things as the representative and embodiment of the family unit itself.

This arises again with the nuptial blessing during the Nuptial Mass. After calling to mind the purpose and dignity of marriage, the celebrant invokes God's blessing on "thine handmaid who is to be joined in wedlock." The celebrant asks God to make her amiable like Rachel, wise like Rebecca, and long-lived and faithful like Sarah, and honoured for her fidelity, modesty, and learning: *doctrinis cælestibus erudita* ("learned in heavenly doctrine"). The blessing refers to the couple in its conclusion, that they may see their descendants to the third and fourth generation, but for the most part the *marriage* is blessed *through* the blessing of the bride.

Wives and children

I have noted above that in the Old Testament the relationship between God and the Chosen People is sometimes compared to that of a husband

---

[239] See Plutarch's *Life of Themistocles.*

and a wife, and sometimes to a father and his children. This variation of imagery is worth noticing as it reinforces something which I have already noted in passing: that Israel the unfaithful wife does not, contrary to the Platonic model, become *more appropriately* under the authority of her husband, but drifts away from him.

When the Chosen People as son or daughter are a prophet's theme, we are told that the bad consequences of Israel's bad behaviour are a loving father's punishment.

> For what shall I strike you any more, you that increase transgression? the whole head is sick, and the whole heart is sad. From the sole of the foot unto the top of the head, there is no soundness therein: wounds and bruises and swelling sores: they are not bound up, nor dressed, nor fomented with oil. Your land is desolate, your cities are burnt with fire: your country strangers devour before your face, and it shall be desolate as when wasted by enemies. And the daughter of Sion shall be left as a covert in a vineyard, and as a lodge in a garden of cucumbers, and as a city that is laid waste. (Isa 1:5–8)

With the faithless wife, most notably in Hosea, the wife's punishment takes the form of *separation* from the husband, a separation she has initiated. What happens when a wife joins herself to adulterers, and places her trust in them to provide for her? The wife says: "I will go after my lovers, who give me my food and my water, my wool and my linen, my olive oil and my drink" (Hos 2:5). Naturally they betray her, and she is left completely desolate.

> And she did not know that I gave her corn and wine, and oil, and multiplied her silver, and gold, which they have used in the service of Baal. Therefore will I return, and take away my corn in its season, and my wine in its season, and I will set at liberty my wool, and my flax, which covered her disgrace. . . . And I will destroy her vines, and her fig trees, of which she said: These are my rewards, which my lovers have given me: and I will make her as a forest, and the beasts of the field shall devour her. . . . Therefore I am now going

to allure her; I will lead her into the wilderness and speak tenderly to her. (Hos 2:8–9, 12, 14)

The desolation of Israel is God's punishment, to be sure, but through the husband-wife analogy this works in a slightly different way from the punishment of a son. God is not, even metaphorically, a wife-beater, though he exercises corporal punishment of his son. He repudiates the faithless wife, but he is ready to take her back.

The postconciliar magisterium

The reformed liturgy avoids the asymmetrical symbolism of husband and wife. Annibale Bugnini explained his changes to the Nuptial Mass saying that he wished to make the blessing apply to both bride and bridegroom,[240] and a novel prayer was composed to make pointed reference to the couple's *equality*, as if in apology for the Epistle traditionally assigned to the Nuptial Mass, which begins: "Brethren, let women be subject to their husbands as to the Lord" (Eph 5:22).[241]

The *Catechism of the Catholic Church* displays a similar hesitation about the traditional teaching of the Church. It makes only one reference to the complementarity of the sexes: homosexual acts "do not proceed from a genuine affective and sexual complementarity" (2357). The word does not appear at all in the section on marriage, although this twice asserts that men and women are equal (1605, 1645).

This equality of men and women is found in their equality as creatures of God and heirs of heaven. However, the postconciliar "complementarian" account of marriage seems to lack a conception of paternity to balance that of maternity. Egalitarians tend to ignore the contribution represented by childbirth: for them, having children is a lifestyle choice with no profound significance. For postconciliar Catholic complementarians, however, it

---

[240] Bugnini, *Reform of the Liturgy*, 704.

[241] On the contrast between traditional and reformed readings at Nuptial Masses, see Peter Kwasniewski, "The New Lectionary and the Catholic Wedding," *OnePeterFive*, May 22, 2019, https://onepeterfive.com/lectionary-wedding.

does have significance. Pope John Paul II tells us about the "naturally spousal predisposition of the feminine personality," which is related to "self-giving."[242] The Catechism quotes St Paul's admonition "Husbands, love your wives, as Christ loved the Church," placing the mother in a special place of honour as the heart of the family, a role connected with femininity and maternity—but skipping over the preceding verses where St Paul says wives should obey their husbands.[243] What neither Pope John Paul nor the *Catechism* can do is tell us anything about *men*.

Giving women an important role and giving men nothing is an unsatisfactory kind of complementarity. Perhaps men can take the rubbish bins out.

Authority and the feminist critique

A wide variety of cultural forms point to a single idea, which is not a Platonic idea but is congruent with Catholic teaching. The traditional hierarchical ordering of the family is not about women being intellectually or morally deficient, but about a symbolic complementarity of the sexes, in which the husband has authority, and the wife represents in her own person the whole of what the husband has authority over: the family or household. This position was pithily expressed by Pope John XXIII in 1959, just before the storm broke: "Within the family, the father stands in God's place. He must lead and guide the rest by his authority and the example of his good life."[244]

Feminists make two kinds of objections to the authority of the husband and father.

One focuses on the question of "opportunities" for women to engage in paid work, entrepreneurial activity, political engagement, and education. Whatever the situation on these fronts might have been in the 1950s, however, these issues are not centrally relevant to the traditional family on a wider historical perspective. Wives took part in the labour force up until the Industrial Revolution, and it is certainly a good idea for them to be educated, particularly in *doctrina cælestia*. Readers of the *Book of*

---

[242] John Paul II, Apostolic Letter *Mulieris Dignitatem* (1988), §20.
[243] Ephesians 5:25–26, leaving out 22–24.
[244] John XXIII, *Ad Petri Cathedram*, §50.

Margery Kemp can see for themselves that this fifteenth-century woman of middling social status had financial independence and entrepreneurial initiative. A little earlier Christine de Pizan was one of the foremost scholars of Europe, Yolande of Anjou one of its most active political figures, and Yolande's *protégé* St Joan of Arc, one of its most remarkable military commanders. Yes, these women were unusual, and the vast majority of their female contemporaries sought and found their status as wives and mothers. The point is that the hierarchical conception of the family did not put rules in place which prevented them from doing what they did. We should not confuse the traditional family with the precise form it took under the influence of a decadent, industrialised Protestantism.

On the other hand, what the vast majority of fifteenth-century women wanted, like women throughout history, namely participation in a traditional family, is itself an opportunity, and as already noted, it is an opportunity which feminists do not want women to have.

Still more to be rejected is the extreme version of this feminist argument: that pre-modern patriarchal societies were founded on fear or hatred of women. This is not to say that medieval society was entirely free of misogyny. The idea that females were inferior to males in various ways, found in the ancient pagan writers, is often repeated, and given a Christian spin. Memorably, one of Geoffrey Chaucer's characters, the Wife of Bath,[245] complained that one of her husbands used to read aloud from a book which collected together all the bad things women had done in history, starting with Eve. But Chaucer's attitude is instructive: the whole episode, in which the Wife of Bath's husband throws the book at her in exasperation, and is then persuaded to burn it, is satire. Equally satirical is Chaucer's account of being hectored by a ghostly throng of historical females into writing about their heroism, to make amends for his depiction of the infidelity of Cressida, in his *Troilus and Cressida*.[246]

In Chaucer's day criticisms of female weakness, exemplified by Eve, were balanced by praise for female piety, exemplified by the Blessed Virgin

---

[245] Geoffrey Chaucer, *The Wife of Bath's Prologue*.
[246] Recounted in his *The Legend of Good Women*.

Mary, the new Eve. The idea of the woman as temptress was balanced by the holy women on Mount Calvary. The idea of the woman as ignorant and irrational was balanced by the triumph of St Catherine of Alexandria over the pagan scholars sent to browbeat her into abandoning Christ.[247]

Indeed, Leon Podles, in his discussion of the feminisation of Christianity, presents many examples of medieval writers taking for granted the idea that women were more pious than men, to such an extent that he argues that religion became feminised in the thirteenth century, at the time of St Bernard of Clairvaux's promotion of "bridal mysticism."[248] For reasons I have discussed in chapter 13, this conclusion, I believe, goes too far, but there is no doubting the strand in medieval thinking Podles has identified. The nuance and freedom of debate in medieval Catholic culture on the subject of femininity is, indeed, something largely lacking in pagan antiquity and Protestant modernity alike.

The other kind of feminist objection focuses on status. A great deal of polemic has been devoted to the position of women in traditional families, to the effect that they were exploited and downtrodden, and above all not appreciated.[249] Feminists themselves do not value the work of childrearing, keeping house, feeding, clothing, and in part educating a family, and contributing to household income, and many feminists have written about housewives as infantile and feeble-minded (Frieden), parasitic (de Beauvoir, Gloria Steinem), and even tantamount to prostitutes (Elizabeth Wurtzel). However, feminists' lack of esteem for this work is not shared by either men or women in traditional societies. The description of the valiant woman, the *mulier fortis*, who exemplifies housewifely virtues, in Proverbs 31, forms the long Epistle on many feasts of holy women in the traditional Catholic liturgy. I recently discovered that Jewish husbands and children traditionally sing this passage to the mother of the family every Friday evening.

---

[247] See her entry in Jacobus de Voragine's *The Golden Legend*, trans. William Granger Ryan (Princeton, NJ: Princeton University Press, 1993), vol. 2, 334–41.

[248] Podles, *The Church Impotent*, 102ff.

[249] The American TV series *Desperate Housewives* is especially focused on this.

Even more fundamentally, the hierarchical household does not deprive women of authority. In the traditional family, the wife is the second in command, and in the absence of the husband she is, simply, in command. Such absence may be regular, prolonged, or, for widows, permanent; for unmarried women, especially heiresses, it is temporary, and terminable at their own will. Not for Catholic women the requirement of classical paganism or Islam that she be under the authority of a man in the absence of a husband. The exercise of authority in the absence of a husband gave rise in the fullness of time to the female monarchs of the late Middle Ages and early modern period, and female voters prior to the Great Reform Act of 1831.

The Catholic priest and psychologist Thomas Verner Moore compared the roles of husband and wife to those of the abbot and the cellarer of a monastic community.[250] The cellarer is not the slave of the abbot, but exercises a crucial role under the abbot's ultimate purview, the authority necessary to provide for the feeding and care of all members of the community. This is no mere detail in the running of a household, but absolutely central to the comfort, health, and happiness of every member, including the head.

Conclusion

I am not going to persuade a convinced feminist that for a woman to submit to the authority of a husband is anything other than an unbearable contradiction of her dignity, but I will conclude this discussion with two observations.

The first is that unlike the other forms of authority to which we are subject in this life, the relationship between husband and wife in a Christian marriage is based on consent. This fact makes it very difficult to claim that it is intrinsically unjust, unless one adopts the Victorian conception of womanhood after all, according to which women are too frivolous and dim-witted to be allowed to determine their own fate.

My other closing observation is that for women considering what sort of family they wish to form, the alternative to a traditional household in

---

[250] Moore, *Sanctity and Insanity*, 10.

which they exercise authority, but not always the ultimate authority, is a household based on the theory of the equality of the sexes, in which there is no authority: not even authority over the children.

This is so for both abstract and practical reasons. In abstract terms, it is difficult to reject the hierarchically ordered household and then make an exception for the children, and progressive parents are characterised by a deep embarrassment about any exercise of authority, and even more so about the punishment of children.

In a practical way, and to generalise, fathers tend to find it easier to exercise authority without really trying, and can also be less affected than mothers by misbehaving children. Even today they tend to spend more time out of the house and away from the children, and tend to be less emotionally invested in whether the house looks like a rubbish tip. The progressive mother can no longer convincingly warn the children about what will happen when daddy gets home. From being the patriarch, the father can turn into an irresponsible and indulgent uncle, who gets the children over-excited when they should be going to bed.

We have all heard the progressive family in action: on public transport, and in parks and pubs. One hears parents *begging* small children to behave themselves, or appealing, unavailingly, to reason. More worryingly, one can witness parents engaging in emotional manipulation to get their way: sulking, blanking, and withdrawing approval.

How did parents control their children in past ages, these parents may wonder? The answer is not far to seek, but ideology has put it out of their reach.

~୬୦~

Appendix: The New Testament on Headship

Colossians 3:18: "Wives, submit yourselves to your husbands, as is fitting in the Lord."

1 Corinthians 11:3: "But I want you to realize that the head of every man is Christ, and the head of the woman is man, and the head of Christ is God."

1 Corinthians 11:7–10: "A man ought not to cover his head, since he is the image and glory of God; but woman is the glory of man. For man did not come from woman, but woman from man; neither was man created for woman, but woman for man. It is for this reason that a woman ought to have authority over her own head, because of the angels."

Ephesians 5:22: "Wives, submit yourselves unto your own husbands, as unto the Lord."

1 Timothy 2:12: "But I suffer not a woman to teach, nor to usurp authority over the man, but to be in silence."

1 Peter 3:1: "Likewise, ye wives, [be] in subjection to your own husbands."

1 Peter 3:5: "For after this manner in the old time the holy women also, who trusted in God, adorned themselves, being in subjection unto their own husbands."

Titus 2:3–5: "Older women likewise are to be reverent in their behaviour, not malicious gossips nor enslaved to much wine, teaching what is good, so that they may encourage the young women to love their husbands, to love their children, to be sensible, pure, workers at home, kind, being subject to their own husbands, so that the word of God will not be dishonoured."

16

Feminism, Patriarchy, and Regretting
the Sexual Revolution

Since the sexual revolution of the 1960s, in Western Europe and North America, divorce has increased to a level at which it ends almost half of all marriages; family formation, marriage, and the birth rate have collapsed; half of births now take place outside wedlock; women of childbearing age are overwhelmingly using some form of contraception, but despite this abortion ends the lives of hundreds of thousands of unborn infants each year.

These things matter for many reasons, most obviously because of their effect on children. Chronic family instability and homes without fathers create an environment, for those children who survive their time in the womb, which disadvantages them in every measurable way compared to those brought up in a stable relationship by both biological parents living together: school work, stress levels, their chance of getting a criminal conviction, and their chance of premature violent death.

Even in the narrowest possible terms, namely those of sexual pleasure, it seems that the sexual revolution has not achieved its goal. Younger women complain that they are required to undertake acts inspired by pornography which are humiliating, painful, and physically harmful. The use of pornography has also led to young men suffering impotence, and an inability to form attachments to real women.

Louise Perry's *The Case Against the Sexual Revolution: A New Guide to Sex in the 21st Century* (Cambridge: Polity Press, 2022) is self-consciously addressed to young women, and specifically to those who regard themselves

Published in *The European Conservative*, Winter 2022.

as feminists. The traditional family, monogamy, indissoluble marriage, the restriction of sex to marriage—the things damaged or destroyed in the sexual revolution—are usually said by feminists to be aspects of a patriarchal power-structure which exists (or existed) to control and subjugate women. This claim generally doesn't seem open to rational debate; it is the axiomatic basis of everything else feminists believe. The writer and activist Kellie-Jay Keen-Minshull (who also goes by the *nom de guerre* Posie Parker) has given up calling herself a feminist. As a married mother of four, the feminist movement, she feels, has no room for her.

Perry takes a different tack, calling herself a "post-liberal feminist," the "post-liberal" qualification indicating her opposition both to anti-family social liberalism and to the economic liberalism of corporate capitalism. She quotes Patrick Deneen making the link between the two, and writes: "Liberal feminism promises women freedom—and when that promise comes up against the hard limits imposed by biology, then the ideology directs women to chip away at those limits through the use of money, technology and the bodies of poorer people."[251] And she goes on to say: "I don't reject the desire for freedom—I'm not anti-liberal, and goodness knows that women have every reason to chafe against the constraints imposed on us by our societies and our bodies, both in the past and in the modern world."[252] This sets the scene for her arguments, which say, essentially, that if her female target audience wants freedom, opportunities of various kinds, and sexual satisfactions, the sexual revolution has manifestly failed them.

At the most fundamental level, Perry explains, the sexual revolution has "disenchanted" sex: it has convinced people that sex has no meaning. The new social understanding of sex has presented it simply as a fun activity, one among others, with no further significance. The problem, Perry argues, is that this is a particular understanding of sex and an invitation to a particular kind of sexual lifestyle which works best for people described by psychologists as having high (or "unrestricted") sociosexuality. This

---

[251] Perry, *Case Against the Sexual Revolution*, 8.
[252] Perry, 8–9.

is a measure of willingness or desire to engage in casual sex. What has happened is that one set of norms, suited to people of relatively low sociosexuality, have been replaced by a new set of norms, suited to people of relatively high sociosexuality. Furthermore, it is a scientifically established fact that women are on average significantly lower on this scale than men.

Were the distribution to be plotted on a graph, with men and women separated, it would be represented as two partially-overlapping bell curves. If one thinks of a particular set of sexual *mores* as best suited to people at a particular point on this graph, moving these sharply in the direction of higher sociosexuality benefits men at the expense of women. To put it another way, and a little crudely, the old social norms were better for women than men; the new ones are better for men than women.

It is not difficult to explain why this might be. As Perry points out, the risks and burdens of pregnancy and child-rearing fall disproportionately on the females of mammal species, and humans are no exception. Technology can mitigate but not eliminate these risks and burdens. Even if technology were more effective, however, it would not change what Perry calls the differences between men and women "above the neck." The female psychology which evolved to deal with pre-modern conditions is here to stay.

It is true, of course, that there are some women who are high in the sociosexual scale, who chafed under the old rules and feel liberated by the new, and there are men low on sociosexuality who feel the opposite. But the overall effect is undeniable: the sexual revolution is massively to the advantage of men, as a group, and to the disadvantage of women, as a group.

I labour Perry's point here because it is devastating for a feminist defence of the sexual revolution. Insofar as feminism is an ideology which seeks to benefit women by freeing them from old-fashioned, repressive sexual norms, it is devastating for feminism as well.

Feminism has typically dealt with the problem by claiming that women low in sociosexuality are repressed and suffering from false consciousness. If social norms are changed, then, it is claimed, these women will move smoothly up the scale and enjoy themselves. No doubt people do move around the scale a bit in response to various influences, but this does nothing to negate the reality that the average man has a much higher score than the average woman, a feat he achieves without having to change anything. What the liberal feminists have been saying, in fact, is that women should model themselves on *men*. They have promoted a man's world, and have told women to be more like men in order to make their way in it.

Perry's argument is a feminist one in the sense that it bases itself on the interests of women. But—although Perry does not draw this conclusion—it reveals the truth of what feminism has historically sought to deny: that, however imperfect and even corrupt the pre-revolutionary patriarchal structure may have been at this or that historical moment, it was not fundamentally about controlling and oppressing women. It was, rather, about protecting them. This is less surprising than it sounds, because for a patriarchal society—if we may be allowed to use this term literally and unironically—the protection of women is critical to the interests of the family, and therefore to the interests of the patriarch: the father.

It is not young women who are sent to war, or deep-sea fishing, or down the coal mines, by patriarchal societies: it is the more expendable young men. Restrictions on women's opportunities in patriarchal societies derive from attempts to protect them, attempts which may be exaggerated or misguided, and should always be open to renegotiation and debate, but should not be misrepresented as being inspired by hatred or fear of women.

Feminists often claim that social restrictions on female sexual activity were motivated by "fear of female sexuality." This deserves the same ridicule as is heaped on some liberal feminists' more recent suggestion that separate male and female categories in sporting events are motivated by a fear that women would humiliate men by outcompeting them. A parallel and disturbing claim heard today is that opposition to the premature sexualisation of children is motivated by "fear of children's sexuality."

It may be objected that, if things are as bad as Perry suggests, women can simply adopt a more sexually restrictive lifestyle, without the need for socially recognised and enforced rules. However, unilaterally adopting traditional sexual norms is not as easy as it sounds.

For one thing, before the sexual revolution, it was possible to have romantic relationships with members of the opposite sex, with a view to possible marriage, without being expected to sleep with them. Such relationships are still theoretically possible, but it will be hard work to find another party willing to have one.

The familiar temptations of the flesh are only part of the problem. Much of what young women might resist, but do not, in the end, resist, are *unwelcome* sexual propositions. Indeed, an entire industry has arisen to deal with sexual harassment, inappropriate relationships, and subtle forms of coercion, although apparently with little to show for its efforts. Perry quotes the veteran feminist Virginia Ironside, talking about the effect of the introduction of the contraceptive pill: "It often seemed more polite to sleep with a man than to chuck him out of your flat."[253]

Ironside's point in context is that the danger of pregnancy had provided women with a strong argument against extramarital sex, and this seemed to disappear with the advent of the Pill. That kind of argument against sex could be employed without invoking personal dislike, religious conviction, or anything else which might reflect badly on the person using the argument.

The key development, in fact, was not the Pill; it was the disappearance of the social valuation of chastity, which left fear of pregnancy as the *only* argument against extramarital sex. The game was lost when saying "no" began to violate a new social norm, namely that against being a "prude." As Perry notes, virginity is now stigmatised for young people of both sexes.

As a result, for all the problems of the modern dating scene, it is very difficult to swim against the tide unless strongly motivated by religious conviction, and preferably as part of a religious subculture where these norms at least get some comprehension and respect. Perry's practical suggestions come down to not sleeping with a man on the first few dates. This is not the stuff of which counterrevolutions are made.

Part of the problem is that it is all too natural for Perry, as a feminist, to see the issue in terms of men *vs.* women. Good heterosexual relationships are not, however, about getting the better of the other party, but joining with them in a common project. Cooperation between the sexes is something entirely missing from this book.

[253] Perry, 166.

Some feminists suggest that the current "sexual marketplace" amounts to a new phase of patriarchy, which should be combatted by hypervigilance about sexual harassment. Maximising female sexual availability certainly appeals to a lot of men, but so do pornography and drugs. Most men, even at the higher levels of sociosexuality, like the idea of settling down eventually, and the sexual revolution has made this incomparably more difficult than before. In doing so, it has deprived many men, particularly at the lower reaches of the social and educational scale, of the ultimate goal of traditional male ambition: a stable family life. Directly traceable to this are the facts that boys underperform girls in school, are outnumbered by them at university, and vastly outstrip them in deaths of despair. Men may enjoy the sexual free-for-all, but it is no basis for a meaningful life.

This is not a society designed and controlled by patriarchs, but one implacably opposed to fatherhood, in any sense but the bare biological one. If the sexual revolution is to be countered, even if only for a small subculture, we need to find a place for fathers.

17

The Family and Culture

The family home is the dominant locus of culture. By "culture," I mean cultural practices: the things people in a particular culture *do*, which mark them out as being of that culture, such as the songs people sing, the food they cook, and the jokes they tell.

The Vatican Museum's extensive collection of ancient Etruscan artefacts tells us a lot about ancient Etruscan culture, but it does not keep that culture alive. Ancient Etruscan culture is dead because no living people are doing the things which ancient Etruscans used to do. Fine paintings and music and the like are important in European culture not because they comprise it, but because of the cultural practice of seeing and listening to these things, a practice which incorporates them, as shared reference points, into the further cultural practices of conversation and the creation of new art. These non-living things have a role in what we call cultural *life*.

If culture is a matter of how people live, and not a matter of artefacts in museums, it is clear that a great deal of it goes on in the family home. Some cultural practices can be performed alone, but others require a social setting, or simply seem pointless without one. Again, some of these group activities can take place outside the home—in the context of education and sport, for example—but the home is the most important *locale*, and for some of the most important cultural practices it is an indispensable one.

First published in German translation as "Die kulturelle Zukunft liegt in der Familie" at corrigenda*, December 5, 2022, www.corrigenda.online/leben/die-kulturelle-zukunft-liegt-der-familie.

It would hardly seem worthwhile to spend many hours cooking a Christmas dinner for one. Telling jokes is pretty difficult for a person on his own, and the game of charades, I would say, is simply impossible. The ideal Christmas described by Charles Dickens in *A Christmas Carol*, which incorporates these elements, is necessarily a *family* Christmas.

The period of time spent by a young adult between leaving home and forming a new family will tend, therefore, to be thinned out, culturally. Many people in this state don't have the time or inclination to cook properly; they spend little time in the place where they sleep at night, and so don't bother to decorate it with care or keep it looking nice; many cease the practice of their religion.

They don't tend to live like this out of a conscious choice: it is simply difficult not to live like this when living alone. It is common for such people to return to the old family home for culturally significant events, and when they come to form a family of their own, they usually make an effort to restore their cultural lives, sometimes in a bit of a scramble. They suddenly feel the need to have a presentable place to live; they realise, perhaps, that they had better learn how to cook; when children arrive, they rediscover the children's literature they themselves had enjoyed; religious practice can be resumed; and so on.

It is telling that it is the period of living alone which forms the ideal for some people, who are even eager to extend it indefinitely, because, as they would say, it is a lifestyle of maximum freedom. What they are idealising, essentially, is a radically impoverished culture, one characterised by mass-market entertainment and short-term sexual relationships.

It is often said that parents, or those wanting to become parents, do a lot of the things I have mentioned as examples of cultural practices, "for the children." This is true; but even for the parents' own sake, the setting of the family home is often indispensable for a satisfying cultural life.

We can also consider the connection from the other direction. Young people who have not been inducted as children into a rich culture will not miss it while living alone, and will not be motivated to form a family to regain it, unless they have been able to rediscover their culture for themselves somehow. They will have nothing to give their children, culturally, and this being so, they may well think that there is no point having children at all.

This is connected with another phenomenon of modern life: even those who do become parents often disclaim responsibility for their raising of their children. Parents blame schools, for example, for shortcomings in their children's education, whether it be a lack of knowledge of geography, or an experience of sexual abuse. They are encouraged in this attitude by an educational establishment which tends to limit choice and parental input, and schools do, of course, deserve blame. There remains, however, plenty of blame to go round.

T.S. Eliot identified one aspect of the problem in his *Notes Towards a Definition of Culture*, when he complained that schools were being expected to be the main conduits of culture to the young, in place of the family. He identifies many problems with this, but an obvious one for us today is simply that schools are bad at it. A society that places its cultural future in the classroom, instead of in the family home, is inevitably going to lose all those aspects of culture which can happen only in the family home.

Downgrading the role of the family in the formation of children also undermines family life itself. The more the state, or any other outside institution, arrogates to itself the family's functions, the more impoverished family life becomes, and the less attractive family formation is. In the developed world, parents are regarded with permanent suspicion by an array of experts ever ready to take over one or another aspect of the parental role, in a way which is progressively destroying the cultural coherence of the home.

The reasons given in online lists for not having children, leaving aside prophecies of impending environmental catastrophe, tend to be trivial: parents lose sleep, gain weight, have to tidy up, find travel more difficult, and so on. These are reasons, one would think, that would motivate only people whose desires are entirely bound up with material possessions and the pleasures of the flesh. It is not simply that such people are egoistical or selfish, but that relationships and the satisfactions of family life are not among the things they want from life. They are not necessarily to blame for this, however. They are the victims of a progressive degradation of family life, which has for many people made it something which does not offer the comfort and satisfaction confidently aspired to by earlier generations.

The direction we need to travel to get out of this problem may be clear, but the path is not an easy one. Parents, and those who aspire to have children, must do what they can to enrich their home lives with the cultural practices which can alone be continued there, and which alone can make the life of the home stimulating and satisfying. This will mean a reassertion of the principle of subsidiarity—resisting the state's takeover of the family's functions—and taking on both hard work and a daunting responsibility. The effort, however, is a necessary one.

18

The Family and the Defence of the Faith

Just over a century ago, in 1907, the convert priest Msgr Robert Hugh Benson published an extraordinary and prophetic book, *Lord of the World*, which is set more or less today. Like most prophetic books, it is really about Msgr Benson's own time, and it is interesting to see which of the trends of his day, that he extrapolated into the future, have continued, and which have petered out or gone into reverse. Even where he has turned out to be wrong, it is interesting to see where he thought threats were coming from, and what form of defence he thought would prove effective.

Msgr Benson's image of the Church is that of Pope St Pius X: archaic, embattled, unyielding, and ever more centralised. The centralisation of the Church, he explains, is the natural and correct response to an increasingly centralised world. Where the threat is centralised—notably, in Benson's imagined world, by a united and secularised Europe—so must the defence be.

This part of Benson's vision has not aged well. We know, with hindsight, that the centralisation of the Church has made her painfully vulnerable to the capture of central institutions by corrupt individuals or misguided ideas. It is no new thing in the history of the Church for there to be corruption in Rome (as I write, the trial of Cardinal Becciu is ongoing). What is new, and disastrous, is the diminishment of alternative sources of influence, initiative, and prestige, from which Roman problems could be

First published in *Calx Mariae*, Winter 2020, under the title "The Family in the Defence of the Faith."

addressed without being cut off immediately by the very people causing the problems. I have in mind things like monastic reformers, reforming bishops, fearless preachers, or even the Holy Roman Emperor.

In the secular realm, the invader of a centralised state like the ancient Persian Empire will face a powerful and united army, but if the army is defeated and the central apparatus of control captured, then success—like that of Alexander the Great—could be complete in a bewilderingly short time. By contrast, when England's King Edward III, and later Henry V, invaded France, they quickly had disaffected French lords as allies, but faced an apparently endless task in tackling one local centre of power after another, while ceaselessly beset by small rebellions and counter-attacks. Their brilliant victories apparently counted for little in dealing with the hydra-like resilience of a state where power was widely diffused.

Benson, for all his prophetic insight, was wrong on this issue: what the Church needs in dealing with a unified threat is not the brittle strength of the centralised control centre, but the flexible resistance of ten thousand little platoons with the self-sufficiency and initiative to carry on guerrilla warfare even when the enemy has won the big battles. What it needs, in fact, is the family.

Why did popes like St Pius X think that centralisation was the way forward? It was because they could not trust local centres of authority. The autonomy of religious orders and the independence of bishops had to be restricted because, under intense political and intellectual pressure from protestantising and secularising influences, they could not be trusted to hold the line otherwise. To prevent the appointment of Modernist bishops, the appointment of bishops had to be centralised. To prevent the teaching of Modernism in seminaries, seminary syllabuses had to be centrally approved. And so it went on, inevitably, perhaps, but ultimately unsuccessfully.

This isn't the place to go into exactly how and why things worked out as they did, but just to note that a different approach is needed, if only because the central authority in the Church today has no interest in engaging in a campaign against heresy like that carried on by St Pius X. The final capture of the Church as a human institution by her enemies will not be prevented by clever and zealous men in Rome with their hands on the levers of centralised power. It will be prevented, if it is prevented, by the refusal of ordinary Catholics to go along with it.

I am not, however, thinking of an atomised collection of individuals. Not only does resistance still have to be coordinated to some extent but, even more importantly, the spirit of resistance, the spirit of truth, must be inculcated in us and in the next generation. In this, magazines, associations of the faithful, parishes, dioceses and religious orders, schools, and so on, all have great importance, but the importance of the family is paramount. Let me explain why.

First, the family is a natural institution. While we have seen all kinds of attempts to weaken and belittle the family, and attempts to create parody-families, it is to the traditional family that people are drawn most strongly by nature. Young men and women, despite many temptations and distractions, are strongly drawn to a life-long monogamous and exclusive relationship ordered towards children. They see this instinctively as fulfilling and wholesome. We have moved into a time where this instinct is often frustrated, and even made to seem impossible, but these dystopian conditions serve to emphasise the fundamental and irreplaceable quality of this yearning. While our approach to relationships and child-rearing owes much to our own upbringing and experiences, they have a foundation which is not learned, but arises from the depths of human nature.

This means that the family can never be erased. The other things I mentioned—magazines, associations, parishes and so on—can be, and from time to time are, destroyed. For three centuries England had no dioceses or parishes. Every now and then the French state sees fit to abolish religious orders and Catholic schools. The time may come when one can read Catholic magazines only on the "dark web." But even the Soviet Union could not abolish the family.

The bonds of family life, between spouses, between children and their parents, and between siblings, are not invincible, but they are extremely powerful, and they create and sustain an environment where the whole person can be nourished—emotionally, intellectually, and physically.

Secondly, the family is not only a natural institution. Marriage has been raised to the dignity of a sacrament by Christ, and the Christian family is a powerful means of grace for its members. Its prayer in common is a microcosm of the Church at prayer. The authority exercised in the family—paradigmatically, by the *paterfamilias*—is a reflection of the authority of our Heavenly Father. The effect of the sacrament is to make the natural bonds of marriage unbreakable, to sanctify the natural love of spouses, and to reinforce with divine assistance their natural efforts in raising their children.

This is familiar stuff which can be found in every orthodox catechism, but reflect for a moment: these things are not given to lay associations, to magazines, or even to parishes. Even religious orders are not sacramentally established, and as noted, even dioceses are not an essential feature of the life of the Church.

Not everyone, at every stage of life, can identify a family of which they are a member, and not all families are open to grace. The family is the building block of society not because everyone is in one, or must fulfil their personal vocation through one, but in a different sense. It is the normal and ideal environment for the raising of children, and for this reason has the vocation of passing on to each new generation religion, culture, and even language. These things can be acquired in other ways, certainly, but only with difficulty. It is the family which is the proper instrument for this task—by nature and in the sacramental economy—and it is the task of other social institutions, and of the Church, to assist the family in its work, and never to displace it.

To return to the question of the resilience of the Church, considered as a society here on earth, the family has a key role because it is extraordinarily robust, and because it is the family which has the task of passing on the spirit of truth to each new generation. By this I mean, not only an intellectual grasp of the truths of the Faith, important as that is, but the practice of the virtues: natural virtues, passed on through example and training, and supernatural virtues, whose giving by God is prepared for and facilitated by the family environment.

I would like briefly to mention two practical implications of this. First, parents like myself have a very serious burden of responsibility. This should not be felt as a crushing one—we are, after all, promised divine assistance—but it is one that may come as a bit of a shock for those whom popular culture has conditioned to see romantic relationships solely as means to self-fulfilment. The state, the school, and the parish are not going to do this work for you, especially not today.

Secondly, the family environment in which one can relax and breathe freely, in which one can find solace and pass on wisdom and experience to one's children, is sustained by sacramental graces, for Christian families, but, as always, God prefers to work through secondary causes where possible. An environment in which parents and children can truly feel at home is not built exclusively on prayer and the sacraments. The family needs culture. It needs a tradition of cooking, of clothing, of architecture, of home decoration; it needs Christmas carols and fairy stories. In today's world, not everyone can have a very meaningful connection with the soil, and many are separated from the experiences of their parents and grandparents by space as well as time, but we can still sustain a world of shared reference points, attitudes, and affections. Catholic culture is a natural culture as well as a supernatural one, and it is the family's task to maintain it, to develop it, and to pass it on.

The family is the ultimate bulwark of Christian society. It is our task to strengthen our own families, and to help to strengthen other families as well, against this storm which seems to gain greater and greater power. We know, however, something that our opponents do not: that Christ has already gained the victory.

Acknowledgements

Chapter 1 of this collection, "Discovering and Rediscovering the Traditional Mass," first appeared in Polish translation in Tomasz Rowiński, ed., *Odwieczna Msza Świadectwa* (Rosa Mystica, 2021).

Chapter 4, "Understanding Liturgical Participation," is a slightly developed version of my contribution to Jaime Alcalde, ed., *Fidem servavi. Escritos en homenaje al Prof. Julio Retamal Favereau* (Valencia: Tirant lo Blanch, 2023).

Chapter 5, "Traditions and the Narcissism of Consumer Capitalism," first appeared in *The European Conservative* online, March 6, 2022.

Chapter 6, "Tradition, Liberation, and Meaning," first appeared in *The European Conservative* online, October 31, 2021.

Chapter 9, "The Traditional Latin Mass and Diversity," first appeared on the blog *OnePeterFive*, October 11, 2021, with the exception of part 2.

Chapter 16, "Feminism, Patriarchy, and Regretting the Sexual Revolution," first appeared in *The European Conservative* print edition, Winter 2022.

Chapter 17, "The Family and Culture," first appeared online at corrigenda*, December 5, 2022.

Chapter 18, "The Family and the Defence of the Faith," first appeared in *Calx Mariæ*, Winter 2020, and was subsequently published online in *Voice of the Family Digest*, December 15, 2021.

I am grateful to the editors and publishers for their permission to reprint these pieces, and to the editors of *The European Conservative* for editorial work on the two pieces reprinted from their journal. The remaining chapters are published here for the first time. I am also grateful to the various live audiences who helped me develop my thoughts in relation to other pieces collected in this volume.

About the Author

Joseph Shaw was born in London; his university studies culminated in a Doctorate in Philosophy, and he was a member of Oxford University's Philosophy Faculty for eighteen years. During that time he taught moral philosophy, Aristotle, Aquinas, and the philosophy of religion, and published academic papers on philosophy of religion and ethics. He is the Chairman of the Latin Mass Society of England and Wales, and President of the International Una Voce Federation (FIUV). He is the editor of *The Case for Liturgical Restoration* (Angelico Press, 2018), and blogs at lmschairman.org. He is married, lives outside Oxford, and home educates his nine children.

Os Justi Press specializes in publishing Catholic classics and new works that support the Church's traditional Faith. Check out some of our other titles:

Os Justi Studies in Catholic Tradition
John Joy, *Disputed Questions on Papal Infallibility*
Fr. Réginald-Marie Rivoire, *Does "Traditionis Custodes"*
Pass the Juridical Rationality Test?

Translations of Dr. Kwasniewski's *True Obedience*
La Verdadera Obediencia en la Iglesia
A Verdadeira Obediencia na Igreja
Wahrer Gehorsam in der Kirche

Dogmatic Theology
Lattey (ed.), *The Incarnation*
Lattey (ed.), *St Thomas Aquinas*
Pohle, *God: His Knowability, Essence, and Attributes*
Pohle, *The Author of Nature and the Supernatural*
Scheeben, *A Manual of Catholic Theology* (2 vols.)
Scheeben, *Nature and Grace*

Spiritual Theology
Doyle, *Vocations*
Guardini, *Sacred Signs*
Leen, *The True Vine and Its Branches*
Swizdor, *God in Me*

Liturgy
A Benedictine Martyrology
The Life of Worship
The Roman Martyrology (Pocket Edition)
Chaignon, *The Sacrifice of the Mass Worthily Offered*
Croegaert, *The Mass: A Liturgical Commentary* (2 vols.)
Kwasniewski (ed.), *John Henry Newman on Worship, Reverence, and Ritual*
Parsch, *The Breviary Explained*
Pothier, *Cantus Mariales*

Language & Literature
The Little Flowers of Saint Francis (illustrated)
Brittain, *Latin in Church*
Farrow, *Pageant of the Popes*
Kilmer, *Anthology of Catholic Poets*
Walsh, *The Catholic Anthology*

Printed in Great Britain
by Amazon

18871673R00171